GUIDE TO THE USE OF BOOKS AND LIBRARIES

GUIDE TO THE USE OF BOOKS AND LIBRARIES

FOURTH EDITION

JEAN KEY GATES
University of South Florida

McGraw-Hill Book Company

New York/St. Louis/San Francisco/Auckland/Bogotá/Düsseldorf/Johannesburg
London/Madrid/Mexico/Montreal/New Delhi/Panama/Paris/São Paulo
Singapore/Sydney/Tokyo/Toronto

GUIDE TO THE USE OF BOOKS AND LIBRARIES

Copyright © 1979, 1974, 1969, 1962, by McGraw-Hill, Inc.
All rights reserved. Printed in the United States of America.
No part of this publication may be reproduced, stored in a
retrieval system, or transmitted, in any form or by any means,
electronic, mechanical, photocopying, recording, or otherwise, without the prior written permission of the publisher.

2 3 4 5 6 7 8 9 0 D O D O 7 8 3 2 1 0 9

This book was set in Binny Old Style by Black Dot, Inc.
(ECU). The editors were Richard R. Wright and Susan Gamer;
the designer was Anne Canevari Green; the production super-
visor was Donna Piligra. The cover was designed by Scott
Chelius.
R. R. Donnelley & Sons Company was printer and binder.

Library of Congress Cataloging in Publication Data

Gates, Jean Key.
    Guide to the use of books and libraries.

    Includes index.
    1. Reference books. 2. Libraries—Handbooks, manuals, etc. I. Title.
Z710.G27 1979   028.7   78-11076
ISBN 0-07-022986-4
ISBN 0-07-022985-6 pbk.

For Sherwood

CONTENTS

Preface   ix
Introduction   xi

PART ONE
THE LIBRARY

    1 A Brief History of Books and Libraries   3
    2 The Parts of the Book   22
    3 Academic Libraries   26

PART TWO
THE ORGANIZATION AND ARRANGEMENT OF LIBRARY MATERIALS

    4 Classification   35
    5 The Card Catalog   51

PART THREE
GENERAL INFORMATION SOURCES

    6 Reference Sources   65
    7 Dictionaries   71
    8 Encyclopedias   80

9 Indexes 87
10 Biographical Dictionaries 101
11 Atlases and Gazetteers 111
12 Yearbooks and Handbooks 116
13 Bibliographies 122
14 Nonbook Information Sources and Government
   Publications 129

PART FOUR
INFORMATION SOURCES IN THE SUBJECT FIELDS

15 Subject Reference Sources 151
16 Philosophy and Psychology 156
17 Religion and Mythology 163
18 The Social Sciences and Education 171
19 Language (Philology) 187
20 Science and Technology 195
21 The Fine Arts 211
22 Literature 228
23 History and Geography 246

PART FIVE
USING THE LIBRARY FOR A RESEARCH PAPER

24 The Undergraduate Research Paper 261

Index 275

PREFACE

The purpose of this book—as was the purpose of the three previous editions—is to provide a brief but comprehensive treatment of libraries, with emphasis upon the many kinds of library materials, their organization and arrangement, and their usefulness for specific purposes. Particular attention is paid to academic libraries and to ways of using them most effectively.

I have given attention to the historical development of the book and the library and have emphasized the usefulness of each type of library material for particular purposes.

The chapters are arranged in logical sequence, and the reader who follows straight through the text should gain a full-length picture of the academic library and a reasonably clear picture of any library. There is some repetition of ideas and information. This repetition is by design: each chapter, while it is a necessary part of the whole, has been planned to stand alone so that the instructor who has only a limited time in which to teach the use of the library can select the chapter or parts of chapters best suited to the requirements and purposes of a given situation.

In this book emphasis is placed upon *how to use information sources* rather than upon *the number of titles* included. The selection of titles to illustrate the several kinds of library materials was based on a critical study of the basic reference materials reviewed in a number of selective and evaluative bibliographies, including:

"The Book Review," *Library Journal.* New York: R. R. Bowker Company, 1876– . (Semimonthly September through June; monthly in July and August.)

The Booklist. Chicago: American Library Association, 1905– . (Semimonthly; monthly in August.)

Bunge, Charles A. "Current Reference Books," *Wilson Library Bulletin.* New York: The H. W. Wilson Company, 1972– . (Monthly, except July and August.)

Choice. Chicago: American Library Association, 1964– . (Monthly except August.)

RQ. Chicago: American Library Association, 1961– . (Quarterly.)

"Reference Books of . . . ," annual feature of *Library Journal* (April 15 issue).

Sheehy, Eugene P. "Selected Reference Books of . . . ," *College and Research Libraries.* Chicago: American Library Association. (January and July of each year.)

––––––. *Guide to Reference Books.* 9th ed. Chicago: American Library Association, 1976.

Also included are materials which I have used and evaluated in my own college teaching and reference work. The titles listed are thus only a selected sample of those now available, and each person will undoubtedly wish to add titles and to replace, with new editions and new titles, some of those which have been included. Listings of titles have been brought up to date by substituting new editions, adding titles omitted in the third edition, or adding titles published since 1974.

This book is not a manual for the study of a particular library. It is designed to serve as a textbook for college freshmen and other students who require instruction in the use of libraries and library materials. It will provide supplementary material for introductory courses in library science and can be used to advantage not only by reference librarians but by any person who is interested in learning what a library is and how to use it.

I am indebted to many authors, publishers, and holders of copyrights for permission to use their material. I should like to express my appreciation to my family and to my friends for their support; to my professional colleagues who answered questions or volunteered suggestions regarding this revision; to numerous users of the first, second, and third editions, both teachers and students, who have made helpful comments; and to cooperative librarians in many libraries who helped locate needed materials.

Jean Key Gates

INTRODUCTION

The college library contributes to the program of the college by providing the materials which are required in the various phases of that program. The more diversified the college program, the greater the quantity and variety of library materials.

Students entering college find a library which was planned and developed for work and study. They soon learn that the library is to become a part of their way of life. How much a part of their college experience it will become and how effectively it will contribute to their college years and to the years after college will depend upon their competence in using it.

Competence in the use of the library is a combination of attitudes, knowledge, and skills. It is dependent upon an awareness of the importance of books and libraries in our cultural heritage and in our daily life, a desire to use them, a knowledge of the kinds of materials which the library provides, and the development of skill in locating, selecting, using, describing, and evaluating these materials.

With the ever-increasing number, variety, and complexity of library materials and the emphasis upon teaching methods which place greater responsibility for learning upon the student, it becomes imperative that the college student begin in the freshman year to achieve a measure of competence in the use of the library. This competence should increase year by year while the student is in college.

Some of the basic attitudes, knowledge, and skills which it is desirable for the student to achieve are:

1 Acquaintance with the history and development of books and libraries,

appreciation of their importance in our history and in our daily life, and the desire to use them

2 Understanding of the purpose of the college library, the kinds of materials it includes, and their physical arrangement and organization

3 General idea of classification systems as an aid in the use of libraries

4 Knowledge of the purpose of the card catalog, the meaning for the student of each item of information on the catalog card, and the ways in which this information can be used

5 Ability to search for material beyond the catalog

6 Familiarity with the major reference sources, both general and specialized: what they are and how to use them

7 Experience in the use of printed bibliographies

8 Experience in taking notes, compiling bibliographies, and making footnotes for term papers and research papers

9 Ability to decide what kinds of books and materials are needed to answer a given question or to develop a given subject

10 Understanding of the importance of using a variety of sources

In general, each chapter includes (1) a definition of terms, (2) a brief statement of historical development, (3) discussion, and (4) appropriate examples.

Information sources are discussed as general or subject (specialized), according to kinds: dictionaries, indexes, handbooks, microforms, and others. Emphasis is placed on what they are, the purposes they serve, and the kinds of questions they are designed to answer, rather than on a mere listing of titles.

Since students learn by doing, rather than by being told, all phases of their instruction should be accompanied by learning experiences, with each experience built upon the preceding ones but introducing new materials.

Technical library terminology is used only when it seems to be essential. The language is, with few exceptions, that of the student and nonspecialist.

PART ONE
THE LIBRARY

CHAPTER ONE
A BRIEF HISTORY OF BOOKS AND LIBRARIES

The earliest and greatest system for storing information and transmitting it from one person to another was language. By the use of words, history, rituals, stories, prayers, and medical and other knowledge were passed on from one generation to another. When people realized that spoken words could be represented by visual symbols, they invented their second means for the preservation and transmission of knowledge: writing—the chief medium used for this purpose for more than 5,000 years.

The first writings were crude pictures carved on rocks, stone, bark, metal, clay, or whatever materials were at hand. They were of three kinds: (1) pictographic, representing an object; (2) ideographic, representing the idea suggested by the object; and (3) phonographic, representing the sound of the object or idea. Some of these ancient inscriptions can be interpreted. Crude picture writing was done on other materials which were at hand: vegetable fiber, cloth, wood, bark, animal skin, clay, and metal. However, only the writings on clay, metal, and stone have survived.

Most historians agree that all our systems of writing came from these crude carvings and picture writings.

The story of books and libraries from earliest times to the present is closely interwoven with the story of writing and other methods of preserving and transmitting information and knowledge, with the materials and the physical forms which have been used for these purposes, and with the methods of preserving them and of making them accessible for use. For with the first "book" came the necessity for a place to keep it, to make it accessible for use, and to pass it on to succeeding generations.

WRITING, BOOKS, AND LIBRARIES

ANTIQUITY

The Sumerians, Babylonians, and Assyrians

From about 3600 to 2357 B.C. the Sumerian civilization flourished in the Tigris-Euphrates Valley, and as early as 3100 B.C. Sumerian historians began to record their current history and to reconstruct the story of their past.

The system of writing of the Sumerians—perhaps their greatest contribution to human culture—is the oldest system known. The word "cuneiform," which describes their style of writing, is from *cuneus*, the Latin word for "wedge." The materials used were soft clay and a wedge-shaped stylus of metal, ivory, or wood. When the scribe had finished writing, the clay was baked until it was hard as stone. These pieces of baked clay, small enough to be held in the hand of the scribe, are called "tablets" and were the first books.

To the Sumerians, writing was first of all a tool of trade and commerce. In addition, it was an instrument for recording religious works: prayers, ritual procedure, sacred legends, and magic formulas. On these clay tablets are also preserved the records of the first schools, the first social reforms, the first tax levies, and the first political, social, and philosophical thinking. It was several hundred years before the Sumerians produced literature, but among the tons of tablets and cylinders removed from the ruins of Sumer's ancient cities are some containing literary works almost 1,000 years older than the *Iliad*. They constitute the oldest known literature.

By 2700 B.C., the Sumerians had established private and religious, as well as government, libraries. Among these libraries was one at Telloh which had a collection of over 30,000 tablets.

Sumer's culture passed to Babylonia in Lower Mesopotamia, a civilization which lasted until 689 B.C. and which produced Hammurabi and his notable code of laws. Both Sumerian and Babylonian characters represented syllables rather than letters.

The Babylonians used writing in business transactions and in recording noteworthy events; thus their books were devoted to government, law, history, and religion. It is believed that there were many libraries in the temples and palaces of Babylonia. While none of these survives, the tablets of one of the most important ones, the library of Borsippa, were copied in their entirety by the scribes of Assurbanipal, King of Assyria (d. ca. 626 B.C.), who preserved them in his library at Nineveh. These duplicates of the tablets from Borsippa are the chief sources of our knowledge of Babylonian life.

The Kingdom of Assyria, which also inherited its language and method of writing from Sumeria but modified the written characters until they resembled those of the Babylonians, existed at the same time as Babylonia. The most important library in Assyria was established at Nineveh by Assurbanipal. Tens of thousands of clay tablets were brought to this great royal library by the king's scribes, who traveled throughout Babylonia and Assyria to copy and translate the writings they found. The catalog of the Nineveh Library was a listing of the contents of each cubicle or alcove, painted or carved on the entrance, where the clay tablets were arranged according to subject or type. Each tablet had an identification tag.

Among the most famous surviving specimens of cuneiform writing are the Code of Hammurabi,[1] now in the Louvre Museum in Paris, and the Gilgamesh Epic, part of which is the Babylonian story of the Flood. The key to this system of writing is the Behistun Inscription, which is located on the side of a mountain in Iran (Persia). Written in three languages (Persian, Babylonian, and Elamite), it was deciphered by Sir Henry Rawlinson when he was consul at Baghdad in 1844.

The Egyptians

The civilization of ancient Egypt flourished simultaneously with the Sumerian, Babylonian, and Assyrian civilizations. The earliest known writings of the Egyptians date from ca. 3000 B.C. The writing material was the papyrus sheet,[2] and the instrument for writing was a brushlike pen made by fraying the edges of a reed.

Papyrus was far from satisfactory as a writing material, for there was constant danger of punching through it in the process of writing. Also, it was susceptible to damage from water and dampness, and when it was dry, it was very fragile and brittle. In spite of these limitations, however, papyrus was the accepted writing material throughout the ancient Mediterranean world and is known to have been used as late as A.D. 1022.

The form of the book in ancient Egypt was the roll, usually a little more than 12 inches high and about 20 feet long, made from papyrus sheets pasted end to end. The style of writing was hieroglyphic, a word derived from the Greek *hieros*, meaning "sacred," and *glyphein*, meaning "to carve." Hiero-

---

[1]The Code of Hammurabi was not written on clay but was carved on a diorite cylinder. Diorite is a granular, crystalline, igneous rock.

[2]To make a papyrus sheet, the marrow of papyrus stalks was cut into thin strips and laid flat, side by side, one layer crossways over the other. The two layers were treated with a gum solution, pressed, pounded, and smoothed until the surface was suitable for writing, and then sized to resist the ink.

glyphic writing, as old as the earliest Egyptian dynasty, was used as late as A.D. 394.

The Egyptians developed an alphabet of twenty-four consonants, but they did not adopt a completely alphabetic style of writing. They mixed pictographs, ideographs, and syllabic signs with their letters and developed a sketchy kind of writing for manuscripts, but the sacred carvings on their monuments were hieroglyphic.

Egyptian scribes were trained in the temple schools to learn to draw at least 700 different characters (hieroglyphs).

Writing was done in columns without spaces between words, without punctuation marks, and usually without titles; the text began at the extreme right and continued right to left, and Egyptian rolls included religious, moral, and political subjects. The Prisse Papyrus in the Bibliothèque Nationale in Paris—the oldest Egyptian book known—is believed to have been written before the end of the third millennium (2880) B.C.; it contains the proverbial sayings of Ptahhotep. The longest Egyptian manuscript in existence, more than 130 feet long, is the Harris Papyrus, a chronicle of the reign of Rameses II.

The key to hieroglyphic writing is the Rosetta Stone, which was discovered near the mouth of the Nile in 1799 by a young officer of Napoleon's expeditionary force in Egypt. In 1821 this flat slab of slate, bearing an inscription in three styles of writing—hieroglyphic, demotic (popular), and Greek—gave to Jean François Champollion, the French Egyptologist, the clue needed to decipher the Egyptian hieroglyphics. It is now preserved in the British Museum in London.

Little is known about Egyptian libraries. There may have been private and temple libraries as well as government archives. Records indicate that a library existed at Gizeh in the 2500s B.C., and it is known that Rameses II founded one at Thebes about 1250 B.C. Rolls were kept in clay jars or in metal cylinders with an identifying key word on the outside or on the end, or they were stacked on shelves.

Other Semitic Peoples

In addition to the Babylonians and the Assyrians, other Semitic peoples inhabited that part of the Near East known as the "Fertile Crescent."[3] Among them were the Phoenicians. Phoenicia was the name given in ancient times to a narrow strip of land about 100 miles long and 10 miles wide between Syria and the sea.

The Phoenicians were traders, and an important item in their wares was papyrus, which they imported from Egypt and exported to all of the

[3]The region bounded by the Taurus and the mountains of Armenia and Iran, the Persian Gulf, the Indian Ocean and the Red Sea, Egypt and the Mediterranean (*Cambridge Ancient History*, I, 182).

countries along the Mediterranean. It is believed that, wherever the Phoenicians took papyrus, they also took the Egyptian alphabet. History gives them major credit for spreading the knowledge and use of the alphabetic characters which had been developed in Egypt, Crete, and Syria and which form the basis of Greek and of all European writing. The Phoenicians were not a literary people; writing and books were to them merely means of keeping their numerous commercial accounts, and in time they developed a cursive, flowing style of writing and replaced the cumbersome clay tablets with papyrus sheets.

The Chinese

The art of writing was known in China as early as the third millennium B.C. Materials on which the Chinese wrote included bone, tortoiseshell, bamboo stalks, wooden tablets, silk, and linen, and their writing instruments were the stylus, the quill, and the brush pen, depending upon the particular writing material used. The style of writing involved the use of characters, mainly ideographic, and book forms were the tablet and the roll. Little is known about their libraries.

The Greeks

In the early part of the second millennium B.C., Crete became the center of a highly developed civilization which spread to the mainland of Greece and, before the end of the fifteenth century B.C., throughout the entire Aegean area. The Cretans developed the art of writing from a pictographic system to a cursive form, now called "Linear A," and by the fifteenth century B.C. to a system now called "Linear B." Many scholars believe that the language of Linear B tablets is an early form of Greek which was spoken by the Mycenaeans who occupied Knossos about 1460 B.C. and eventually overthrew the Minoan kingdom. After 1200 B.C. the Mycenaean world ceased to exist and the script disappeared. A period of illiteracy is believed to have existed from this time until the Greeks adopted the consonantal twenty-two-letter alphabet of the Phoenicians in the eighth century B.C.

Of the seventh and sixth centuries B.C., only fragments of literature remain, but these fragments show the beginnings of new forms of poetry, notably the elegy and the choral lyric, and the birth of philosophy and scientific research. The fables of Aesop date from this period.

The fifth century was the golden age of Greek civilization, a period characterized by the highest form of literary creativity: the tragedies of Sophocles, Aeschylus, and Euripides; the lyric poetry of Pindar; the histories of Thucydides and Herodotus; the comedies of Aristophanes; and the philosophy of Socrates. This period, also referred to as the "Classical Age," extended through the fourth and into the third centuries B.C., finding expression in the works of Plato and Aristotle, as well as in drama, poetry, oration, and music.

The Hellenistic period, dating from the death of Alexander in 323 B.C. to the Roman conquest, saw a continuation of the literary activities of the preceding century and a new emphasis on scientific knowledge (in the works of Euclid and Archimedes), on art, and on rhetoric.

In ancient Greece the materials used to receive writing were leaves or bark of trees, stone or bronze for inscriptions, and wax-coated wooden tablets for messages or notes. From the sixth century B.C., papyrus, which the Phoenicians brought from Egypt, was the usual writing material. In Hellenistic Greece, parchment and vellum came into use.[4]

The use of parchment and vellum made necessary the development of a new kind of writing instrument, the broad-pointed pen made from a reed or a quill. Parchment proved to be a better medium for writing than papyrus because it was smooth on both sides and was less likely to tear. Papyrus competed with it for three centuries, however, and only in the fourth century after Christ did parchment become dominant.

The forms of Greek books were the roll, the wax tablet, and the codex, in which the papyrus or parchment leaves of the manuscript were fastened together as in a modern book. The subject matter of Greek books included literature, history, science, mathematics, philosophy, religion, politics, and all of the other facets of their civilization and culture.

Early Greek writing resembled that of the Phoenicians, who had brought them the alphabet, but gradually the Greeks changed the form of the letters, added vowels, changed some consonants to vowels, developed lowercase letters, and began writing from left to right. The first books did not have spaces between words or punctuation marks of any kind. Change from one topic to another was indicated by a horizontal dividing stroke called the *paragraphos*, and if the roll had a title, it was located at the end. Before the conquest of Greece by the Romans, Greek grammarians had introduced some forms of punctuation.

There are evidences of private libraries in the fifth century B.C. The important library of Euripides was followed by other private libraries, notably that of Aristotle. In Hellenistic Greece there were private, governmental, and royal libraries.

The greatest libraries were in Alexandria in Egypt. The Museion, founded by Ptolemy I (323–285 B.C.), as an essential part of the academy of scholars under his patronage, is reported to have reached a total of 200,000 rolls within five years. It is said that foreigners were required, upon entering the Alexandria harbor, to surrender any books in their possession, later receiving copies in exchange for the originals. By the time of the Roman conquest, it contained 700,000 rolls, including manuscripts from all parts of

[4]Parchment was the skin of animals, principally that of the sheep or the calf, prepared for writing. Vellum, which is made from the skin of calves, is heavier than parchment and more expensive. It is probably the most beautiful and the most lasting material ever used for books.

the known world, written in Egyptian, Hebrew, Latin, and other languages. The second library, the Serapeum, founded by Ptolemy III (r. 246–221 B.C.), grew to more than 100,000 volumes. Although there is not complete agreement regarding the fate of the Alexandrian libraries, many historians date the destruction of the Museion from Julius Caesar's campaign in Alexandria in 47 B.C. and that of the Serapeum from the reign of Theodosius the Great (A.D. 379–395), whose edicts against paganism resulted in the destruction of many pagan temples.

Second in importance to the libraries at Alexandria was the one at Pergamum, founded by Eumenes II (197–159 B.C.). Pergamum became outstanding for patronage of arts and letters, and book production was so intense that an embargo was placed by the Egyptians on the exportation of papyrus, with the hope of discouraging the copying of books. This act led to the increased production of parchment for use as a writing material.

According to Plutarch, Calvisius, a friend of Caesar, charged that Antony gave to Cleopatra the entire library at Pergamum, which contained 200,000 distinct volumes.[5]

The Romans

Through commerce with Greece, Rome had early adopted the Greek alphabet, and Greek culture became important in Rome following the first Punic war (264–241 B.C.). By the time of the Roman conquest of Greece, the Romans were under the influence of the Greeks to the extent that they read and studied their literature, philosophy, and science, sent their sons to Athens to be educated, and at times spoke Greek. Thus, having adopted the Greek tradition in books, the Romans continued it. Latin literature began in the second century B.C..

The materials which the Romans used for writing were papyrus, parchment, vellum, wood tablets coated with wax, the stylus, the split-point reed, and the split-feather quill.

The Romans developed a style of handwriting unlike the ordinary cursive writing for use in literary works. Much like the Greek, it consisted largely of capital letters. By the end of the fourth century after Christ, another style, called "uncial script," which involved the use of large, somewhat rounded letters, was the standard book script and continued as such until the end of the eighth century.

The forms of the book in ancient Rome were the roll, the wax tablet, the diptych (two boards hinged together at one side with waxed surfaces on the inside for writing), and the codex.

Since the roll was relatively inconvenient to write upon and to read, it was superseded inevitably by the more usable form, the codex, which was

[5]*Plutarch's Lives of Illustrious Men*, corrected from the Greek and revised by A. H. Clough (Boston: Little, Brown & Company, 1930), p. 674.

used to some extent by the Greeks and which is known to have been in use among the Christians in the second century after Christ. From that time the codex generally was used for Christian works, even though the papyrus roll was continued in use for pagan works.

Roman books included all known fields of knowledge: law, science, mathematics, philosophy, politics, and religious and secular literature. The earliest known fragment of a manuscript book is the Papyrus Rylands, a tiny piece of a papyrus leaf of the Gospel according to St. John, dated (from the style of writing) in the first half of the second century after Christ. The Codex Vaticanus of the fourth century after Christ is the oldest extant manuscript of antiquity.

Roman generals brought back entire libraries from the campaigns in Greece, and these libraries, considered spoils of war, became their private collections.

Julius Caesar drew up plans for public libraries, but his plans were not carried out until the reign of Augustus, when Asinius Pollio established the first public library in Rome between 39 and 27 B.C. By the middle of the fourth century after Christ there were at least twenty-eight public libraries in Rome, and they were used by any person, slave or free, who could read.

The Ulpian Library, founded by Trajan—a scholarly collection housed in two structures, one for Latin and one for Greek works—was second in importance among ancient libraries only to those at Alexandria and Pergamum. In Roman libraries, Greek works were kept on one side of the library, and Latin works were placed on the other side; they were arranged according to subject on shelves or in bins. Except in rare cases, books had to be used in the reading rooms.

THE MIDDLE AGES

Monasteries

With the disintegration of the Western Roman Empire[6] came the decline of classical literature, and all libraries, including Christian collections, suffered at the hands of the barbarians. It was in the monasteries that literature was preserved and developed during the Middle Ages.

In the last half of the sixth century, under the leadership of Cassiodorus, the monastery became a center for all studies and for the preservation of all writings, both religious and secular. In southern Italy, Cassiodorus established the monastic community of Vivarium. He set up a great library which included manuscripts of the great literature of the past—Greek and Latin,

[6]Emperor Diocletian (A.D. 284–305) had divided the Roman Empire into Eastern and Western spheres. In 330, Constantine, then Emperor of both the East and the West, moved the capital from Rome to Constantinople. When the Western part of the Roman Empire fell in 476, the Eastern part (called the Byzantine Empire) was entering upon a period of progress which was to last a thousand years.

pagan and Christian—and established a scriptorium (writing room) for the copying of Christian and secular literature, thus assuring the preservation of much ancient writing which would otherwise have been lost during those troubled times.

After Cassiodorus, intellectual activity came to a standstill in Western Europe, except in Ireland. In the sixth century, numerous Irish monasteries came into existence in whose scriptoria a national script and a national art evolved and the first great development of manuscript books was begun—books which were characterized by superb calligraphy and illumination[7] and fine workmanship. Irish manuscript art reached its height in the *Book of Kells*, a manuscript of the Gospels, written in the eighth century and believed to be the most richly decorated manuscript ever produced in an Irish scriptorium.

Irish missionaries established monastic centers in Scotland, northern England, and continental Europe, including Lindisfarne in Northumbria, Luxeuil in France, and Bobbio in northern Italy.

During the eighth century, missionaries from the English church also established monasteries on the continent. Most notable of the English missionaries was St. Boniface, whose greatest monastery was at Fulda in Germany.

The reign of Charles the Great, or Charlemagne (768–814), marked by his efforts to raise the educational level of his subjects, brought to Western Europe a period of educational and cultural growth. Alcuin, master of the school at York in Northumbria, was chosen by Charlemagne to direct his educational program. In 782, as head of the Palace School in Aachen, Alcuin began the task of establishing educational centers and disseminating learning throughout the Frankish Empire. Scriptoria were established in monasteries and a carefully planned system of selecting, collecting, and copying religious and secular literature was begun. When Alcuin retired from the Palace School to the monastery of St. Martin at Tours, he made the monastery a center of learning, and the works copied in the scriptorium served as models for copyists for many generations. This revival of learning during the time of Charlemagne is called the "Carolingian Renaissance."

In the scriptoria of countless monasteries in continental Europe, Ireland, and England, as well as in the Byzantine Empire and the Moslem world, manuscripts were copied and recopied by the monks and by secular scribes who were often brought in for special tasks. These manuscripts tell us much of what we know of the ancient world. In these institutions were preserved the books of the Bible, the epics of Homer, the poetry of Virgil, the Greek dramas, and the scientific, legal, and philosophical works of the great minds of antiquity.

---

[7]Decorations of ornamental letters, scrolls, and miniatures—small paintings in color.

The chief materials used by the monks for writing were plain or dyed parchment or vellum, quill pens, and many kinds of colored inks. The forms of the book were the roll and the codex.

Early monastic libraries were small. Manuscripts were expensive: a large Bible was bought for 10 talents (about $10,000), and a missal was exchanged for a vineyard. A monastery library would have many copies of the Bible, the service books of the church, lives of the saints, early Christian writings, law, poetry, and some classical works.

Books were kept in chests or cupboards, or they were brought out and chained to desks for safety. Most of the reading was done standing up. In general, books were arranged by subject or kind—religious or secular, Greek or Latin. At first, catalogs were rough checklists. Later, a fuller and more precise description of the book and its contents was given in the listing.

Universities

From the fall of Rome to the twelfth century, education was in the hands of the monastery, and instruction was chiefly theological. Some instruction was given to sons of noblemen and, in some cases, to promising children of the poor. In trading centers there were schools to train clerks.

By the middle of the twelfth century, men were going to school to study Latin grammar and other basic subjects. The rise of cathedral schools, the study of Latin grammar, the appearance of writing in the vernacular (the language of the masses), and the increasingly favorable social and economic conditions gave rise to the universities.

The university of this period was a group of teachers organized as a kind of guild and empowered by either religious or civil government to grant degrees. The outstanding universities of the Middle Ages were the universities of Bologna, Paris, Prague, Heidelberg, Oxford, and Cambridge.

Book dealers *(stationarii)* and their scribes were an important part of every medieval university. They were appointed or controlled by the university to guarantee the authenticity of texts. They kept in stock correct editions of books used for instruction and rented them to the students. Dealers in parchment and vellum were licensed by the university. Since the universities constituted both the chief supply of books and the chief demand for them, they became the main centers of the book trade and of the publishing (copying) business. Book forms were the roll and the codex.

There was little need for libraries as long as the students could rent the texts they needed. However, as the number of students increased, the universities were forced to establish libraries. In time, books were given by individuals to the universities for the use of students.

Each college within a university had its own library. Arrangement and organization were similar to those of the larger monastery libraries except that books were divided according to the subject taught. They were arranged according to size or accession, sometimes on shelves rather than in chests. The more important books were still chained to the desks.

The Renaissance

In Italy during the fourteenth century, Petrarch and Boccaccio were laying the foundations for a new revival of learning. They searched medieval monasteries for old manuscripts, and many long-lost Latin works were recovered. The fall of Constantinople in 1453 aided the revival of learning by dispersing to Europe many works of ancient Greek and Latin literature. This period, the Renaissance (also called the "Age of Humanism"), was characterized by the unceasing search for missing ancient Greek and Latin works and the intense effort to read and understand them and to imitate their style and form. Florence became the center of the Italian Renaissance, and under the Medici saw the most brilliant development of culture since the Golden Age of Greece.

Printing with Movable Types

The zeal for learning which characterized the Renaissance brought a demand for books which could no longer be satisfied by handwritten copies. The need for a new and faster medium for transmitting knowledge was urgent. In Northern Europe by the middle of the fifteenth century, this medium had been developed: printing with movable types.

The success of printing depended upon a cheap substance on which to print, an ink which would adhere to type, a press which could apply heavy pressure over a large frame, and a general knowledge of metal technology.

By the second quarter of the fifteenth century, these needs had been met. Paper was a cheap and plentiful material on which to print. Discovered in China in the second century but used little by the Chinese, paper had traveled west along the trade routes. It was brought to Persia in the eighth century; it was displacing papyrus in Egypt in the ninth century; the Moslems used it in Spain in the eleventh and twelfth centuries; it was manufactured in southern Italy in 1270; and by the end of the fourteenth century, it was manufactured in France and Germany. The material used in making paper was linen rags. These rags were softened to a pulp and molded into sheets on a wooden frame. The sheets were drained, pressed and pressed again, hung to dry completely, and then sized to make them impervious to ink.

A suitable ink was developed by adapting the oil paints which the artists of the time were using.

The screw presses which were used for pressing olives and grapes and in binding manuscript books were used to apply pressure over a large frame.

The general knowledge of metal technology, which was essential to the success of printing, was borrowed from the goldsmiths and silversmiths. Carving of woodblocks for wood-block printing and engraving on metal by goldsmiths and silversmiths had reached a high degree of perfection. This knowledge was easily transferred to the process of making metal types.

Perhaps no event in human cultural history exceeds in importance the invention of printing with movable types.[8] Learning, which was formerly confined to monasteries or available only to the student, particularly the wealthy student, was now within reach of any person who wished to pursue it.

Movable word types made of clay originated in China but were used very little. It is to Johann Gutenberg, born in Mainz, Germany, about 1400, that credit is given for the development of printing with movable types. His creative genius combined the available materials and supplied the remaining essentials which made possible the printing of the famous 42-line Bible, commonly called the "Gutenberg Bible," between 1450 and 1456. This was the first book printed with movable types.

The printed book was new only in the way it was made; it was not new in appearance. The types were similar to manuscript writing. Space was left for illumination and rubrication, which were done by hand. The first illustrations were woodcuts. This similarity to the handwritten book continued for more than a hundred years.

The first printed works are called "incunabula" (from the Latin *incunabulum*, meaning "cradle"), indicating that printing was in its infancy. The subject matter of early printed books included the Bible and other religious works, textbooks, histories, travel books, and literature of all kinds.

During the last quarter of the fifteenth century, printing spread to all major cities of Europe. More than 20,000 different works and editions of this period survive. The first book printed in the English language was the *Recuyell of the Histories of Troy*, printed between 1474 and 1476 by William Caxton, who learned the art of printing in order to be able to print his own translation of this work.

The sixteenth century is notable for the rise of a large number of printing families, each with its own specialty. The House of Estienne, for example, printed Greek and Latin classics. The French printer Geoffroy Tory was responsible for introducing the accent, the apostrophe, and the cedilla into the French language; and in Venice, Aldus Manutius developed a system of punctuation marks. By 1700 the printed book had reached its

---

[8]The Babylonians and the Egyptians had used metal or wooden seals to print on soft clay or on wax; the Romans printed symbols on coins and stamped official documents with a carved seal; as early as the fifth and sixth centuries, the Chinese used carved seals to print short mottoes and charms. The full-page woodcut, printed from a wooden block on which the text and illustrations had been carved, was the next step in printing. By the ninth century, the Chinese produced a complete book printed in this manner. This kind of book was called a block book. The *Diamond Sutra*, a block book printed in A.D. 868, has survived. By the tenth century, printing in this manner was common in China. In Europe there were woodcut prints by the fourteenth century.

present form, with a title page, illustrations, a table of contents, and even a kind of index.

The invention of printing provided an unparalleled and effective impetus to the rebirth of learning. Precious manuscripts of the past, formerly copied one at a time by hand, could be reproduced in multiple copies and passed on to those who eagerly sought them. By making written works quickly available, the printing press also encouraged the production of new literature, and in this way it helped to create the "professional literati." The printing press and the increased dissemination of printed materials contributed significantly to the spread of the Reformation, and the stimulus which it gave to mapmaking hastened the era of discovery and exploration.

1500 TO 1900
Europe

Books after 1500 varied widely both in format and in content. There were many large volumes, many very small ones. Bookbindings ranged from ornate, bejewelled, gold-tooled leather to plain vellum and, eventually, paper. Printing types ceased to be copies of manuscript writing and assumed an identity all their own. In the sixteenth and seventeenth centuries periodicals were published; in the late seventeenth century newspapers appeared.

The contents of books during these centuries included religious and classical subjects, as well as science, superstition, travel, and romance.

The nineteenth century brought new mechanical developments, including stereotyping and the cylinder press. The first successful effort to set type mechanically and thus speed up printing was the invention of the linotype machine by Ottmar Mergenthaler in 1866. Other inventions followed.

In the nineteenth century there was much fine printing, especially in England. Wood came into use as a material for paper, books were bound with cloth, and copyright legislation was enacted.

In Europe, libraries flourished during the period from 1500 to 1900. Italy was outstanding for the number and quality of libraries in the sixteenth century. The Laurentian Library in Florence, the Ambrosian Library in Milan, and the Vatican Library in Rome were the most important.

In France, the Bibliothèque Nationale (which had its origins in the collections formed by the kings of France and dates from Francis I) was moved to Paris by Charles IX (1560–1574) and was greatly expanded and enlarged by Louis XIV (1643–1715).

Germany had the finest libraries of the nineteenth century. State libraries and university libraries were outstanding for size, content, and organization. There were also circulating libraries with catalogs, popular reading rooms, and children's collections.

The libraries of Oxford University, Cambridge University, and the British Museum (the National Library) were the most important in England.

The Austrian Royal Library, the royal library at Brussels, and the university libraries at Ghent and Louvain were other important libraries founded between 1500 and 1900.

America

Among the valued possessions which the early settlers brought to America or imported as necessities as soon as they were settled were books. Even though a printing press was in operation in Massachusetts as early as 1639, books had to be imported from England and the Continent for many generations. The earliest book known to have been printed in Colonial America was *The Bay Psalm Book*, printed in 1640.

Important private libraries of the early colonial period were those of Elder Brewster of the Plymouth Colony (about 400 different works), John Winthrop (over 1,000 volumes), and John Harvard (more than 300 volumes). Outstanding eighteenth-century libraries were those of Cotton Mather of Boston (between 3,000 and 4,000 volumes), James Logan of Philadelphia (more than 2,000 volumes), and William Byrd II of Virginia (3,600 titles).

In 1731, Benjamin Franklin and a group of his friends in Philadelphia established the first subscription library, a voluntary association of individuals who contributed to a common fund to be used for the purchase of books, which every member had the right to use but whose ownership was retained by the group. Subscription libraries (also called "social libraries") of several forms and names flourished for more than a century. Their collections, at first largely moral and theological in content, in time included history, biography, literature, travel, and scientific materials.

The first colleges in the American Colonies—Harvard (1638), William and Mary (1695), Yale (1700), and Princeton (1746)—began with, or were accompanied by, gifts of books. Although the Massachusetts General Court voted in 1636 to set aside £400 for the establishment of a "schoole or colledge," Harvard was not opened until 1638, when John Harvard bequeathed to the new college one-half of his estate and his entire library of 320 volumes. Yale College began with forty books. Each of the eleven clergymen who met in 1700 for the purpose of forming a college brought a number of books which he gave "for the founding of a college in this colony" (Connecticut). Most of the volumes in the early college libraries were books on theology, but there were also copies of the classics and of philosophical and literary works. By 1725 the Harvard Library had 3,000 books, and was the largest college library in the Colonies.

Before the Revolution nine colleges were formed in the Colonies, and by the time of the Civil War more than 500 colleges and twenty-one state universities had been established.

In the early college libraries there was no effort to make books available to students; rather, it seemed, books were protected from the students. This protective attitude continued throughout the nineteenth century, and as late as the 1850s, some college libraries were open only one hour every two weeks, others one hour twice a week, and a few one hour a day. In some libraries, attempts were made to classify books into three groups: memory, judgment, and imagination; or history, philosophy, and poetry. In others, books were arranged according to appearance, accession, or donor. The location symbol for books gave the physical location only and did not indicate the class to which the book belonged. Catalogs were printed lists, with little information about the books.

Following the Revolution, historical societies were formed to collect materials important in the history of the state or territory and a library was an essential part of each society. The Library of Congress was established in 1800 to serve the needs of the Congress,[9] and in the following decades state and territorial libraries were organized to collect and preserve publications of the state or territory and to serve the needs of the state or territorial government.

The first tax-supported town library in the United States was established in Peterborough, New Hampshire, in 1833. But it was not until 1854, when the Boston Public Library was opened to the public, that the free, public, tax-supported library became a part of American life.

By 1890 the public library had become an established institution in America, and the organization and development of libraries was given added impetus after that time by the state library commissions, which were established to aid in founding libraries and in improving and extending their services.

In 1876 the American Library Association was organized to promote libraries and librarianship throughout the United States. That same year Melvil Dewey published the first edition of his *Decimal Classification*, and eleven years later organized—at Columbia University—the first library school for the training of professional librarians, which he served as director.

MODERN ERA: THE TWENTIETH CENTURY

In the twentieth century, all libraries have been characterized by enormous growth in size and in importance. This growth has been made possible by increased local interest, by a recognition of the importance of libraries in the educational, social, and cultural life of a democratic society, and by the munificent gifts of private philanthropy. The greatest individual benefactor of libraries was Andrew Carnegie, whose gifts totaled over $41 million. Other benefactors include the Rockefeller and Ford Foundations and individual philanthropists who have opened their collections of rare books to the public. Examples of rare-book libraries are the Pierpont Morgan Library in New York City and the Folger Shakespeare Library in Washington, D.C.

[9]See pp. 42–43.

Each state has made legal provision for public library service, and the state library commission is authorized to aid in founding local, county, and multicounty libraries. The public library is now recognized as a valuable complement to the public school in educating for democratic living. In carrying out this function, it provides special services for children and young people; promotes educational, civic, and cultural programs; makes special materials available to the handicapped; supplements school library collections; and carries library materials to rural and isolated areas via the bookmobile.

The Library Services Act, enacted in 1956,[10] promoted the extension of public library services to rural areas only and included funds for materials and services, but not for buildings. This act, amended in 1964 and thereafter called the Library Services and Construction Act, extended federal aid to urban as well as to rural public libraries for materials, equipment, salaries, and also for construction. It provided funds for interlibrary cooperation, state institutional library service, and library services to the physically handicapped. During the ten-year period from 1964 to 1974, federal funds brought public library service to more than seventeen million people for the first time and 1,980 public library buildings were built, remodeled, or expanded.

In an effort to provide more and better library services, state library commissions are developing library systems. These are cooperative endeavors in which a number of local libraries join together and, under the direction of a separate board, form a system. The resources of all libraries in a system are available to member libraries. Access is by means of telephone, teletypewriter, photocopying, or interlibrary loan. In a network of public libraries, access to resources of member libraries is by means of computers, telefacsimile, and other forms of communications technology.

In 1965 Congress passed the first bill providing for federal aid to public education, the Elementary and Secondary Education Act of 1965, which included a five-year program of grants for the acquisition of library resources and other instructional materials, for setting up model school library programs, and for strengthening school library supervision. By 1973, the act had aided more than 60,000 public and private elementary and secondary schools.

The American academic library has entered upon a period of growth also—not only in terms of number of volumes but also in terms of its importance in the instructional program. The Higher Education Facilities Act of 1963 authorized federal grants and loans to institutions of higher education for the construction of various facilities, including libraries. By

---

[10]LSCA and ESEA have been extended, with some amendments, through 1983; HEA and the Higher Education and Facilities Act, through 1979.

1975, 605 separate library buildings were completed and 414 other buildings having a library were constructed.

The Higher Education Act of 1965 provided financial aid to libraries in institutions of higher education for the acquisition of materials, for the educational preparation of librarians, and for research projects and demonstrations relating to libraries, such as the use of computers in library operations. By 1975 almost $135 million dollars had been spent for library resources, providing about ten million volumes.

Emphasis on research has accelerated since World War II and has resulted in greatly expanded research facilities in universities, government agencies, large public library systems, and existing research libraries, and also in the development of an increasing number of independent private research libraries and centers. Examples of privately endowed research libraries are the John Crerar Library in Chicago, the Henry F. Huntington Library in San Marino, California, and the Linda Hall Library in Kansas City, Missouri.

Special libraries, which have as their sole purpose the providing of information resources vital to the parent organization's specialized clientele, are developments of the twentieth century. The special library may serve an industry, a business firm, a newspaper, a church, an art museum, or an association. Depending on the nature of the group it serves, the special library's collection may be varied, containing books, pamphlets, reports, periodical publications, translations, research and laboratory notebooks, patents, sheet music, audiovisual materials, microforms, etc.—whatever is required to meet the needs of its clientele.

The increasing importance and use of information is seen in the rapid development of facilities, called "information centers," for the purpose of identifying, collecting, analyzing, and disseminating information and in the new methods which are being used to speed up these processes. Special libraries and information centers have pioneered in the development and use of mechanization for the improvement of library service, especially in the field of information retrieval, using electronic computers and auxiliary mechanized equipment. As of 1978, there were approximately 14,000 special libraries and information centers in the United States and Canada.

The form of the book in the last quarter of the twentieth century is no longer limited to the printed form. Among its many new forms are film, filmstrip, transparency, programmed book, disk and tape recording, microform,[11] video tape, and sound track. The book assumes whatever form is most effective in recording, preserving, using, and disseminating information and knowledge.

[11]Microforms include microfilm, microfiche, and other forms of microphotography. (See pp. 132–135.)

In the expanding field of librarianship there are still the traditional and essential positions of library director, reference librarian, catalog librarian, acquisitions librarian, and circulation librarian. But there are many new positions: library consultant, medical cataloger, rare-book librarian, systems analyst, minority services librarian, editor of publications, etc. Librarianship is, as Francis Keppel, a former Commissioner of Education, said, "a profession whose future is unlimited."[12]

BIBLIOGRAPHY

Bieler, Ludwig. *Ireland, Harbinger of the Middle Ages.* London: Oxford University Press, 1963.

Bury, J. B., Cook, S. A., and Adcock, F. E. (eds.). *The Cambridge Ancient History.* 2d ed. Vol. I: *Egypt and Babylonia to 1580 B.C.* New York: Cambridge University Press, 1924.

Clark, Kenneth. *Civilisation: A Personal View.* New York: Harper & Row, Publishers, 1970.

Evans, Joan (ed.). *The Flowering of the Middle Ages.* New York: McGraw-Hill Book Company, 1966.

Gates, Jean Key. *Introduction to Librarianship* 2d ed., (The McGraw-Hill Series in Library Education). New York: McGraw-Hill Book Company, 1976.

Grant, Michael (ed.) *The Birth of Western Civilization: Greece and Rome.* New York: McGraw-Hill Book Company, 1964.

Herodotus. *The History of Herodotus.* Translated by George Rawlinson. New York: Tudor Publishing Company, 1941.

Hessel, Alfred. *History of Libraries.* 2d ed. Translated by Reuben Peiss. New York: Scarecrow Press, 1955.

Hobson, Anthony. *Great Libraries.* New York: G. P. Putnam's Sons, 1970.

Knight, Douglas M., and Nourse, E. Shepley. *Libraries at Large: Tradition, Innovation, and the National Interest.* New York: R. R. Bowker Company, 1969.

Laistner, M. L. W. *Thought and Letters in Western Europe, A.D. 500 to 900.* Rev. ed. Ithaca, N.Y.: Cornell Paperbacks, Cornell University Press, 1957.

McMurtrie, Douglas C. *The Book: The Story of Printing and Bookmaking.* New York: Oxford University Press, 1943.

[12]Francis Keppel, "Libraries: Future Unlimited," *ALA Bulletin* LVIII (December, 1964), 994.

Piggott, Stuart (ed.). *The Dawn of Civilization*. New York: McGraw-Hill Book Company, 1961.

Plutarch's Lives of Illustrious Men. Corrected from the Greek and revised by A. H. Clough. Boston: Little, Brown & Company, 1930.

Rice, David Talbot (ed.). *Dawn of European Civilization*. New York: McGraw-Hill Book Company, 1966.

Shera, Jesse H. *Foundations of the Public Library: Origins of the Public Library Movement in New England from 1629–1855*. Chicago: The University of Chicago Press, 1949.

Thompson, James Westfall. *Ancient Libraries*. Berkeley: University of California Press, 1940.

———. *The Medieval Library*. New York: Hafner Publishing Company, 1957.

Tierney, Brian, and Painter, Sidney. *Western Europe in the Middle Ages 300–1475*. New York: Alfred A. Knopf, 1970.

Ver Steeg, Clarence L. *The Formative Years: 1607–1763* (The Making of America Series). New York: Hill and Wang, 1964.

CHAPTER TWO
THE PARTS OF THE BOOK

In order to understand and appreciate the importance, significance, and usefulness of each of the physical parts of a book, one needs only to recall the lack of aids to the reader in the early forms of the book.[1] Each of the parts of the book has been added because it contributes to the usefulness of the book.

PHYSICAL DIVISIONS OF THE BOOK

The physical divisions of the book can be grouped as follows: (1) the binding, (2) the preliminary pages, (3) the text, and (4) the auxiliary or reference material.

BINDING

The binding holds the leaves of the book together, protects them, and makes them easy to handle. It may be plain or decorated, and it may bear the author's name and the title. It has two important parts, the spine and the endpapers.

The spine is the binding edge of the book and carries the title or a brief form of it, the author's name, the publisher, and the call number if it is a library book.

The endpapers are pasted to the covers to make them stronger; they may carry useful information, such as tables, maps, graphs, and rules.

[1]See Chapter 1.

PRELIMINARY PAGES

The preliminary pages precede the body of the book and include the flyleaves, the half-title page, the frontispiece, the title page, the copyright page, the dedication, the preface, the table of contents, lists of illustrative material, and the introduction.

The flyleaves are blank pages next to the end papers; they are the first and last leaves in the book.

The half-title page precedes the title page and serves as protection for it; it gives the brief title of the book and the series title if the book belongs to a series.[2]

The frontispiece is an illustration relating to the subject matter of the book; it precedes the title page.

The title page is the first important printed page in the book; it includes the following items:

1   Title; that is, the name of the work
2   Subtitle, a descriptive phrase which clarifies or explains the main title
3   Author's name and, usually, facts concerning his or her status, such as academic position, academic degrees, or the titles of other works by the same author
4   Name of the editor, if there is one
5   Name of the illustrator or translator, if there is one
6   Name of the person who wrote the introduction, if other than the author
7   Edition,[3] if it is other than the first
8   Imprint, which includes the place of publication, the publisher, and the date of publication

The back (verso) of the title page gives the date of the copyright[4] and the names of the copyright owners.

[2]A series is a number of separate works issued successively and related to each other in subject, form, authorship, or publication.

[3]An edition is the total number of copies of a book or other publication printed from one set of type. A revised edition is a new edition in which the text of the original work has been changed or new material has been added. A revised edition will have a new copyright.

[4]Copyright is the exclusive right to publish, reproduce, and sell a literary or an artistic work. The new copyright law, which took effect January 1, 1978, provides that for works already under statutory protection (created before January 1, 1978) the copyright term is twenty-eight years, renewable for forty-seven years. For works created after January 1, 1978, the new law provides a term lasting for the author's life and an additional fifty years after the author's death. (See Public Law 94–553 for additional information about copyright. See also p. 28)

The dedication page follows the title page and bears the name or names of the person or persons to whom the author dedicates the book.

The preface introduces the author to the reader and gives his or her reasons for writing the book; it indicates those for whom the book is intended, acknowledges indebtedness for services and assistance, and explains the arrangement, symbols, and abbreviations used, as well as any special features.

The table of contents is a list of the chapters of the book with page numbers; it may be so detailed that it serves as an outline of the book.

The lists of illustrative material may include illustrations, maps, or tables.

The introduction describes the general subject matter and plan of the book.[5]

TEXT
The text is made up of the numbered chapters and constitutes the main body of the book.

AUXILIARY OR REFERENCE MATERIAL
The auxiliary or reference material follows the text and may include an appendix or appendixes, notes, a glossary, a bibliography, and one or more indexes.

An appendix contains material referred to, but not explained, in the text.

A bibliography may be a list of the books, articles, and other materials which the author has used in writing the book, or it may be a list of materials recommended for further reading.

The glossary is a section which lists and explains all technical or foreign words not explained in the body of the book.

All footnotes, if they are not placed at the bottom of each page, may be placed in a section for notes. This section may contain explanations of certain passages in the text.

An index is a list of the topics discussed in the text, arranged alphabetically with page references. An index may have subdivisions of the topics and cross references.

Not all books have all the parts which have been discussed in the preceding paragraphs, nor do the parts always follow the order given in this chapter.

---

[5]The introduction may be written by the author, by a person of importance who has encouraged the author to write the book, or by one who considers the book an important contribution. It may be an elaboration of the preface, or it may be the first chapter in the book.

CARE

Care in opening a book when it is new and careful handling of the book at all times will add to its years of usefulness and to the reader's enjoyment of it.

SUMMARY

Some of the parts of the book are useful from the standpoint of the book, such as the binding which holds it together. From the user's point of view, the binding is useful also because it usually gives brief information about the book which makes it easy to locate on the shelf.

By reading the preface and introduction, the researcher may be able to tell whether the book will be useful for a particular purpose. The table of contents will give the scope of the book and the items covered, and the reader can see whether or not the topic under study is included. The index also helps on this point, especially if it gives subdivisions of a topic as well as broad topics.

On the title page—and only on the title page—the user will find the correct bibliographical information about the book. One item, the copyright date, is found on the verso of the title page. If this page should be lost, it would be very difficult to establish and verify a book's identity (see p. 123).

Other parts of the book provide additional sources for study (the bibliography) or explain, clarify, or expand upon items in the text (the glossary, notes, maps, and illustrations). The habit of looking at these parts before beginning to read a book can be both useful and timesaving.

CHAPTER THREE
ACADEMIC LIBRARIES

L ibraries in institutions of higher learning—academic libraries—are as varied and distinctive as the institutions which they serve. There are the libraries in junior colleges and in four-year colleges, and there are the central libraries in the universities and the more specialized libraries in the colleges within the universities. In each kind of institution, the purposes, staff, buildings, program of services, equipment, and physical facilities of the library are determined by the extent and nature of the curriculum, the size of the faculty and student body, the methods of instruction, the variety of graduate offerings, the needs of faculty and graduate students for advanced research materials, the amount of financial support, and whether or not the library is a part of an area, state, or regional cooperative system in which certain materials, equipment, and services may be shared.[1]

FUNCTION AND ORGANIZATION

Academic libraries differ from each other in many respects but they all have the same basic function, which is to aid the parent institution in carrying out its objectives. The library contributes to the realization of these objectives and supports the total program by acquiring and making available the books, materials, and services which are needed.

[1]See p. 18.

In carrying out its responsibility in the academic program effectively, the library[2] performs certain activities and offers certain services:

1   It selects books and materials. This selection is based upon study and evaluation of available materials and upon requests from the faculty and other members of the college community. It acquires these materials chiefly through purchases and gifts.

2   It prepares these materials for the use of students, faculty, and others who require them. This preparation includes:

    a   Stamping, pasting, typing, and lettering.

    b   Classifying materials according to the classification system in use by the library and assigning book numbers. (The classification number and the book number make the call number of a book.)

    c   Cataloging these materials; that is, providing descriptive information about each one as to author, title, facts of publication, number of pages, illustrative material, and other information; assigning subject headings and making cross references; and maintaining the card catalog and other necessary files.

3   It makes these materials easily accessible physically through open shelves or other efficient means and bibliographically through catalogs, bibliographies, indexes, and thesauri.[3]

4   It circulates materials from the general collection and from the reserve collection. (Reserve materials are those in which class assignments have been made; they are kept together in one place and administered under special rules and regulations.)

5   It gives reference service, answering questions and preparing bibliographies and reading lists.

6   It borrows and lends materials on interlibrary loan. Many college and university libraries participate in interinstitutional cooperative systems to strengthen and improve library resources and services. Under this cooperative arrangement, certain materials and services of each participating library are made available to all member libraries. Interlibrary loans are made from member libraries in the system and from libraries outside the cooperative system.

7   It gives instruction in the use of the library in formal courses which carry college credit, in lectures on specific topics and types of materials, and in aid to readers in the use of the card catalog, reference books, and other materials and facilities; it encourages students to develop lifelong habits of good reading, inquiry, and research.

8   It interprets library services to the administration, faculty, students, and community.

[2]"The library" refers to the professional staff and the personnel under its direction.

[3]A thesaurus (*plural*, thesauri) is a detailed list of subject headings.

9 It supplements and continues classroom instruction.

10 It provides adequate and comfortable physical facilities for study, including carrels for private study and such aids as typing facilities and photocopying devices which are operated by users or by the library staff.[4]

11 It may make bibliographical searches by computer; this is referred to as a "computer-assisted reference search," or as an "automated reference service." (See pp. 135–136 for a discussion of this subject.)

12 It administers the total library program, including the budget, the organization and supervision of the various library activities, the maintenance of the building and equipment, and the public relations activities.

In most libraries, these activities are divided into departments such as the acquisitions department, the cataloging department, the circulation department, and the reference department, all of which are under the administrative head of the library. These departments may be subdivided according to specific activities, such as technical processes, or according to specific materials, such as audiovisual and other nonbook materials; they may be combined; and they may be given different names. Many academic libraries have departmental branches in the respective departments, such as a collection of materials in the Humanities Division. Others, especially university libraries, are organized departmentally according to subject areas, such as the Education Library or the Engineering Library, each with its own staff, collection, catalog, and services. In this type of organization, materials in each departmental catalog are also entered in the main catalog of the university library. Academic libraries may have other special departments or divisions, such as the rare-book room, the periodicals department, the government documents room, the curriculum laboratory, and so on.

Whatever the nature of the administrative organization of the library, varying as it does according to the size and purpose of the institution, the size of the staff, the nature and adequacy of the physical facilities, and other

---

[4]The new copyright law established the conditions under which photocopies or reproductions of copyrighted works may be made. One specified condition is that the photocopy or reproduction is not to be "used for any purpose other than private study, scholarship, or research." If a user makes a request for or uses a photocopy or reproduction for any other purpose, that user may be liable for copyright infringement. Libraries are required by law to place a notice to this effect on photocopying machines, at places where orders for copies are accepted by libraries, and on all printed forms supplied by libraries for ordering copies. Other conditions of copyright are found in Section 107 and Section 108 of PL 94-553. The librarian will be able to explain the user's responsibility as well as the library's responsibilities in the matter of photocopying.

factors, its aim is to serve efficiently the participants in the instructional program.[5]

KINDS OF MATERIALS PROVIDED

The quantity and diversity of library materials will vary according to the size, purpose, and the program of the college, but in most college libraries materials will include:

1   Reference books of a general nature and reference books in the subject fields, with emphasis upon the subject areas included in the instructional program. These reference books include dictionaries, encyclopedias, indexes, yearbooks, handbooks, atlases, gazetteers, bibliographies, and some reference histories like the *Cambridge Ancient History* and the *Cambridge History of American Literature.*
2   A collection of books containing:
    a   Books which relate to and supplement each curriculum offered, such as history, education, and foreign languages, including those books which cover the entire field and those which relate to the specific courses offered in that field.
    b   Important general books not relating to a specific subject area, and important books in subject fields not included in the college curriculums.
    c   Books for voluntary and recreational reading.
3   Periodicals and newspapers—current issues, bound volumes, and in some libraries, those on microfilm, microcards, and microfiche.
4   Pamphlets and clippings.
5   Audiovisual materials, which include pictures, motion picture films, slides, filmstrips, music, phonograph records, tape and wire recordings, maps, globes, videotapes, and cassettes.
6   Microfilm, microcards, microfiche, and other microforms.
7   Government publications.
8   Programmed materials.
9   Archival materials pertaining to the institution.
10 Equipment for the use of these materials, such as microreaders and listening and viewing equipment.

The academic library must support not only the traditional programs, but also such new programs as independent study, tutorial, honors and

[5]In some institutions, the library is a department of a larger learning resources division which has, in addition, a language laboratory, large-group and small-group facilities, classrooms, audiovisual department, and television studios.

seminar-type experiences, programs of study abroad, residence-hall libraries, year-round study, off-campus courses, and advanced research.

STAFF

The academic library is administered and staffed by professional librarians who have a broad, general education and the specializations which are required in each area of service offered by the library, such as specialties in the subject fields, in languages, in audiovisual and other nonbook materials, in guidance of readers, and in technology. They have an understanding of the educational philosophy and teaching methods of the institution and work with the faculty in selecting and evaluating materials to support the instructional program. They keep up with trends in higher education, curriculum development, methods of teaching, and new materials and new sources of materials. They may teach a course in their specialty and they may participate in team teaching.

TYPES OF ACADEMIC LIBRARIES

Each kind of academic library—the junior college, the college, and the university—in addition to the characteristics which it shares with all other academic libraries, serves certain purposes and has certain features peculiarly its own which grow out of the particular character and scope of the institution of which it is a part.

JUNIOR COLLEGE LIBRARY

The public junior college (often called a "community college") is designed to meet the needs of the high school graduate who does not choose to go to a four-year college but must have additional education and training to prepare for a vocation, to update occupational skills, or to acquire new skills. It also provides for the needs of the student who will continue formal education at a four-year institution.

The junior college library must provide the materials and services to support each of the programs offered—general education, vocational, technical, semiprofessional, and adult education—and to serve the needs of the widely different students who enroll in these courses and the faculty members who teach them. The junior college library also provides cultural activities for the entire community and often serves as a center for community affairs.

COLLEGE LIBRARY

The name "college" is given to any institution of higher learning that is not divided into separate schools and faculties, that offers a four-year curriculum leading to a bachelor's degree in arts and sciences, and that requires for admission graduation from an accredited secondary school or its equivalent. The name, however, does not indicate the wide variation among colleges in purposes, programs, and size. There are liberal arts colleges, colleges for the preparation of teachers, technical colleges, professional colleges, agricultural colleges, and so on.

Since it is the basic function of the college library—as it is of all academic libraries—to serve to the fullest extent possible the program of the parent institution, each college library is in some ways different, but basically they all strive to meet the needs of all their patrons, from the professor engaged in advanced research to the freshman just entering college.

UNIVERSITY LIBRARY

A university has a liberal arts college; it offers a program of graduate study; usually it has two or more professional schools or faculties; and it is empowered to confer degrees in various fields of study.

The program of the university library ranges from the needs of the freshman student to those of the doctoral candidate engaged in scholarly research and the research professors. For the undergraduate students, the university library provides materials and services specifically designed to meet their requirements. The university library may be a central library which serves all students—undergraduate as well as graduate. Some universities provide a library for undergraduates in a separate building with all the materials, facilities, and services necessary to meet their basic needs. In other universities the undergraduate library is not in a separate building but occupies one or more floors of the central library; in still other universities, the central library makes special provisions for undergraduates, such as reading rooms with special reserve and reference collections. In any case, the central library and the undergraduate collection are open to all students.

RULES AND REGULATIONS

In order that all students will have an equal opportunity to use the library materials, certain rules and regulations are established in all libraries. These rules govern the kinds of materials which are circulated, the length of time they can be borrowed, the fines charged for overdue books, the use of library facilities—reading rooms, listening rooms, conference rooms, and other special areas—and the hours of service.

ORIENTATION VISIT

A part of the freshman orientation program in most colleges and universities is a visit to the library. In many libraries students are given a handbook which includes information about the physical arrangement of the library, the kinds of materials it provides, the classification system in use, the nature of the card catalog, the rules governing the use of the library, and the schedule of the hours the library is open.

The orientation visit to the library and the library handbook will have greater and more lasting meaning for the student who follows it with a personal survey of the library, fixing in mind the arrangement and purposes of the several rooms, taking stock of the kinds of reference books which are provided and their location, and learning firsthand the many kinds of books, materials, and services which are available.

SUMMARY

The size of the academic library varies from the small community college or college library with a centralized collection of 60,000 to 100,000 volumes and two professional librarians to the large university library with a central library of several hundred thousand volumes, a research library, an undergraduate library, departmental libraries, and learning laboratories and a staff large enough to operate all these facilities.

A student entering a given college or university can have an idea of the size of the library and the services it offers before arriving on the campus by reading the description of the library in the college or university catalog. This brief preacquaintance with the library can—to some extent—eliminate some of the fear the student may feel in approaching a library which differs in almost every way from his or her high school library. It will not explain how to use the library, but it will tell something of what to expect and will make the orientation lectures more meaningful.

PART TWO

THE ORGANIZATION AND ARRANGEMENT OF LIBRARY MATERIALS

CHAPTER FOUR
CLASSIFICATION

Classification is the systematic arrangement of objects, ideas, books, or other items which have like qualities or characteristics into groups or classes. The "like" characteristics may be size, color, type, form, content, or some other feature.

HISTORICAL DEVELOPMENT OF THE CLASSIFICATION OF BOOKS

Ever since there have been books, there has been the problem of organizing and arranging them so that they can be used easily and conveniently. Clay tablets were arranged on narrow shelves according to subject or type. Papyrus rolls were placed in clay jars or metal cylinders and labeled with a few key words describing their content. Parchment rolls were divided by author or title or by major subject or form groups and were placed in bins or on shelves. In medieval monasteries, manuscripts were classified as religious or secular, Latin or Greek; or they were divided according to subject matter, and all books on a subject were kept in the same chest. Books in medieval university libraries were divided according to the subjects taught and were arranged by size and accession on shelves or in chests. After the advent of printing, books were classified as manuscript books or printed books or as Latin, Greek, or Hebrew. In the college libraries of Colonial America, the organization was by location symbol—alcove 1, shelf A, book 6—with subject or language divisions within the alcoves.

Since the time of Aristotle, philosophers and nonphilosophers alike have been devising schemes for the classification of knowledge. In his *Advancement of Learning*, published in 1605, Sir Francis Bacon developed a plan for classifying knowledge into three large divisions: history, poetry, and philosophy; these large divisions were then subdivided into specific classes, with further subdivisions within the classes.

Thomas Jefferson adapted Bacon's plan for the classification of knowledge for use in his personal library at Monticello; and when he sold his library of 6,700 volumes to the United States to replace the Congressional Library which had been destroyed by the British in 1814,[1] his classification system went along with it and was used by the Library of Congress until 1864—and, with modifications, until the end of the nineteenth century, when the development of a new classification system was begun.[2]

When Melvil Dewey, a student library assistant at Amherst College in 1872, decided to organize the contents of the college library, his first step was to develop a classification system. After studying the schemes for classifying knowledge which had been devised by Aristotle, Bacon, Locke, and other philosophers, as well as some recently published library classification schemes, he decided to group books according to subject matter. Like his predecessors, Dewey divided all knowledge into main classes which he subdivided into specific classes and into further subdivisions within each class, always proceeding from the general to the specific.

PURPOSES AND CHARACTERISTICS OF LIBRARY CLASSIFICATION SYSTEMS

The chief purpose of a classification system in a library is to provide a basis for organizing books and materials so that they can be found quickly and easily by those persons who use the library; it is also a means of bringing books on the same subject together so that they can be used easily and conveniently. Since ease of use is the basic concern, library classification schemes place materials in those categories from which they are most likely to be called for by those who need them. In addition, such schemes provide for the form of the material as well as for the subject matter; for example, dictionaries, encyclopedias, handbooks, periodicals, and other book forms have particular notations.

The first step in classifying according to subject is to arrange all knowledge into major classes, bringing together into one class the parts

[1]The Library of Congress was housed in the Capitol building when it was burned by the British in 1814.
[2]See p. 42.

which are related and arranging the parts in some logical order, usually from the general to the particular. The several classes so formed constitute the classification scheme.

To be used, these classes must follow a definite and established plan so that they can be referred to again and again. Such a plan is called a "schedule." Classes and subdivisions within the classes are arranged in logical order.

Each class of the schedule and each subdivision within each class must be given a symbol so that all the books in which a particular subject is discussed can have the same notation and be kept together on the shelves of the library. The symbols used are letters of the alphabet, Arabic numerals, or a combination of these.

Library classification systems follow the generally accepted ideas of what major classes of knowledge are: philosophy, religion, science, history, language, literature, art, and so on. A general class number or letter is assigned to these large classes; for example, in the Dewey Decimal Classification System, 900 is General Geography and History; 973 is History of the United States; and 975 is History of the Southeastern United States. The smallest numbers belong to the largest subjects, and the longest numbers are assigned to the smallest or most specialized areas. Thus, 600 is Technology (Applied Sciences), 620 is Engineering and Allied Operations, 629.134 is Aircraft Components and General Techniques, and 629.1343537 is Fan-jet Engines.

In addition to a definite and established schedule of classes, there must be an index to all materials which are classified according to this schedule so that these materials can be found quickly and easily. The index to all the classified materials in a library is the card catalog,[3] which gives the location symbol for each publication. This location symbol is the call number, composed of the classification number and the book number (see pp. 41, 45).

Theoretically, a classification system should be so organized that material on any one subject can be found in only one place. Some subjects, however, have so many aspects, so many phases, so many contributing factors that it may not be possible to place all material relating to such a subject in only one class. For example, on a given subject, historical information may be found in the History class, economic data in Economics, sociological facts in Sociology, cultural information in Literature.

It is important to remember that even though books are classified according to the subject which is given the greatest emphasis, they may, to some extent, treat other subjects.

[3]The card catalog may be supplemented by other catalogs, files, bibliographies, and indexes.

DEWEY DECIMAL CLASSIFICATION SYSTEM[4]

HOW THE DEWEY DECIMAL SYSTEM WORKS

In the Dewey Decimal Classification System, Arabic numerals are used decimally to signify the various classes of subjects.

Dewey divided all knowledge, as represented by books and other materials, into nine classes which he numbered 100 to 900. Materials too general to belong to a specific group—encyclopedias, newspapers, magazines, and the like—he placed in a tenth class, which preceded the others as the 000 class. Each of the nine subject classes was organized as follows: the first of the ten divisions of every subject class was given to the general books in that subject; the remaining nine divisions were assigned to specific subject areas. The 800 class, Literature, illustrates this general-to-particular organization. Some numbers, such as 804, have been unassigned to allow for expansion.

800 CLASS, *Literature (general divisions)*[5]

800 Literature (Belles lettres)	806 Organizations
801 Philosophy and theory	807 Study and teaching
802 Miscellany about literature	808 Rhetoric (Composition) and collections
803 Dictionaries and encyclopedias	809 History, description, critical appraisal
804	
805 Serial publications	

810 CLASS, *American literature (specialized divisions)*

810 American literature in English	815 Speeches
811 Poetry	816 Letters
812 Drama	817 Satire and humor
813 Fiction	818 Miscellaneous writings
814 Essays	819

In 1876 Dewey's *Classification and Subject Index for Cataloging and Arranging the Books and Pamphlets of a Library* was published anonymously. Today a substantial majority of all libraries in the United States, including most school libraries and many public libraries, follow Dewey's

---

[4]Certain selections in this section have been reproduced from Edition 18 (1971) of *Dewey Decimal Classification and Relative Index* by permission of Forest Press Division, Lake Placid Club Education Foundation, owner of copyright. Each quoted selection is documented.

[5]Dewey, *op. cit.*, classes 800–809 and 810–819 from The Third Summary, Vol. 1, p. 459.

system.[6] It has been translated wholly or partly into scores of languages and is now in the eighteenth edition.

The Dewey Decimal Classification System provides for the form as well as for the subject matter of the materials to be classified. The standard subdivisions are:[7]

01 Philosophy theory
02 Miscellany
03 Dictionaries, encyclopedias, concordances
04 General special
05 Serial publications

06 Organizations
07 Study and teaching
08 Collections
09 Historical and geographical treatment

The classes of the Dewey Decimal System, as listed in the Second Summary: Divisions, follow.

SECOND SUMMARY: *The 100 divisions*[8]

000 Generalities
010 Bibliographies and catalogs
020 Library and information sciences
030 General encyclopedic works
040 (Unassigned)
050 General serial publications
060 General organizations and museology
070 Journalism, publishing, and newspapers
080 General collections
090 Manuscripts and book rarities

100 Philosophy and related disciplines
110 Metaphysics
120 Knowledge, cause, purpose, man

130 Popular and parapsychology, occultism
140 Specific philosophical viewpoints
150 Psychology
160 Logic
170 Ethics (Moral Philosophy)
180 Ancient, medieval, Oriental
190 Modern Western philosophy

200 Religion
210 Natural religion
220 Bible
230 Christian doctrinal theology
240 Christian moral and devotional
250 Local church and religious orders
260 Social and ecclesiastical theology

[6]*Ibid.*, p. 15.
[7]*Ibid.*, Standard subdivisions, The Third Summary, Vol. 1, p. 115.
[8]Dewey, *op. cit.*, The Second Summary, Vol. 1, p. 450.

270 History and geography of
church
280 Christian denominations
and sects
290 Other religions and
comparative

300 The social sciences
310 Statistics
320 Political science
330 Economics
340 Law
350 Public administration
360 Social pathology and
services
370 Education
380 Commerce
390 Customs and folklore

400 Language
410 Linguistics
420 English and Anglo-Saxon
languages
430 Germanic languages
German
440 Romance languages
French
450 Italian, Romanian,
Rhaeto-Romanic
460 Spanish and Portuguese
languages
470 Italic languages Latin
480 Hellenic Classical Greek
490 Other languages

500 Pure sciences
510 Mathematics
520 Astronomy and allied
sciences
530 Physics
540 Chemistry and allied
sciences
550 Sciences of earth and
other worlds

560 Paleontology
570 Life sciences
580 Botanical sciences
590 Zoological sciences

600 Technology (Applied
sciences)
610 Medical sciences
620 Engineering and allied
operations
630 Agriculture and related
640 Domestic arts and
sciences
650 Managerial services
660 Chemical and related
technologies
670 Manufactures
680 Miscellaneous
manufactures
690 Buildings

700 The arts
710 Civic and landscape art
720 Architecture
730 Plastic arts Sculpture
740 Drawing, decorative
and minor arts
750 Painting and paintings
760 Graphic arts Prints
770 Photography and
photographs
780 Music
790 Recreational and
performing arts

800 Literature (Belles lettres)
810 American literature in
English
820 English and Anglo-Saxon
literatures
830 Literatures of Germanic
languages
840 Literatures of Romance
languages

850 Italian, Romanian,
Rhaeto-Romanic

860 Spanish and Portuguese
literatures

870 Italic languages literatures
Latin

880 Hellenic languages
literatures

890 Literatures of other
languages

900 General geography and
history

910 General geography
travel

920 General biography and
genealogy

930 General history of ancient
world

940 General history of Europe

950 General history of Asia

960 General history of Africa

970 General history of North
America

980 General history of South
America

990 General history of other
areas

CALL NUMBER IN THE DEWEY DECIMAL SYSTEM

The class number and the book or author number make up the call number of a book. A book is classified according to the subject matter it covers and is given the number in the classification schedule which stands for that subject. The class number for ancient history is 930; since many books are written on that subject, and since all of them will be placed in the 930 class, it is necessary to have a means of distinguishing one book about ancient history from another book on the same subject. This distinction is made by assigning a *book number* (or author number) as well as a class number, using the initial of the author's last name plus Arabic numerals. Author numbers are usually taken from a table in which numerals, used decimally, are assigned to letters of the alphabet in the order of the alphabet, thus providing for alphabetical arrangement by author.[9] The title of a publication may be represented in the call number by the first letter of the title, excluding articles. This letter, in lower case, is placed immediately following the book number and serves to distinguish between books on the same subject written by the same author. Thus the call number for *Ancient History* by Allen Cable is 930 C11a, whereas the call number for *A Survey of Ancient History* by Allen Cable is 930 C11s.

The arrangement of books on the shelves follows the outline of the classification system. Books with the following call numbers will appear on the shelves in this order:

[9]Many libraries use a table which was developed by C. A. Cutter about the time Dewey was devising his classification system. This accounts for the fact that the author or book number is also referred to as the "Cutter number." Adaptations of this and other tables are in use. All are used for the purpose of arranging books within a class alphabetically by author.

338	338	338.095	338.1	338.1247	338.15
Am3a	H46s	B38m	Am3m	J13s	B21m

In some libraries, fiction and biography are not classified. Books of fiction may be given the designation F or Fic plus an author number and arranged alphabetically on the shelves by author. An example is Fic L488a for *Arrowsmith*, by Sinclair Lewis.

Biography, instead of being given a class number, may be marked B and arranged in alphabetical order by the subject of the biography—for example, B C56, a biography of Winston Churchill.

Special symbols are sometimes added to the call number to indicate that the book is shelved in a particular location or that it is a particular kind of material. For example, the symbol R or Ref with the call number signifies that the book is a reference book and that it is located in the reference collection. J or C above or below the call number might mean that the book is in the children's collection. H.H. or a similar symbol with the call number may indicate that the book is one of a memorial gift collection which is kept together in one place.[10]

LIBRARY OF CONGRESS CLASSIFICATION SYSTEM

The Library of Congress was founded in 1800 by and for the Congress of the United States. The earliest classification of books in the library—as in many other libraries of the time—was by size. When Congress purchased Thomas Jefferson's private library in 1815,[11] his classification system and catalog were included. Jefferson's classification, based on a modification of Francis Bacon's division of knowledge, was used by the Library of Congress until 1864, and with some adaptations until the end of the century.

In 1897, when the Library of Congress was moved from the Capitol building to its own building, the collections contained more than 1½ million items and the library was receiving more than 100,000 items each year. It was then that a new system of classification was begun, designed specifically for the Library of Congress.[12] This system of classification is still being developed; it is under constant study, classes are revised whenever it is necessary, and new classes are added.

The functions of the Library of Congress, the nature of its collections at that time and its expected acquisitions, and the ways the collections were to

[10]See also Figure 14.

[11]See p. 36.

[12]See L. E. La Montagne, *American Library Classification with Special Reference to the Library of Congress* (Hamden, Conn.: The Shoe String Press, 1961).

be used, determined the organization and the details of the classification system. Since the library was to serve the Congress, it was assumed that the holdings in the branches of knowledge most used by lawmakers—the social sciences—would be very large and diverse, and adequate provision had to be made for these fields. It was also expected that the library would receive, through purchase, national and international exchange, gifts, copyright deposit, and other sources, much material which university and other scholarly libraries would not ordinarily acquire. Therefore, because of the range and diversity of materials, a comprehensive and minute classification system was needed. The primary concern in devising the new system was that it should meet the requirements of Congress. In addition, it must provide for the organization of large amounts of diverse material, both scholarly and popular.

In spite of the fact that it was designed specifically for the Library of Congress collections and is particularly suited to very large collections, the Library of Congress Classification System is used widely in America and in other countries and, increasingly, academic and public libraries are adopting it.

HOW THE LIBRARY OF CONGRESS SYSTEM WORKS

The Library of Congress Classification System combines letters of the alphabet with Arabic numerals. Starting from a base of twenty-six letters, it offers, in theory, 676 subject divisions—compared with 100 divisions (from a base of 10) in the Dewey Decimal Classification System. At the present time, the letters *I, O, W, X,* and *Y* are not used but are reserved for further expansion.[13]

Unlike the Dewey Decimal Classification System, in which each class follows the same form, no two classes of the Library of Congress Classification System are identical in their divisions. Each subject class has been given individual treatment and has been developed according to the kind of material which the Library of Congress had or expected to acquire in that subject area. There are not any mnemonic or constant form numbers because not all classes have all forms of materials. Each class is, in fact, a separate classification. There are, however, some basic features which are characteristic of all classes.

1 The Library of Congress classification, like other classification systems, proceeds from general to particular. General materials, such as periodicals, dictionaries, directories, and so on, appear early in the class.

2 Main classes are marked with a single letter:
   P Language and literature

[13]See pp. 46–49 for a listing of the main classes and selected subdivisions.

3 Principal subdivisions are denoted by an added letter:
PN Literary history and collections (General)
PR English literature
PS American literature

4 Further subdivision is by use of Arabic numerals in ordinary sequence,
begining at 1 in each of the main divisions and going as high as 9999 in
some classes:[14]
PN 1 International periodicals
PN 2 American and English periodicals
PN 3 French periodicals
PN 86 History of criticism
PN 101 American and English authorship
PN 6413 Collections of Greek proverbs

5 Decimal letters and numbers may also be used in the class number to
subdivide a subject alphabetically by subject or form or by state or
country:
PN 6110 Special collections of poetry by subject and form
PN 6110.C7 Collections of college verse
PN 6110.H8 Humor
PN 6110.S6 Sonnets
PN 6511 Oriental proverbs
PN 6519.A7 Arabic
PN 6519.C5 Chinese
PN 6519.J3 Japanese
A class number may have both a decimal number and a decimal letter and
numeral:
PN 1993.5 History of motion pictures
PN 1993.5 A 1 General history of motion pictures
PN 1993.5 U65 History of motion pictures in Hollywood, California

6 The decimal letter and Arabic numeral combinations are used for persons
as subjects and authors as well as for subjects which are not persons:
PS 708.B7 William Bradford (author of the colonial period)
PS 595.C6 Collection of cowboy verse

In no other classification is alphabetical suborder within the class so
commonly used. But the alphabetical designation is not uniform in every
class; for example, C7 in another class is not college verse, and in another
class J3 is not Japanese.

Usually two letters and four figures are the limit of the length of a class
number, but the class number may be expanded by the use of decimal letters
and numbers, as has been noted.

[14]Numbering may not be continuous since one or more numbers are frequently left for
expansion.

Through the combination of letters and numerals, the Library of Congress classification provides for the most minute grouping of subjects. In general, because of the specificity of the class number, only a brief author number is used. It is taken from a modified Cutter table[15] and allows for alphabetical arrangement by author within a subject class. Author numbers, used decimally, may be made up of a letter and one numeral or a letter and two or three numerals.

CALL NUMBER IN THE LIBRARY OF CONGRESS SYSTEM

The Library of Congress classification numbers range in length from one letter and one numeral (P 1) to two letters, four numerals, one decimal number, and a decimal letter and number combination (PN 1993.5.U65). The classification proceeds from general to specific, and the longest numbers belong to the most specialized subjects.

All numbers before the decimal are read in ordinary sequence; all those following the decimal are read decimally. Therefore, PN1993.5.U65S4 will come before PN1994.C5. Class number and author number make the call number. The last letter-and-numeral combination is the author number. Examples of class numbers and author numbers are:

PN1	PN86	PN86	PN1993.5.U65	(class number)
A86	K57	K7	S4	(author number)
PN1994	PN6099	PN6099	PN6110.C7	(class number)
C5	L27	L4	T47	(author number)

Books are arranged on the shelf according to the classification and, within each class, alphabetically by author. The following examples show the way the call number looks on the spine of a book and how the books would be arranged on the shelf:

PN	PN	PN	PN	PN	PN	PN	PN
1	86	86	1993	1994	6099	6099	6110
A86	K57	K7	.5	C5	L27	L4	.C7
			U65S4				T47

Because of the length and the complexity of Library of Congress classification numbers, and because collections in which the system is used are generally quite large, it saves time to begin with the card catalog. In fact, as library collections increase and become more diversified and as all classification systems become more complicated, the necessity for using the card catalog increases. However, if library users will learn the letter designations and the range of numbers for the fields in which they are

[15]See p. 41.

working and will remember the general to specific arrangement, they can soon be able to go directly to those sections and browse. In all literatures, a large number of the subdivisions are devoted to individual authors; for example, the subclasses in English literature (PR) from PR1509 through PR6076 are devoted to individual authors from the beginning to about the middle of the twentieth century.

A listing of the classes and a selected list of subclasses from the Library of Congress Classification System follows.[16]

A   General Works.
     AE Encyclopedias (General)
     AI Indexes (General)
     AY Yearbooks. Almanacs. Directories

B   Philosophy. Psychology. Religion
     B   Philosophy (General)
     BF Psychology
     BL Religions. Mythology. Rationalism
     BM Judaism
     BP Islam. Bahaism. Theosophy, etc.
     BR Christianity (General)

C   Auxiliary sciences of history
     C   Auxiliary sciences of history (General)
     CB History of civilization and culture (General)
     CC Archaeology (General)
     CR Heraldry
     CT Biography

D   History: General and Old World
     D   History (General)
     DA Great Britain
     DC France
     DD Germany
     DE The Mediterranean region. Greco-Roman world
     DK Russia
     DS Asia
     DT Africa
     DU Oceania (South Seas)

E-F   History: America
     E   America (General)
          51–99 Indians. Indians of North America

[16]From the Library of Congress, Subject Cataloging Division, *LC Classification Outline*, 3d ed. (Washington, D.C.: U.S. Government Printing Office, 1975).

186–199 Colonial history
456–655 Civil War

F   1–975 United States local history
1001–1140 British America. Canada
1201–1392 Mexico
2201–2239 South America (General)

G   Geography, Anthropology. Recreation
G Geography (General)
GB Physical geography
GN Anthropology
GT Manners and customs (General)
GV Recreation

H   Social Sciences
H Social Sciences (General)
HB Economic theory
HC Economic history and conditions. National production
HG Finance
HJ Public finance
HM Sociology (General and theoretical)
HQ The family. Marriage. Woman
HX Socialism. Communism. Anarchism

J   Political science
JA Collections and general works
JC Political theory. Theory of the state
JF Constitutional History and Administration
General works. Comparative works
JK United States

K   Law
KF Law of the United States
KFA-KFW Law of individual states

L   Education
L Education (General)
LA History of education
LB Theory and practice of education
LH College and school magazines and papers

M   Music and books on music
M Music
ML Literature of music
MT Music instruction and study

N   Fine Arts
N Visual arts (General)

NA Architecture
ND Painting
NX Arts in general

P Language and literature
P Philology and linguistics (General)
PA Classical languages and literatures
PB Modern European Languages
PC Romance languages
PD Germanic languages
PG Slavic. Baltic. Albanian languages and literatures
PJ Oriental languages and literatures
PN Literary history and collections (General)
PQ Romance literatures
PR English literature
PS American literature
PT Germanic literatures
PZ Fiction and Juvenile literature

Q Science
Q Science (General)
QA Mathematics
QB Astronomy
QC Physics
QD Chemistry
QE Geology
QH Natural history
QK Botany
QL Zoology
QM Human anatomy
QP Physiology
QR Microbiology

R Medicine
R Medicine (General)
RB Pathology
RK Dentistry
RT Nursing

S Agriculture
S Agriculture (General)
SB Plant culture
SD Forestry
SF Animal culture
SK Hunting

T Technology
T Technology (General)

TA Engineering (General). Civil engineering (General)
TJ Mechanical engineering and machinery
TK Electrical engineering. Electronics. Nuclear engineering
TP Chemical technology
TS Manufactures
TX Home economics
U   Military Science
U   Military Science (General)
UA Armies: Organization, description, facilities, etc.
UD Infantry
UH Other services
V   Naval Science
V   Naval Science (General)
VA Navies: Organization, description, facilities, etc.
VD Naval seamen
VE Marines
VK Navigation. Merchant marine
Z   Bibliography and Library Science
         4–8 History of books and bookmaking
         40–115 Writing
         116–265 Printing
         662–1000 Libraries and library science
         1001–8999 Bibliography

The library user should keep in mind that some types of materials may be arranged by some method other than by subject, e.g., a numbering system indicating the order in which the library received the materials, 1, 2, 3, 4, etc. In depository libraries, government publications are arranged according to the Superintendent of Documents Classification System (see pp. 145–146). The Educational Documents number is used for materials in the ERIC files (see p. 185). The library user may need to look into several kinds of catalogs, indexes, or files in order to locate all the materials in the library on a given subject.

SUMMARY

An understanding of library classification systems in general, and of the ones used in a particular library, aids in using that library efficiently.

The user should remember that a class number does not embrace all the materials on a given subject, that books and other materials are classified according to the subject which is given the greatest emphasis, and that additional material on a subject may be found in some or in all the major classes of the classification system.

The classification system provides an introduction to the generally accepted divisions of knowledge, and the classification schedule is an illustration of the process of limiting a subject, of proceeding from a large general subject to smaller specialized areas of that subject.

An understanding of the classification system helps the user locate quickly the books and materials in any reference room or in an open-shelf library. It makes it easier to locate the general books—encyclopedias, periodical indexes, etc.—and to go directly to those sections of the library where books on given subjects are shelved.

CHAPTER FIVE
THE CARD CATALOG

O riginally, the word "catalog" meant a list or an enumeration. It has come to mean a systematic or methodical arrangement of items in alphabetical or other logical order, with the addition of brief descriptive information such as price, size, and color. A library catalog, then, is a systematic listing of the books and materials in a library with descriptive information about each one: author, title, edition, publisher, date, physical appearance, subject matter, special features, and location. It is an index to the library materials which it includes just as the index of a book is the key to the contents of that particular book.

Not all the materials in a library are listed in the main card catalog; for example, individual articles in periodicals are not listed in the card catalog but are located by using indexes;[1] periodicals may not be listed in the card catalog but may be in a special file called the "serials file";[2] government documents, pamphlets, clippings, audiovisual materials, microforms, and other special types of materials are generally not included in the main catalog but are located by means of bibliographies, lists, or special catalogs and files.[3]

The function of all these bibliographical tools—card catalog, indexes,

[1]See pp. 89–98.

[2]A serial is a publication issued in successive parts, usually at regular intervals, and, as a rule, intended to be continued indefinitely. Examples are periodicals, newspapers, yearbooks and annual reports, and so on.

[3]See Chapter 14, Nonbook Information Sources; Government Publications.

bibliographies, and special catalogs, lists, and files—is to make the total resources of the library fully and easily accessible to the users.

LIBRARY CATALOGS IN BOOK FORM AND OTHER FORMS

Some library catalogs are in the form of printed books. This form of catalog has always been in use to some extent and was at one time the generally accepted form. It was discarded because, as libraries grew in size, the printed catalog was soon out of date since cards for new materials could not be interfiled alphabetically. With the advent of photocopying devices, the card-punch or key-punch machine, and other mechanized devices, the book catalog is again being used in some libraries.

Book catalogs may be used for books, for nonbook materials, or for both. They may be divided—author-title or subject—or all entries may be filed in one alphabet. Some libraries use a book catalog for only one kind of material, e.g., periodicals.

In a book catalog which is reproduced photographically, the entries are simply photographic reproductions of printed or typed catalog cards. In computer-produced catalogs, the entries may consist of full information or of only two lines, depending upon the amount of information which was fed into the computer. The computer not only can make multiple copies of a catalog but can also interfile new entries in the old alphabet with each printing.

Advantages claimed for the book catalog are that it is easier to use; a large number of entries can be seen at a glance (e.g., all books by an author follow each other on one or more pages); duplicate copies of the catalog can be made and put in every room of the library; and so on. Disadvantages are the difficulties in keeping it up-to-date and the necessity for consulting more than one volume.

Some library catalogs are on microfilm or microfiche. In these kinds of catalogs, the catalog cards are microphotographically reproduced on film or film cards and must be read with the aid of a device which enlarges the image. (See pp. 132, 134.)

The library card catalog may be in machine-readable form with on-line access by means of a cathode-ray tube. (See pp. 135, 136.)

LIBRARY CATALOGS IN CARD FORM[4]

GENERAL CHARACTERISTICS
Most library card catalogs are on 3- by 5-inch cards, printed, typewritten, or mimeographed, and are filed alphabetically in trays. Other characteristics that library card catalogs have in common are:

[4]This discussion is concerned with the main card catalog.

1 They provide aids for the user: labels on the outside and guide cards on the inside of the trays.

2 They have many cross references: a *see* reference refers from a heading that *is not* used to one that *is* used; a *see also* reference refers from a heading that *is* used to another that *is also* used.

Education—Colonies	Literature—Anthologies
see	*see*
Education, Colonial	Anthologies
Education, Medieval	Education, Art
see also	*see*
Universities and colleges— Europe	Art—Study and teaching
Literature, Aesthetics	Literature—Evaluation
see also	*see*
Style, Literary	Books—Reviews

3 The catalog cards in all library catalogs give the same kinds of information about books: author, title, imprint, collation,[5] notes, subject headings, and other entries.[6] At the present time, catalog cards are available from several sources: Library of Congress, commercial firms, Ohio College Library Center (which prints cards by computer), and local processing centers. Therefore, catalog cards do not always look alike, but they give the same kinds of information. (See Figures 1 to 6.)

The card catalog is the reader's chief means of discovering and locating material in the library.

1 It points out the location of the books and other types of materials it includes by giving the location symbol or call number.

2 It lists in one place, in alphabetical order, all books by a particular author or on a particular subject, regardless of their locations in the library.

3 It provides several ways of finding materials, listing them by author, title, subject; by coauthor, translator, or illustrator, if there is one; and often by series, if the book belongs to a series.

There are several kinds of library catalogs, but few libraries have all of them.

1 A *subject* catalog is made up exclusively of subject cards.

2 An *author* catalog includes only the author or main entry cards.

[5]The collation indicates the number of volumes or pages, the number and kind of illustrations, and the size of the book.

[6]The same kind of information is given about audiovisual materials. (See pp. 130, 132.)

3 An *author and title* catalog is made up of these two kinds of entries.

4 A *title* catalog is made up of only title cards.

5 A *dictionary* catalog, which is the most common, has all cards—author, subject, title, and other entries—filed in one alphabet.

Large libraries may have three catalogs: author, subject, and title.

KINDS OF ENTRIES (CARDS) IN THE CARD CATALOG

An entry is a single listing of a publication. Most publications have at least two entries in the card catalog. (1) They are entered under author and (2) they are entered under title or subject. Most books other than fiction are listed under author and subject. In addition, books may be entered in the catalog under coauthor, editor, translator, and illustrator.

Author Card

The author card (Figure 1) is the basic card and is called the "main entry". In general, it gives the following information:

1 Author's full name, inverted, and usually date of his or her birth, and date of death if applicable

2 Title and the subtitle

3 Edition, if it is not the first

4 Coauthor, illustrator, translator

5 Imprint, which includes place of publication, publisher, and date of publication

6 Collation, which includes number of pages or volumes, illustrative material, and size of the book in centimeters

7 Series to which the book belongs, if it is one of a series

8 Subjects which are treated fully in the book

9 Full name and usually the dates of the coauthor, translator, editor, or illustrator

The catalog card may give other pertinent information about the book, such as a note concerning the contents or the pages on which bibliography is located. (See Figures 1, 2, 3, 5, and 6.)

The author or main entry for a publication may be:

1 An individual

2 An individual who edits rather than writes the work (Figure 2)

3 An institution or an organization (Figure 3)

   a U.S. Office of Education

   b American Academy of Political and Social Science

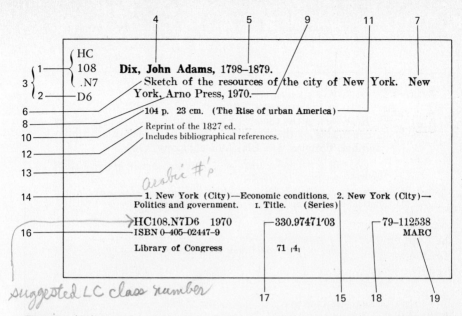

HC
108
.N7
D6

1
3 {
2

6
8
10
12
13

14

16

Dix, John Adams, 1798–1879.
Sketch of the resources of the city of New York. New
York, Arno Press, 1970.

104 p. 23 cm. (The Rise of urban America)

Reprint of the 1827 ed.
Includes bibliographical references.

arabic #'p

1. New York (City)—Economic conditions. 2. New York (City)—
Politics and government. I. Title. (Series)

HC108.N7D6   1970
ISBN 0-405-02447-9

Library of Congress

330.97471'03

71 [4]

79-112538
MARC

suggested LC class number

4 5 9 11 7

17 15 18 19

Figure 1 Author card or main entry: (1) Class number. (2) Author or book number. (3) Call number. (4) Author's name, inverted. (5) Author's dates. (6) Title of book. (7) Place of publication. (8) Publisher. (9) Date of publication. (10) Collation. (11) Series note. (12) Explanatory note. (13) Bibliographical note. (14) Subject heading (the subject treated fully). (15) Another subject treated. (16) Identifying number of book—International Standard Book Number. (17) Dewey Decimal class number. (18) Library of Congress catalog card number (to be used to order the card). (19) The information on this catalog card is available in machine-readable format (MARC means "Machine Readable Cataloging").

(14) + (15) Tracings

Figure 2 Editor as main entry.

817.44
Sc425   **Scott, Arthur Lincoln,** 1914–   *ed.*
Mark Twain, selected criticism. Edited with an introd.
Dallas, Southern Methodist University Press [1955]

xii, 289 p. 22 cm.

"Guide to Mark Twain bibliographies": p. 286–289. Bibliographical footnotes.

1. Clemens, Samuel Langhorne, 1835–1910. I. Title.

PS1331.S3   817.44   55—12080

Library of Congress   [62t1]

HG
221
.A46   **American economic association.**
         **Readings in the theory of income distribution, selected by
         a committee of the American economic association. Phila-
         delphia, Toronto, The Blakiston company, 1946.**

xvi, 718 p.   diagrs.   22 cm.   ₍Blakiston series of republished
articles on economics, vol. ɪɪɪ₎

"Classified bibliography of articles on national income and distribution, compiled by Frank E. Norton, jr." : p. 661–710.

1. Income.   ɪ. Norton, Frank E.   ɪɪ. Title.

HB601.A46   339.3   46—6895

Library of Congress   ₍62h³₎

Figure 3   Organization as author or main entry.

4 A committee
   a Committee on Higher Education
   b Committee on the Teaching of English
5 A title or a publication
   a The Bible: Old Testament
   b *The National Geographic Magazine*

Title Card

A title card (Figure 4) is made for a book which has a distinctive title. The
title is typed at the top of the card in black, above the author's name. If the
title of the book is used as the author or main entry, there will not be a title
card in the catalog for that book.

Subject Card

There is no set number of subject cards for each book; a subject card (Figure
5) is made for every subject which is discussed fully in the book. A subject
card differs from all other types of entries in that the subject is typed at the
top of the card in red letters, or in black capital letters. No other kind of
heading is typed in this manner. The remainder of the card is an exact
duplicate of the main entry card. *Try to limit to three.*
    Subject headings describe the contents of a book and therefore indicate
to the reader the usefulness of that book for a particular purpose. Subject
headings in a given card catalog are uniform and are used consistently
throughout the card catalog. The subject headings used for one book on a

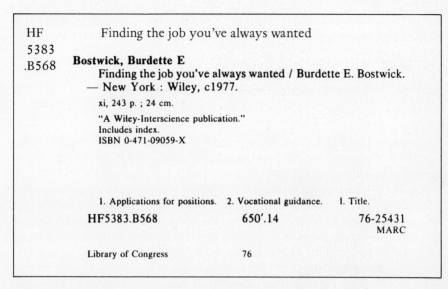

<table>
HF
5383
.B568

Finding the job you've always wanted

Bostwick, Burdette E
Finding the job you've always wanted / Burdette E. Bostwick.
— New York : Wiley, c1977.

xi, 243 p. ; 24 cm.

"A Wiley-Interscience publication."
Includes index.
ISBN 0-471-09059-X

1. Applications for positions.   2. Vocational guidance.   I. Title.

HF5383.B568   650'.14   76-25431
                                                              MARC

Library of Congress   76
</table>

Figure 4 Title card.

given subject will be used for *all* the books in the library which deal fully
with that same subject. A reader who is searching for material on "libraries,"
will find that all the books in the library in which this subject is discussed
fully are listed under the heading "libraries." They will be filed together in

Figure 5 Subject card.

```
K           LAW—PHILOSOPHY
237
.H3         Hart, Herbert Lionel Adolphus.
1976            The concept of law / by H. L. A.
            Hart. New York : Oxford University
            Press, 1961 [i.e. 1976]
                263 p. ; 21 cm.
                Preface: Mar. 1972.
                Bibliography: p. 257-258.
                Includes index.




                1. Jurisprudence.  2. Law--
            Philosophy.  I. Title

FTS     14 NOV 77     2808160   FHMMsl       76-379015
```

the catalog, alphabetically by author. A subject heading may be a word, a phrase, or a compound heading, inverted to emphasize the important words:

Literature

Learning and scholarship

Paintings, American

The subject heading may be determined by the form of the work (American poetry—Collections) or by location (Education—U.S.), or it may be a location subdivided by subject (France—Politics and government).

A knowledge and understanding of subject headings is essential to the efficient use of the catalog. If the student knows the author or title of a book, it is relatively simple, if the library has the book, to find it in the catalog. If, however, the assignment is to find material *on a subject*, the student must have an understanding of the nature of subject headings—how they are determined and how they are phrased—in order to know how to look for the topic in the card catalog. For example, if the topic is "social life in the United States," the student will look in the catalog for U.S.—Social life and customs. If the topic is "compulsory education," the student will look for Education, Compulsory.

Examples of other topics and their subject headings are:

Topic	Subject heading
The American novel	American fiction—History and criticism
The history of contemporary England	Great Britain—History—Twentieth century
The history of music	Music—History
The American Revolution	U.S.—History—Revolution
The government of France	France—Politics and government

Careful reading of the subject headings listed on each card will result in the discovery of related subjects under which material can be found (see Figures 1 to 6).

To ensure consistency in the subject headings used in the card catalog, most libraries follow the headings used by the Library of Congress and listed in the publication *Library of Congress Subject Headings* (8th ed., 1975).[7] This volume is useful also to researchers because (1) it tells them under what headings a given subject may be found in the card catalog; (2) it directs

[7]School libraries and some public libraries follow the *Sears List of Subject Headings* (11th ed.; New York: The H. W. Wilson Company, 1977), which is also based on the Library of Congress subject headings.

them to other headings under which material can be located and to other useful aspects of a subject; and (3) it breaks a subject down into its several parts, thus aiding the researchers in limiting their subjects. In some libraries, this volume is kept near the catalog to be used by the public. Other sources which may be useful in deciding how to phrase a subject or which give subdivisions of a subject are indexes to encyclopedias and to periodicals and thesauri.

An understanding of subject headings (called "descriptors" in the field of computers) is essential to the successful use of any mechanized information retrieval system as well as to the use of the traditional library card catalog. Information is fed into the computer under given subject headings (descriptors) and retrieved by using the *same* subject headings. In general, a list of descriptors is referred to as a "thesaurus." (See p. 136.)

Other Entries

If a book has a joint author or an important editor, illustrator, or translator, a card is made for each one. The name of such a person is typed at the top of the card, above the author's name, in black. These cards are called " added entries" (Figure 6). *Roman numerals*

When a title card and an author card are made for each of the stories, plays, or essays in an anthology, each card is called an "analytical entry," and the cards are referred to as "analytics" (Figure 7). Analytics may be made for each important subject discussed in a yearbook or for each biographee in a biographical work which includes several persons.

Figure 6 Joint author as added entry.

```
QA          McCluskey, Sidney Wilcox,   joint author
300    Crowder, Harold K
.C7         Topics in higher analysis ₍by₎ Harold K. Crowder ₍and₎
            S. W. McCuskey.  New York, Macmillan ₍1964₎

               xi, 545 p.  illus.  24 cm.  (A Series of advanced mathematics texts)
               Bibliography: p. 528–531.




               1. Mathematical analysis.      I. McCuskey, Sidney Wilcox, joint
               author. II. Title.

            QA300.C7                517                      64–12861

               Library of Congress         ₍14–1₎
```

added entries

```
914.03
E92f   Hunt, Richard.

          The sum of knowledge: universities
       and learning.  (In Evans, Joan, ed.
       The flowering of the middle ages.
       New York, 1965.  pp. 179-202.)
```

Figure 7   Analytical entry

ARRANGEMENT OF CARDS IN THE CATALOG

Rules for arranging cards in the catalog are adopted by each library. There are some variations, but in general these practices are followed:

1 Alphabetical arrangement is word-by-word rather than letter-by-letter. Examples are:

Word-by-word	*Letter-by-letter*
New Guinea	Newcomer
New Hampshire	Newfoundland
New Mexico	New Guinea
New Orleans	New Hampshire
New products	Newman, John
New thought	New Mexico
New York	New Orleans
Newcomer	Newport
Newfoundland	New products
Newman, John	News agencies
Newport	Newsboys
News agencies	News broadcasts
News broadcasts	Newsome, Mary
Newsboys	Newspapers
Newsome, Mary	New thought
Newspapers	Newton, Robert
Newton, Robert	New York

2 Definite and indefinite articles at the beginning of titles and other headings are ignored.

The academic library
Addition and subtraction
Airports
The All American team
An American Primer
American speech
An annual review

3 Abbreviations are filed as if they were spelled out: "St." is filed as "Saint," "Mr." is filed as "Mister," and so on.

Mr. Mack
Mrs. Miniver
Money and banking
Mt. Olympus
Mountie

St. Augustine
St. Joan
Saint Nicholas
School days
Spelling bee
Strong, John

4 Names beginning with "Mc" are arranged as if they were spelled "Mac."

McHenry, William
machines
McNeill, Richard
mammals

5 Numbers are filed as if they were spelled out.

1984
Odyssey World Atlas
100 Days
Origins

20th century
twins
200 gold pieces

6 Historical subheadings are filed in chronological order.

UNITED STATES—HISTORY—COLONIAL PERIOD
UNITED STATES—HISTORY—REVOLUTION
UNITED STATES—HISTORY—1789-1801
UNITED STATES—HISTORY—WAR OF 1812
UNITED STATES—HISTORY—1821-1823
UNITED STATES—HISTORY—CIVIL WAR

7 Books *by* persons are filed before books *about* them.

Shaw, George Bernard, 1856–1950 (as author)
SHAW, GEORGE BERNARD, 1856–1950 (as subject)

An example of the simplest form of arranging catalog cards in a dictionary catalog, following these practices, is as follows:

The a capella chorus book	Mr. Mack
Aaron, Daniel, editor	Monetary fund
The Abbey Theater	100 days
Ability	Only a rose
Ability—Testing	St. Augustine
Accent on teaching	School days
Accents on opera	Shaw, George Bernard,
Education—History	1856–1950 (as author)
Educational psychology	SHAW, GEORGE
Literature	BERNARD,
Literature—Dictionaries	1856–1950 (as subject)
Literature—History	U.S.—History—Colonial
McHenry, William	period
Machines	U.S.—History—Revolution
McNeill, Richard	U.S.—History—Civil War

SUMMARY

The catalog card stands for the book it describes. The main card gives the items which appear on the title page of the book. In addition, it describes the book as to size, number of pages, and kinds and amount of illustrative material. It indicates whether the book has a bibliography, and it may list the contents. It gives the subject or subjects treated in the book in the order of emphasis, the first subject heading listed being the one which is treated most completely. It is often possible to select or to reject a book by reading and understanding the catalog card.

PART THREE
GENERAL INFORMATION SOURCES

CHAPTER SIX
REFERENCE SOURCES

The word "reference" comes from the verb "refer," which means "to turn to for aid or information." Thus any person or thing referred to for these purposes is a reference. A source which is consulted for aid or information on a topic, a theme, an event, a person, a date, a place, or a word is a reference source. In this sense, the entire library is a reference collection, because it was selected, organized, and arranged for study and reference.

In any library there are some books which are consulted more frequently than others for certain kinds of information; there are books which, because of their organization and arrangement, lend themselves to quick and easy use; and there are other publications which were planned and written to be *referred to* for pieces of information rather than to be read completely. In most libraries these kinds of materials are brought together in one room or area and constitute what is called the "reference collection," the "reference room," or the "reference department." The use of these materials is restricted to the library. Questions may be answered completely from the resources in the reference collection, or a given source may only indicate other books and materials which the information seeker must consult to secure the full answer to a question. The other sources may be in another part of the library or in another library.

The reference collection, room, or department is not a separate library within itself but is only one of the parts of the total library that students will use in their search for material.

REFERENCE BOOKS

The term "reference book" has come to mean a specific kind of publication which has been planned and written to be consulted for items of information, rather than read throughout. It contains facts that have been brought together from many sources and organized for quick and easy use, either in an alphabetical or chronological arrangement or by the use of detailed indexes and numerous cross references.

Using reference books effectively and advantageously depends upon developing a facility in using them independently. An understanding of what reference books are, the kinds that are available, the types of questions each kind will answer, and how each book is arranged will help the user acquire this facility.

There are two types of reference books: (1) those which contain the needed information, such as dictionaries, encyclopedias, handbooks, biographical dictionaries, atlases, and gazetteers; and (2) those which tell the user where the information can be found, such as indexes and bibliographies.

These two types of reference books are of two classes, general and specialized; the latter are referred to in this text as "subject" reference materials.

GENERAL REFERENCE BOOKS

General reference books are those which are broad in scope, not limited to any single subject, but useful for all, or at least for many, subject areas. The kinds of general reference books, according to their form and the material which they include, are dictionaries, encyclopedias, indexes, yearbooks, handbooks, almanacs, biographical dictionaries, directories, atlases, gazetteers, and bibliographies.

Each kind of reference book is designed to do specific things. Theoretically, a given reference book does the specific things it is planned to do better than any other reference book can do them; thus it should be consulted *first* for the kind of information it covers, even though other reference books may include some of the same information. For example, a dictionary or an encyclopedia may give information about a geographical location; but a gazetteer, which is designed for the sole purpose of providing information about geographical names and places, is the first place to look for information concerning a geographical location.

The kinds of general reference books, the purposes they serve, and examples of each kind are listed below.

1 A dictionary provides information about words—meaning, derivation, spelling, pronunciation, syllabication, usage, and current status.

    a Webster's Third New International Dictionary of the English Language

    b Funk & Wagnalls New Standard Dictionary of the English Language

2 An encyclopedia is concerned with subjects. It gives an overview of a topic, including definition, description, background, and bibliographical references.

    a Encyclopedia Americana

    b Encyclopaedia Britannica

3 An index points out *where* information can be found. There are indexes to articles which appear in periodicals and there are indexes to articles, essays, poems, and other writings which appear in collected works.

    a Readers' Guide to Periodical Literature

    b Essay and General Literature Index

4 A yearbook, often called an annual, presents the events of the past year in brief, concise form.

    a Annual Review of Information Science and Technology

    b Britannica Book of the Year

5 A handbook, literally a small book which can be held conveniently in the hand, provides miscellaneous items of information. It may also be called a miscellany, a manual, or a companion. *compendium*

    a Brewer's Dictionary of Phrase and Fable

    b Famous First Facts

6 An almanac, originally a projection of the coming year—days, months, holidays, and weather forecasts—is the name now given to a collection of miscellaneous facts and statistical information.

    a The World Almanac and Book of Facts

    b Whitaker's Almanack

7 A biographical dictionary is a collection of sketches of varying lengths about the lives of individuals, arranged alphabetically by surname.

    a Who's Who

    b Dictionary of American Biography

8 A directory lists the names and addresses of persons, organizations, or institutions. It may provide other pertinent information, such as the purposes, the dues, and the officers of organizations.

    a Directory of Special Libraries and Information Centers

    b The Foundation Directory

9 An atlas is a volume of maps, plates, or charts, with or without explanatory text.

    a The Odyssey World Atlas

    b Goode's World Atlas

10 A gazetteer is a volume which provides geographical information and data about places. It does not define geographical terms.

    a   Columbia-Lippincott Gazetteer of the World
    b   Webster's New Geographical Dictionary

11 A bibliography is a list of books and other materials which have some relationship to each other. The materials listed are described as to author, title, publisher, price, and number of pages. In some bibliographies the materials are evaluated.

    a   Cumulative Book Index
    b   A World Bibliography of Bibliographies

12 Periodical publications—newspapers, magazines, and journals—provide news or material of current interest in a particular field or at a particular time.

SUBJECT REFERENCE BOOKS

Subject reference books are those in which the material is devoted to a specific subject area, such as literature, art, or history. In most subject fields, there are the same kinds of reference books as there are in the general field. Subject reference books are discussed in Chapters 15 to 23.

NONBOOK REFERENCE SOURCES

The many nonbook reference sources include pamphlets; clippings; audio, visual, and audiovisual materials; and microforms. These are discussed in Chapter 14.

DETERMINING THE USEFULNESS OF A REFERENCE SOURCE

The usefulness of a reference source for a particular purpose may be determined by answering some basic questions.

1 Are those who produced the subject matter—the editorial staff as listed on the title page or in the preliminary pages—specialists in their fields, as indicated by the academic position or by some other position which they hold?

2 Is the usefulness of the subject matter of the reference source under consideration affected by time, and if so, is this source out of date?

3 Does it attempt to cover more than can be handled in a work of this size?

4 Is it arranged for quick and easy use, with adequate index and cross references?

5 Does it provide text alone, or does it include illustrative material as well? Is the illustrative material well chosen?

6 Is the treatment of material, as stated in the preface,

    a   Simple for the nonspecialist?

    b Technical for the expert?
    c Scholarly for the scholar?
7 Is there any indication of bias in the treatment of material?
8 Does the source provide bibliographies, and are they up to date?
9 Is the print clear and legible?
10 What kinds of questions will it answer:
    a Factual?
    b Statistical?
    c Historical?
    d Current information?
11 What subject areas are emphasized:
    a Science?
    b Literature?
    c Social science?

CHOOSING A REFERENCE SOURCE

In choosing a reference source to answer a given question most conveniently and effectively, it is necessary to understand the nature of the question and to know the usefulness of the various reference sources in answering given questions. First analyze the question, then decide which reference source or sources provide the kinds of information it requires.

1 What kind of information is needed to answer the question:
    a A definition of terms?
    b Statistical information?
    c An exhaustive explanation or discussion?
    d A brief summary?
2 In what subject area does the question belong:
    a History, economics, geography?
    b An area touching several subject fields?
3 What factors affect the question:
    a Date?
    b Location?
    c Economic conditions?
    d Historical events?
4 What kind of reference source is needed:
    a A general dictionary for definitions?
    b A subject dictionary for specialized terminology?
    c An encyclopedia for an overview or a summary?
    d A periodical article for current information?
    e A yearbook for statistics?
    f A combination of several reference sources?

USING REFERENCE SOURCES

In order to use any reference source intelligently and efficiently, it is necessary to read the preliminary material which explains its distinguishing features. These features include:

1 Plan followed in the organization and presentation of material:
   a Alphabetical, word-by-word or letter-by-letter
   b Chronological
   c Topical, with detailed indexes giving page numbers or some other kind of numerical reference, such as the number of a poem in an anthology or the number of an entry
2 Symbols and abbreviations used in the text
3 Diacritical marking or the phonetic transcription used to indicate pronunciation
4 Kinds of indexes it has

In Chapters 7–14, each kind of general reference source will be discussed, with emphasis upon its usefulness for a particular purpose.

CHAPTER SEVEN
DICTIONARIES[1]

No one dictionary of a language is sufficient: each has its advantages and defects, and the more dictionaries there are, the richer the people.[2]

$\mathbf{T}$he earliest dictionaries were those in which the meanings of the words of one language were given in the words of another. Among the clay tablets recovered from the ruins of the Sumerian civilization are dictionaries which give Sumerian words with their Semitic-Assyrian meanings. The word "dictionarius," meaning "a collection of words," was first used in the English language about 1225 as the title of a collection of Latin terms. Several Latin-English dictionaries, as well as English and other modern language dictionaries, appeared before the end of the sixteenth century. In the seventeenth century, the name "dictionary" was gradually given to works explaining English words in English.

The first general and comprehensive dictionary of the English language was the *Universal Etymological English Dictionary* by Nathan Bailey,

[1]Dictionaries are included in Part Three, General Information Sources, because they cover words in all areas. See also Chapter 19, Language (Philology).

[2]Robert Lewis Collison, *Dictionaries of Foreign Languages* (New York: Hafner Publishing Company, 1955), p. xv.

published in 1721, which gave pronunciation and authority for pronunciation but only very brief definitions.

Comprehensive

Samuel Johnson's *Dictionary of the English Language*, which appeared in 1755, was designed to list all "good" words in the language with their "proper" meanings. There were many quotations to illustrate the uses of words, and these illustrative quotations have been repeated by makers of dictionaries since that time. Johnson's *Dictionary* was used in England and America until 1828, when it was superseded by Noah Webster's *American Dictionary of the English Language*. *Webster's Third New International Dictionary of the English Language*, which we use today, is the successor to the 1828 work.

The next important English dictionary was *A New English Dictionary on Historical Principles*. James Murray, as editor, began the task of publishing this scholarly ten-volume work in 1878. It was not completed until 1928. Reissued in 1933, with some corrections and additions, as *The Oxford English Dictionary*, it is an example of the application of the historical method to words, giving the origin, meaning, and historical development of English words in general use now or at any time since 1150.

15 volumes now

CHARACTERISTICS OF DICTIONARIES

Following the pattern established by the distinguished *American Dictionary of the English Language* and *The Oxford English Dictionary*, the dictionary today is, first of all, a collection of words in which each word is treated as to pronunciation, derivation, usage, meaning, and syllabication. In addition, the dictionary may give synonyms, antonyms, illustrative quotations, maps and plates, biographical facts, and geographical and historical information. Thus a dictionary may be a combination of word book, gazetteer, biographical dictionary, and encyclopedia.

Because most dictionaries are arranged alphabetically for convenience of reference, the word "dictionary" has come to mean any alphabetical arrangement of words or topics. A collection of items of information in a special subject area, arranged in alphabetical order, is often called a dictionary. There are dictionaries of psychology, education, philosophy, music, mathematics, and many other subjects, as well as dictionaries of dates, events, battles, plants, and sports. In fact, dictionaries of subjects and of things surpass in number those of words or language.

When only a few words, a small part of those belonging to a subject, are given, or when these words are only partially explained, the work is a "vocabulary." When it is a list of explanations of technical words and expressions in some particular subject or in a book, it is a "glossary."

DETERMINING THE USEFULNESS OF A DICTIONARY

The primary purpose of any dictionary is to answer questions about words. The usefulness of a dictionary is determined by the way in which it answers them. In order to use a dictionary most effectively, it is necessary to understand what it has to offer and in what manner the material is presented. The user must learn the kinds of dictionaries and the distinguishing characteristics of each kind, in order to decide which one or ones will answer a given question most completely and most satisfactorily.

In judging the usefulness of a dictionary, consider these points:

criteria

1 What part of the language does the dictionary include? Slang, dialect, obsolete, and technical words, as well as standard words?

2 What period of the language does it cover?

3 Is usage indicated?

4 Are plurals, verb tenses, and participles spelled?

5 Is syllabication indicated?

6 In what way is pronunciation shown? If diacritical marks are used, are they explained?

7 Are the definitions clear?

8 Are the definitions given in order of historical or current usage?

9 Is the etymology of the word given?

10 Is illustrative material—quotations, maps, pictures, charts—used? If so, is it adequate and appropriate?

11 Does it give synonyms and antonyms, and are they explained?

12 Are abbreviations and symbols explained?

13 Is encyclopedic information—that is, geographical, biographical, and historical facts and like material—included?

14 Is the dictionary easy to use?

15 How does it compare with other dictionaries on each of these points?

Many of the questions listed above will be answered as one uses the various dictionaries; other answers will be found in the preface and introduction of each dictionary. Making a dictionary is a very complicated and technical task, and any good dictionary will have a large staff of specialists as editors. These editors will explain the steps they have followed in making the dictionary. In order to use a dictionary most efficiently, the student must examine the table of contents, the preface, and the introductory material of the dictionary when consulting it for the first time.

KINDS OF DICTIONARIES

Dictionaries can be divided into (1) general word dictionaries, which provide over-all information such as pronunciation, derivation, syllabication, meaning, etc., about the words of a language; (2) dictionaries which have to do with certain aspects of language such as etymology, synonyms and antonyms, slang, colloquialisms, dialect, and usage; and (3) dictionaries which are concerned with a specific subject area.

General word dictionaries are (1) unabridged, that is, complete—covering all the words of a language; (2) abridged, that is, reduced in content but retaining the features of the unabridged work; or (3) general-purpose desk dictionaries which are not abridgments of a work but which include only a selection of the words of a language. They include both English language and foreign language dictionaries.

Dictionaries which are concerned with certain aspects of language are discussed in Chapter 19, Language (Philology).

Dictionaries in the subject fields are included in Chapters 16 to 23.

REPRESENTATIVE DICTIONARIES[3]

GENERAL WORD DICTIONARIES—UNABRIDGED

Craigie, William A., and others (eds). *A Dictionary of American English on Historical Principles.* Chicago: University of Chicago Press, 1938–1944. 4 vols. Follows the plan of *The Oxford English Dictionary;* continues the story of the English language into Colonial America and to the end of the nineteenth century; indicates which words originated in America; does not include slang and dialect.

Funk & Wagnalls New Standard Dictionary of the English Language. New York: Funk & Wagnalls Company, 1963 (original ed. 1913). Includes all live words of the language; gives current meaning first; provides pronunciation, spelling, etymology; includes many technical terms, illustrative quotations from newspapers and periodicals, and geographical entries; has an appendix of foreign words and phrases.

Murray, James Augustus Henry, and others (eds.). *The Oxford English Dictionary.* Being a corrected reissue, with an introduction, supplement, and bibliography, of *A New English Dictionary on Historical Principles.* London: Oxford University Press, 1933. 12 vols. and supplement. Presents the historical development of each word introduced into the English language since 1150, giving the date it was introduced and

[3]See also Chapter 19, Language (Philology).

the uses which have survived; each meaning illustrated with a quotation from literature; gives pronunciation, etymology, inflectional forms, and synonyms.

A Supplement to the Oxford English Dictionary. Edited by R. W. Burchfield. Oxford: Clarendon Press, 1972-. 4 vols. (In progress.) Vol. I: A–G, 1972; Vol. II: H–N, 1976. The four-volume *Supplement* will incorporate the material in the 1933 *Supplement* and will contain all words that came into common use in English during the publication of the *OED*, 1884–1928, and words which have come into use from 1928 to the present. It aims to record the vocabulary of the twentieth century, including literary, scientific, technical, legal and other professional terminology, and popular, colloquial, and modern slang expressions. Attention is given to American-English words in Vol. II of the *Supplement*. *2,000,000 quotations.*

The Random House Dictionary of the English Language. Editor-in-chief Jess Stein. New York: Random House, 1966. Based solely on current usage, aims to reflect the most up-to-date thinking and usage; emphasizes words and phrases recently in use in our language in all areas; includes "vogue words"; a wide variety of encyclopedic information makes it a general-purpose reference book.

Webster's New International Dictionary of the English Language. 2d ed. Springfield, Mass.: G. & C. Merriam Company, 1959. Gives definitions in historical sequence; features a pronouncing gazetteer and biographical information; includes slang, dialect, obsolete, and technical words; provides pronunciation, etymology, inflectional forms; indicates British pronunciation; includes foreign words and phrases in the main vocabulary. (Now out of print).)

Webster's Third New International Dictionary of the English Language. New, Springfield, Mass.: G. & C. Merriam Company, 1966. Covers current phonics vocabulary of standard written and spoken English; earliest meaning given first; single phrase definitions are based on examples of usage; proposes to be the "prime linguistic aid to interpreting the culture and civilization of today." *500,000 words — language as it is today*

Six Thousand Words: A Supplement to Webster's Third New International Dictionary. 1976.

GENERAL WORD DICTIONARIES—DESK TYPE

Abridged

Funk & Wagnalls Standard College Dictionary. New York: Funk & Wagnalls Company, 1977. Presents a well-selected vocabulary; gives adequate treatment of words; includes usage notes and synonym discriminations; gives population statistics and abbreviations in the appendix; is based on the unabridged *New Standard Dictionary*.

The Random House College Dictionary. Rev. ed. New York: Random House, Inc., 1975. Based on the unabridged *Random House Dictionary of the English Language*, it contains more than 150,000 entries, including many of the latest technical, general, and slang words, in one alphabet.

The Shorter Oxford English Dictionary on Historical Principles. 3d ed. Completely reset, with etymology revised by G. W. S. Friedrichsen and with revised addenda. Oxford: Clarendon Press, 1973. An authorized abridgment of *The Oxford English Dictionary*, has the features of that work; includes some new materials.

Webster's New Collegiate Dictionary. 8th ed. Springfield, Mass.: G. & C. Merriam Company, 1977. The latest in the Collegiate series and based on *Webster's Third New International Dictionary*, it aims to present the English language as it is spoken and written today, including general vocabulary and specialized terminology; contains more than 150,000 entries; offers 22,000 new words and meanings; gives examples of usage and pictorial illustrations, includes a number of appendixes.

Other Desk Dictionaries

The American Heritage Dictionary of the English Language. Edited by William Morris. Boston: Houghton Mifflin Company, 1978. First published in 1969, contains 155,000 entries, 4,000 of which have illustrations; includes new words from science, business, technology; gives clear definitions; includes guides to punctuation, grammar, and word histories; aims to record language and provide guidance in its use.

Funk & Wagnalls Standard Desk Dictionary. New York: Funk & Wagnalls Company, 1977. Based on the *Standard College Dictionary*, has more than 100,000 entries; includes usage notes, discriminated synonyms, idioms, gives encyclopedic information in the text.

Webster's New World Dictionary of the American Language. 2d College ed. Cleveland: William Collins & World Publishing Company, Inc., 1978. Includes scientific and technical terminology, slang and colloquial expressions, and encyclopedic information in one alphabetical list; this edition has many new words and new Americanisms.

FOREIGN LANGUAGE DICTIONARIES[4]—BILINGUAL

French

Harrap's New Standard French and English Dictionary. Ed. J. E. Mansion. Rev. and ed. by R. P. L. Ledésert and Margaret Ledésert. New York:

[4]For additional foreign language word dictionaries, see Robert L. Collison, *Dictionaries of Foreign Languages* (2d ed.; New York: Hafner Publishing Company, 1971).

Charles Scribner's Sons, 1973. *French-English*, 2 vols. Updated, with new entries and new definitions, offers many new words, including scientific and technical terms; gives examples of usage.

―――. *Supplement.* 3d ed. Compiled by R. P. L. Ledésert, with the assistance of P. H. Collen. London: Harrap, 1961.

New Cassell's French Dictionary: French-English, English-French. Completely revised by Denis Gerard and others. New York: Funk & Wagnalls Company, 1973. Includes new words in science, art, and commerce; pronunciation, translations of phrases and expressions; omits obsolete terms.

German

Betteridge, Harold T. (ed.) *Cassell's German Dictionary: German-English, English-German.* Rev. ed. New York: The Macmillan Company, 1977. Includes technical words, geographical and proper names; reflects current usage.

Greek

Liddell, H. G., and Scott, Robert (comps.) *Greek-English Lexicon.* 9th ed. rev. and augmented by Sir Henry Stuart Jones and others. Oxford: Oxford University Press, 1940. *Supplement.* Ed. by E. A. Barber. 1968. The standard English-Greek lexicon, updated by scholars in many countries, includes scientific and technical terms.

Italian

The Concise Cambridge Italian Dictionary. Compiled by Barbara Reynolds. Cambridge: Cambridge University Press, 1975. Based on the unabridged work which is in preparation, is up to date; Italian-English, English-Italian.

Rebora, Piero, and others (comps.). *Cassell's Italian-English, English-Italian Dictionary.* London: Cassell & Co., Ltd., 1967. A general dictionary of the Italian language; includes colloquialisms and new words, as well as obsolete words and words found in the classics.

Latin

Simpson, D. P. (ed.). *Cassell's New Latin Dictionary: Latin-English, English-Latin.* Completely revised. New York: Funk & Wagnalls Company, 1960. Includes new material; useful for beginning students.

Russian

Müller, Vladimir Karlovich (ed.) *English-Russian Dictionary.* 7th ed. New York: E. P. Dutton & Co., 1965. A general dictionary of the Russian spoken language; is modern and up to date.

Smirnitsky, Aleksandr Ivanovich. *Russian-English Dictionary.* Revised ed. New York: E. P. Dutton & Co., 1973. Gives general coverage; is up to date.

Spanish

Cuyás, Arturo (ed.). *Appleton's New Cuyás English-Spanish and Spanish-English Dictionary.* 5th revised and enlarged ed. New York: Appleton-Century-Crofts, 1972. 2 vols. Includes idioms and specialized terms; gives particular emphasis to usage in the United States and Latin America and to scientific and technological terms.

The New Revised Velázquez Spanish and English Dictionary, by Mariano de la Cadena. Newly revised by Ida Navarro Hinojosa and others. New York: Follett Publishing Company, 1967. Has thousands of new terms and idiomatic expressions of general use replacing those no longer in common usage; many encyclopedic features, such as geographical terms, abbreviations, proper names, monetary units.

SUMMARY

The primary purpose of all dictionaries is to give information about words. They differ in the ways this information is presented and in the amount of information given. As Collison said, "No one dictionary of a language is sufficient . . . the more dictionaries there are, the richer the people."[5]

Differences in dictionaries can be seen clearly in the following excerpts from three college dictionaries:

> **re·search** (ri-sûrch′, rē′sûrch) *n. Abbr.* **res.** Scholarly or scientific investigation or inquiry. —*v.* **researched, -searching, -searches.** —*intr.* To engage in or perform research. —*tr.* To study thoroughly. [Old French *recerche,* from *recercher,* to seek out, to search again : *re-,* again + *cerch(i)er,* to SEARCH.] —re·search′er *n.*

(a) *The American Heritage Dictionary of the English Language*

> **re-search** (rē sûrch′), *v.t., v.i.* to search again.
> **re·search** (ri sûrch′, rē′sûrch), *n.* **1.** systematic inquiry into a subject in order to discover or revise facts, theories, etc. **2.** a particular instance or piece of research. —*v.i.* **3.** to make researches. —*v.t.* **4.** to make an extensive investigation into. [< MF *recerch(er)* (v.) (to) seek, OF = *re-*RE- + *cercher* to SEARCH] —**re·search′a·ble,** *adj.* —**re·search′er, re·search′ist,** *n.* —**Syn. 1.** scrutiny, study. See **investigation. 4.** study, inquire, examine, scrutinize.

(b) *The Random House College Dictionary,* revised edition.

[5]Robert Lewis Collison, *Dictionary of Foreign Languages* (New York: Hafner Publishing Company, 1955), p. xv.

¹re·search \ri-'sərch, 're-ı\ *n* [MF *recerche,* fr. *recerchier* to investigate thoroughly, fr. OF, fr. *re-* + *cerchier* to search — more at SEARCH] **1 :** careful or diligent search **2 :** studious inquiry or examination; *esp* **:** investigation or experimentation aimed at the discovery and interpretation of facts, revision of accepted theories or laws in the light of new facts, or practical application of such new or revised theories or laws
²research *vt* **1 :** to search or investigate exhaustively <~ a problem> **2 :** to do research for <~ a book> ~ *vi* **:** to engage in research — **re·search·able** \-ə-bəl\ *adj* — **re·search·er** *n*
re·search·ist \-'sər-chəst, -ısər-\ *n* **:** one engaged in research

(c) *Webster's New Collegiate Dictionary*[6]

They differ in (1) the number of main entries for the word; (2) the method of indicating pronunciation; (3) punctuation and use of symbols; (4) order and extent of etymology; (5) number of meanings; (6) order of meanings (oldest first or current meaning first); (7) number of illustrative examples; (8) number and form of inflectional forms; (9) number of synonyms given; (10) abbreviations given.

[6](a) © 1969, 1970, 1971, 1973, 1975, 1976, 1978, Houghton Mifflin Company. Reprinted by permission from *The American Heritage Dictionary of the English Language.* (b) *The Random House College Dictionary,* Revised edition (New York: © 1975 by Random House). (c) By permission. From *Webster's New Collegiate Dictionary.* © 1977 by G. & C. Merriam Co., Publishers of the Merriam Webster dictionaries.

CHAPTER EIGHT
ENCYCLOPEDIAS

Of all the reference sources in any library, perhaps none is more revered than the encyclopedia—not without reason, for the encyclopedia has a long noble history and a heritage of high and lofty purpose. Since ancient times, it has been the aim and desire of encyclopedia makers to bring together into one work *all* human knowledge.

The first encyclopedias were works of a single author, designed to summarize the knowledge and thinking of the time. Aristotle produced a large number of encyclopedic treatises. The *Historia Naturalis* of Pliny the Elder, dating from A.D. 77, has been called the first encyclopedia because of its method of compilation. It is the oldest encyclopedia in existence.[1]

In general, the encyclopedias of the Middle Ages were devoted to one or another of the sciences; but Isadore, Bishop of Seville, attempted to cover every branch of knowledge in his work *The Etymologiae*, which is sometimes called the "Encyclopedia of the Middle Ages."

In 1630 the first modern encyclopedia (the first work to be given the title "encyclopedia") was published in Switzerland by Johann Heinrich Alsted. French contributions to encyclopedia making in the seventeenth century were the *Grand Dictionnaire* of Louis Moréli and the *Dictionnaire Historique et Critique* of Pierre Bayle.

English encyclopedias began with the two-volume *Cyclopaedia* of Ephraim Chambers in 1728, which became the model for all encyclopedias

---

[1]Translated into English by Philemon Holland in 1601, the *Historia Naturalis* was the standard authority for many centuries on the subjects it included: physics, geography, ethnology, physiology, zoology, botany, medical information, minerals, and art. Forty-three editions were published before 1536. It is now being published in the Loeb Classical Library in ten volumes.

that followed. Translated into French, it provided the working basis for *L'Encyclopédie du XVIIIe Siècle*, which was edited by Diderot and d'Alembert from 1751 to 1772, with all of the savants of France as members of the editorial staff.

The *Encyclopaedia Britannica* was first published in Edinburgh in 1771 in three volumes as a dictionary of the arts and sciences. The next edition, in ten volumes, added history and biography. Other and larger editions followed, including the scholarly ninth and eleventh editions. In 1920 it was acquired by Sears, Roebuck and Company, which gave it to the University of Chicago in 1943. It has been published since that time by Encyclopaedia Britannica, Inc., which was organized for that purpose.[2]

Encyclopedia editing in the United States began with the publication of the *Encyclopedia Americana* in 1829. The *New International Encyclopedia*, which introduced the journalistic style into encyclopedia writing, appeared in 1884.

By derivation, "encyclopedia" means "instruction in the circle of arts and sciences"—considered by the Greeks to be essential to a liberal education. Today, as it has from the beginning, the encyclopedia purports to be a repository of information on all branches of knowledge, presenting the basic general principles and the most essential details of each of the arts and sciences. It gives an overview of each subject, with definition, description, explanation, history, current status, statistics, and bibliography. It is organized, usually in alphabetical arrangement, for rapid and easy use. Most encyclopedias have an index volume. Use of the index enables the researcher to find small items in long articles.

A work of this magnitude calls for the most careful planning and editing and the most experienced writers. Reputable publishers of encyclopedias spare no expense in making their works authoritative and accurate. Because of the amount of work involved, it is not possible to revise an encyclopedia every year. Therefore, the chief means of keeping an encyclopedia up to date is by publishing an annual supplement or yearbook. (The yearbook does not bring the articles in the encyclopedia up to date; it presents topics of interest from the past year.) In addition to publishing yearbooks, the major encyclopedia publishers have programs called "continuous revision." This means that their editorial specialists are always at work on the subjects for which they are responsible and annually a certain number of articles are brought up to date. The new material in the revised articles, and new articles and additions, call for a new copyright. Therefore, each annual issue is a new edition; and instead of appearing as numbered editions, such as the tenth or the eleventh, most encyclopedias are identified by the year, such as the 1978 edition, the 1979 edition, and so on.

[2]See Herman Kogan, *The Great E B: the Story of the Encyclopaedia Britannica* (Chicago: The University of Chicago Press, 1958), pp. 257–258.

There are encyclopedias written for scholars and educated adults, there are some addressed to the general public, and there are others designed for young people and children. In each of these encyclopedias, the basic factual material may be the same; they differ in style of writing, in amount of additional material included, and in manner of presentation.[3]

CHOOSING AN ENCYCLOPEDIA

Encyclopedias are of two types:

1 The dictionary type treats subjects under many specific alphabetically arranged headings.
2 The monographic type presents its subjects under large headings with many subdivisions. The monographic encyclopedia may be arranged alphabetically or by broad topic. In either case, a detailed index and many cross references are needed to locate topics within long articles.

The usefulness of an encyclopedia depends upon the extent to which it fulfills its stated purposes. In order to decide which encyclopedia can most satisfactorily provide material on a given subject, the student should become acquainted with each encyclopedia as to:

1 Its authoritativeness
   a Is the publisher well known and reputable?
   b Is the work dependable, as evidenced by an editorial staff of specialists in each field of knowledge?
2 Its purpose
   a What is the editor attempting to do?
   b For whom is the work intended?
      (1) Scholars?
      (2) The general public?
      (3) Young people or children?
         (a) Is it planned to supplement a curriculum?
         (b) Is it written on grade or age levels?
3 Its scope
   a Is it comprehensive in coverage?
   b Is it limited to one branch of knowledge?

---

[3]The name "encyclopedia" is given also to a work designed to present information on all phases of one particular branch of knowledge. This kind of encyclopedia is usually referred to as a "subject encyclopedia" as distinguished from a "general encyclopedia," which covers all branches of knowledge. Subject encyclopedias are included in Chapters 16–23.

4 Its up-to-dateness
 a Is it a new work?
 b Is it based on an old edition of the same title or of another title?
 c Is the material in the articles, including statistics, maps, and charts, out of date?
 d Are the bibliographies adequate and up to date?
  (1) Are they references for further reading on the subject?
  (2) Are they the sources used in writing the articles?
  (3) Do they follow each article, or are they collected into a single volume?
5 Its strong points
 a What subject areas are emphasized?
 b What features are superior to those in other encyclopedias?
6 Its physical makeup
 a Does the physical makeup—that is, the size of the volumes, the kind of paper, the type, the headings, and the lettering on the spine—add to the ease of use?
 b Is the illustrative material adequate and suitable to the text?

Some of these questions can be answered by reading the preliminary pages in each encyclopedia; others will be answered as the student uses the several encyclopedias.

USING AN ENCYCLOPEDIA

In using an encyclopedia for the first time, it is important to read the preface carefully in order to determine:

1 Organization of the material
 a Are there short articles on small subjects?
 b Are there long articles on large, general subjects?
2 Arrangement
 a Is it alphabetical letter-by-letter or word-by-word?
 b Is it arranged by broad topics?
3 Kind of index provided
 a Is there a detailed index which points out small subjects within the long articles?
 b Is there an index to each volume or a single index for the entire work?
4 Kinds of aids to the reader
 a Is pronunciation indicated? If so, what system is followed?
 b Are cross references provided?
 c Are abbreviations and symbols explained?

SUMMARY

The encyclopedia gives an overview of a subject. Bibliographies which follow each article are sources for further study. The person who writes an encyclopedia article (and signs it) may have written more extensively on this subject—a book or a series of articles—and is therefore a source to consult. Signed articles are an important criterion in judging the quality of an encyclopedia.

The detailed index of the encyclopedia enables the researcher to locate all material on or related to a subject. Indexes are useful also for showing subdivisions of a topic, and they aid the researcher in limiting a topic for a research paper or they suggest headings under which to look for material in the card catalog, periodical indexes, and other sources.

Encyclopedias are written for different levels of readers and in some ways supplement each other.

The authoritativeness of an encyclopedia is of the greatest importance. Librarians base their choice of encyclopedias on reputable review sources[4] as well as on their own experience in using them.

The outstanding features of the general encyclopedias listed below are given in the annotations.

REPRESENTATIVE ENCYCLOPEDIAS

GENERAL ENCYCLOPEDIAS

Chambers's Encyclopaedia. 4th ed. revised. New York: Pergamon Press, 1967. 15 vols. The only major encyclopedia produced in England, presents the British and European viewpoints; covers entire range of human knowledge.

Collier's Encyclopedia. New York: Crowell-Collier Educational Corporation, 1978. 24 vols. Emphasizes modern subjects; includes material to supplement the curriculums of college and secondary school; aims to cover every major area of knowledge; Vol. 24 includes the index, bibliography, and study guide to twenty-three subjects.

The Encyclopedia Americana. New York: American Corporation, 1978. 30 vols. A scholarly work which includes short articles on small subjects, as well as long articles; aims to be comprehensive in scope and depth of material; articles have international orientation; extensive coverage of science and technology.

Encyclopaedia Britannica. 15th ed. Chicago: Encyclopaedia Britannica, Inc., 1977. 30 vols. First published in 1974, the 1977 printing brings the

[4]See the Preface.

Britannica up to date. The new *Britannica* is made up of three parts: the one-volume *Propaedia*, the nineteen-volume *Macropaedia*, and the ten-volume *Micropaedia*. The *Propaedia*, an outline of human knowledge, is a topical guide to the *Macropaedia*. In addition, it provides overviews of the various disciplines. The *Macropaedia* contains more than 4,000 comprehensive articles on thousands of subjects, ranging in length from 750 words to book-length articles. The *Micropaedia* is not a brief version of the *Macropaedia* but is an independent ready-reference source with more than 100,000 articles, ranging in length from a few lines to 750 words. It makes thousands of references to the long articles in the *Macropaedia* and to that extent is an index to it. The *Britannica* does not have a conventional index. The set has thousands of illustrations, many in color, and maps are included in the text rather than in a separate atlas.

The New Columbia Encyclopedia. Edited by William H. Harris and Judith S. Levey. New York: Columbia University Press, 1975. (Distributed by J. B. Lippincott Company.) The third edition of the *Columbia Encyclopedia*, it has about 7,000 short, concise articles covering recent events, persons, problems, and scientific and technological advances; is universal in coverage; includes numerous American writers; gives pronunciation; is a ready-reference source.

The Random House Encyclopedia. New York: Random House, Inc., 1977. 2 vols. Divided into two parts: the *Colorpedia* and the *Alphapedia*. The *Colorpedia* presents human knowledge in text and illustrations; 876 full-color spreads, each beginning with a lengthy essay which is keyed to the illustrations, transmits information by words and pictures as a unit. The *Alphapedia* is a traditional ready-reference volume with entries from one sentence to one column. Cross references are made to the *Colorpedia*. Other kinds of information include a bibliography, illustrations of national flags, and an eighty-page atlas by Rand McNally.

The World Book Encyclopedia. Chicago: Field Enterprises Educational Corporation, 1978. 22 vols. Written for grade and age levels; gives pronunciation and many cross references.

FOREIGN ENCYCLOPEDIAS

Bol'shaia Sovetskaia Entsiklopediia. 3d ed. Moscow: Sovetskaia Entsiklopediia, 1970–1977. 30 vols. and index. Sponsored by the Soviet government; is international in scope. English translation in progress. (See *Great Soviet Encyclopedia.*)

Brockhaus Enzyklopädie in zwanzig Bänden. 17. Völlig Neubearb. Aufl. des Grossen Brockhaus. Wiesbaden: Brockhaus, 1966–1975. Vol. 1–22. New edition of a standard work, has many new entries; provides long articles on countries and continents.

Brockhaus' Konversations-Lexikon. Der Grosse Brockhaus. Wiesbaden: F. A. Brockhaus, 1952–1958. 12 vols. A model for encyclopedias in other languages; has frequent revisions.

Enciclopedia Italiana di Scienze, Lettere ed Arti. Rome: Instituto della Enciclopedia Italiana, 1929–1937. 35 vols. Provides long articles, many bibliographies, illustrations of all kinds, biography; illustrations for travel and art subjects most notable. Vol. 36: *Indici.* 1939. Appendixes I–III cover 1938–1960. 10-year supplements.

Enciclopedia Universal Ilustrada Europeo-Americana. Barcelona: Epasa, 1905–1933. 70 vols., with 10-volume supplement and a 1-volume appendix. *Suplemento Anual.* 1934– . Comprehensive in coverage; gives Spanish and Spanish-American biography and geographical names.

Encyclopaedia Universalis. Paris: Encyclopaedia Universalis, Editeur, 1968–1974. 20 vols. Divided into three parts—the encyclopedia proper (Vols. 1–16), a one-volume summary of human knowledge with long and short articles (Vol. 17), and a thesaurus or analytical index to the encyclopedia (Vols. 18–20)—the *Encyclopaedia* gives long, comprehensive articles with bibliographies and references to related articles, biographical sketches of important figures, and many illustrations, maps, and charts.

Grand Larousse Encyclopédique. Paris: Librairie Larousse, 1960–1964. 10 vols. *Supplement I,* 1960–1968. 1969; *Supplement II,* 1968–1975. 1976. A dictionary as well as an encyclopedia; covers contemporary subjects; vocabulary from contemporary and classical authors; bibliography in each volume.

La Grande Encyclopédie. Paris: Librairie Larousse, 1971–76. 20 vols. Emphasizes twentieth century with special attention given to recent developments in the sciences; offers both long and short articles.

Great Soviet Encyclopedia: A Translation of the Third Edition. New York: Macmillan, Inc., 1974– . 30 vols. (In progress.) Vol. 18 completed 1978. A volume-by-volume translation of the third edition of *Bol'shaia Sovetskaia Entsiklopediia,* it is general in scope but concentrates on the Soviet Union; more than 100,000 articles give comprehensive treatment of Soviet life, including history, peoples, science, technology, economic life, military affairs, institutions, culture, and philosophy—past to present; includes current and past biography; English translation has been verified by the Russian editors. Issued five volumes a year, each five-volume issue has a cumulative index.

CHAPTER NINE
INDEXES

The word "index" comes from the Latin *indicare*, "to point out." Thus an index does not provide the information which is sought; it *indicates* where it can be found.

The index of a book points out the page or pages on which certain information can be found. The card catalog, which is made up of individual catalog cards, is an index to the materials in a library. Each catalog card indicates, by means of a call number, the location of a book or other kind of material. The catalog card may give the pages on which certain material can be found in a given book; for example, the card may have the notation, Bibliography: p. 210–212.

In addition to card catalogs and the indexes of books, three other kinds of indexes[1] are needed by the student who seeks material on a particular subject: (1) indexes to literature appearing in periodicals, (2) indexes to materials appearing in newspapers, and (3) indexes to literature appearing in collections or anthologies.

PERIODICALS

Periodicals appeared in the sixteenth century soon after the invention of printing. They began as pamphlets, grew into a series of related pamphlets,

[1]Libraries compile indexes to special collections or special types of materials to supplement the published indexes, e.g., archival materials, pamphlets, and some nonbook materials. Libraries also have thesauri to be used with certain abstract journals and to gain access to a data base.

and by the seventeenth century had taken on the characteristics of our modern periodicals. Throughout the eighteenth century, the word "periodical" was used chiefly as an adjective, e.g., "periodical literature," "periodical publication." By the end of that century the term was applied to all regularly issued publications except newspapers.

The word "journal" originally meant a daily newspaper or publication; it has since come to mean any publication which contains news or material of current interest in a particular field.

The historical meaning of the word "magazine," deriving from the Arabic *makhāzin*, was "storehouse." The first publication in English with the word "magazine" in the title was the *Gentlemen's Magazine*, founded in London in 1731 and planned as a kind of repository for news, essays, and other outstanding and interesting pieces of literature. The word "magazine" referred at first to content only; it now includes form also, and means a collection of miscellaneous stories, articles, essays, poems, and other material, including illustrations, appearing at regular intervals. Since magazines appear periodically—weekly, monthly, bimonthly, or quarterly—they are often referred to as periodicals. In fact, the words "periodical," "journal," and "magazine" are often used interchangeably.

The first magazine in America was published on February 13, 1741, when Andrew Bradford issued his *American Magazine, or a Monthly View of the Political State of the British Colonies*. Three days later, Benjamin Franklin published his *General Magazine, and Historical Chronicle, for All the British Plantations in America*. Both periodicals carried the publication date January 1741. Bradford's magazine lasted three months; Franklin's, six months. Several other magazines were published before 1775, but none survived the Revolution. Magazine publishing began again in 1779.[2]

From these meager beginnings, magazine publishing has grown until now more than 62,000 magazines, including general-interest magazines, trade journals, vocational and recreational periodicals, and professional journals, are published in the United States and Canada.[3] A certain number of issues, usually covering six months or a year, constitute a volume. Some magazines publish an index for each volume, but many others do not provide an index of any kind.

The search for information on any subject must include the examination of material which appears in periodical publications. The importance of this material cannot be overemphasized.

[2]Frank Luther Mott, *A History of American Magazines, 1741–1850* (Cambridge, Mass.: Harvard University Press, 1938), I, 2–8, and 24.

[3]*The Standard Periodical Directory* 5th ed. (New York: Oxbridge Publishing Company, 1977). See also *Ulrich's International Periodicals Directory*, 17th ed.

1 The most recent material on a subject, especially in the fields of science, technology, statistics, politics, and economics, will be found in a periodical.

2 Subjects too new, or even too obscure or too temporary, to be covered by books are treated in periodicals.

3 The trend of interest or opinion at any given period is traced easily in periodical literature, the current issues giving contemporary information and the old issues giving a record of past ideas, problems, and accomplishments.

4 Books, or parts of books, often appear first in periodicals, before they are published as separate volumes.

5 Professional literature is supplemented by periodicals which keep teachers, scientists, physicians, economists, lawyers, and members of other professions up to date.

Periodical literature can be divided into two classes, general and professional. A general periodical is not limited to one area of interest but touches many interest areas. Examples are *Harper's Magazine*, *Reader's Digest*, and *The New Yorker*. A professional periodical—usually called a "professional journal"—consists of articles on subjects of concern to a particular branch of knowledge, which are usually written by members of the profession. Examples are *College English*, *Journal of Geography*, *American Journal of Psychology*, and *American Historical Review*.

PERIODICAL INDEXES

It would not be possible to make use of the countless pieces of information in periodicals without the aid of indexes.[4] Even the indexes to each volume, when they are provided, may not bring to light all the important topics discussed. To aid the researcher in the use of periodicals, there are indexes to periodical literature. The function of an index to periodical literature is to point out the location of the topics discussed in the periodicals covered by the index. In carrying out this function, the index lists not only the large, general subjects treated, but also the various subdivisions of each subject; it

[4]In general, periodicals are listed in the main catalog with a cross reference to a special file—called the serials file or the periodicals file—for complete information on the library's holdings. This file shows the volumes in the library; it is not an index to individual articles in periodicals. See Chapters 16 to 23 for indexes to periodicals in the subject fields. Not all periodicals are covered by the indexes to periodical literature.

indicates where material can be found on each of the several aspects of a subject. For example, for purposes of indexing, the subject "Literature" includes the following subdivisions:[5]

Literature
Literature—Aesthetics
Literature—Criticism
Literature—Philosophy
Literature—Social aspects
Literature—Technique
Literature, Ancient
Literature, Medieval
Literature, Modern
Literature, Religious
Literature and art
Literature and history
Literature and music
Literature and philosophy
Literature and politics
Literature and science
Literature and social problems
Literature as a profession

This detailed breakdown of a subject and the innumerable cross references which are provided are valuable aids to the student who is trying to choose a subject for a research paper, or who is trying to narrow and restrict a chosen subject.

Each of the indexes to periodical literature covers a group of periodicals of a certain kind—general, scientific, educational, business, and so on. The list of periodicals covered is given in the front of each issue of the index. In general, one index does not include periodicals which have been covered by another index. Note the absence of duplication in the references given for the subject "Literature" in the excerpts from *Readers' Guide to Periodical Literature* (Figure 8), *Education Index* (Figure 9), *Social Sciences Index* (Figure 10), and *Humanities Index* (Figure 11), which cover approximately the same period of time. Note also the absence of duplication in the *see* and *see also* references.

It is necessary, therefore, to consult several indexes in order to locate

[5]Adapted from *Social Sciences and Humanities Index*, April, 1966–March, 1967 (New York: The H. W. Wilson Company, 1967), p. 322.

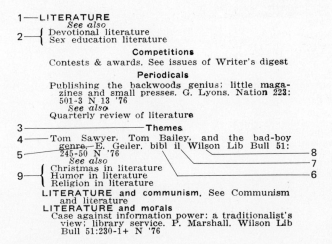

1——LITERATURE
    See also
2——{ Devotional literature
      Sex education literature
          Competitions
    Contests & awards. See issues of Writer's digest
          Periodicals
    Publishing the backwoods genius; little maga-
    zines and small presses. G. Lyons. Nation 223:
    501-3 N 13 '76
      See also
    Quarterly review of literature
3————————**Themes**
4————Tom Sawyer, Tom Bailey, and the bad-boy
    genre.—E. Geiler. bibl il Wilson Lib Bull 51:
5————245-50 N '76———————————8
      See also———————————7
    Christmas in literature
9——{ Humor in literature———————————6
      Religion in literature
    LITERATURE and communism. See Communism
    and literature
    LITERATURE and morals
    Case against information power: a traditionalist's
    view; library service. P. Marshall. Wilson Lib
    Bull 51:230-1+ N '76

Figure 8 Excerpt from *Readers' Guide to Periodical Literature:* (1) Subject. (2) *See also* references—topics under which to look for additional material on the subject "Literature." (3) Subdivision of the subject "Literature—Themes." (4) Title of article on the subject "Literature—Themes." (5) Author of the article. (6) The article has a bibliography. (7) The article is illustrated. (8) Journal in which the article appears—*Wilson Library Bulletin*, Volume 51, pages 245-250, November 1976. (9) *See also* references for the subdivision "Literature—Themes"; additional sources under which to look for material on this subject. (*Readers' Guide to Periodical Literature* Copyright © 1977 by The H. W. Wilson Company. Material reproduced by permission of the publisher.)

the several kinds of periodicals which can be of help in answering a question or in providing material for a research paper.

    The location of a periodical article is given by volume, page, and date of issue. In general, each article is listed under author and subject, with complete information under the author entry. Not all periodical indexes use both forms of listing. Some indexes include a title entry; others index by subject only.

    Some indexes point out only certain kinds of articles appearing in periodicals, such as book reviews (see Figure 12), bibliographies, or biographies.

    In using a periodical index, as in using any other reference book, it is necessary to understand the system of indexing, the kinds of articles covered, the arrangement of items, and the method of abbreviating.

DETERMINING THE USEFULNESS OF A PERIODICAL INDEX
The usefulness of a periodical index depends upon several factors:

1 Number and kind of periodicals covered by the index
2 Inclusion of books or parts of books and other materials

LITERATURE

Aims and objectives

Discussion on school literature teaching; symposium. bibl Soviet Educ 18:3-76 O '76

Curriculum

Theoretical problems of aesthetic education in the study of literature. G. M. Volovnikova. bibl Soviet Educ 18:50-67 O '76

Teaching

Research

Research roundup; ed. by A. J. Petroskey. See issues of English journal December 1976-

Nigeria

What? how? how much? thoughts on university English in Nigeria. A. Mohmed. Eng Lang Teach J 31:52-6 O '76

Russia

Discussion on school literature teaching; symposium. bibl Soviet Educ 18:3-76 O '76

Teaching methods

Discussion on school literature teaching; symposium. bibl Soviet Educ 18:3-76 O '76

Themes, motives

See also

Bible in literature
Dreams in literature
Grotesque in literature
Irony in literature
Negation in literature
Resurrection in literature
Space in literature
Symbolism in literature
Time in literature
Truth in literature

LITERATURE, Comparative

See also

Parallels, Literary

LITERATURE, Medieval

See also

French literature (Old French)

Figure 9 Excerpt from *Education Index*. (*Education Index* Copyright © 1977 by The H. W. Wilson Company. Material reproduced by permission of the publisher.)

Figure 10 Excerpt from *Social Sciences Index*. (*Social Sciences Index* Copyright © 1977 by The H. W. Wilson Company. Material reproduced by permission of the publisher.)

Literature

See also

Autobiography
Chinese literature
Economics literature
Indic literature
Romanticism
Vedic literature
Yugoslav literature

Themes, motifs

See also

City and town life in literature
Forests and forestry in literature
Social values in literature

Literature and society

Criticism and politics: the work of Raymond Williams. T. Eagleton. New Left R no95:3-23 Ja '76; Reply. A. Barnett. no99:47-64 S '76

LITERATURE
See also
Chapbooks
Communism and literature
Folk literature
Local color in literatue
Modernism (literature)
Moving pictures and literature
Naturalism in literature
Picaresque literature
Poetry readings
Religious literature
Russia—Literatures
Sentimentalism in literature
    also
Italian literature
Norwegian literature
Oriental literature

Aesthetics

Ideal presence and the non finito in eighteenth-century aesthetics. E. Rothstein. 18th Cent Stud 9:307-32 Spr '76
Journal of Stephen MacKenna. R. Rosenblatt. Sewanee R 84:133-42 Wint '76
See also
Naturalism in literature
Style, Literary
Sublime, The

Philosophy

About the nature of the word; tr. by S. Monas. O. E. Mandel'shtam. Arion ns2 no4:506-26 '75
Epic, tragedy, and catharsis L. Golden. Class Philol 71:77-85 Ja '76
For a pseudo theory; tr. by M. Ron. J. F. Lyotard. Yale Fr Stud no52:115-27 '75
Graphesis. M. R. Logan Yale Fr Stud no52:4-15 '75
Imagination and repetition in literature: a reassessment. E. Casey. Yale Fr Stud no52:249-67 '75

Psychology

E. E. Cummings as comic poet: the economy of the expenditure of Freud. J. Haule. Lit & Psychol 25 no4:175-80 '75
See also
Study and teaching
Colleges and universities—Foreign language departments
Literary research

Themes, motifs

Fictional encyclopedism and the cognitive value of literature. R. T. Swigger. Comp Lit Stud 12:351-66 D '75
Rags, garbage, and fantasy. R. M. Adams. Hudson R 29:54-68 Spr '76
Some key concepts in the poetry of Yvor Winters. G. E. Powell. Southern R 11:838-54 O '75
See also
Age in literature
Astrology in literature
Authority in literature
Body, Human, in literature
Body and soul in literature
Books and reading in literature
Chess in literature
Circus in literature
Cities and towns in literature
Conspiracies in literature
Curiosity in literature
Disillusionment in literature
Dogs in literature
Drinking in literature
Education in literature
Ethnic attitudes in literature
Expatriation in literature
Feminism in literature
Food in literature
Gems in literature
Heart in literature
Hypocrisy in literature
Interplanetary voyages
Justice in literature
Law in literature
Laziness in literature
Learning and scholarship in literature

Figure 11 Excerpt from *Humanities Index*. (*Humanities Index* Copyright © 1976 by The H. W. Wilson Company. Material reproduced by permission of the publisher.)

93

3 Period of time covered in the index—when it began and whether or not it is still being issued

4 Completeness of the indexing of any periodical—all articles or only certain types of articles

5 Fullness of the information given—author, title, volume, page, date—as well as information about bibliographies and illustrations

6 Method of indexing—by subject as well as by author and title

7 Frequency of issue—bimonthly, monthly, quarterly, less often

8 Ease of use

CHOOSING AND USING A PERIODICAL INDEX

In order to choose the right index for a particular problem, it is necessary to answer the following questions:

1 What is the nature of the question?
  a Does it concern a topic or a person too new to be discussed in books?
  b Is it a topic so limited in appeal that it does not receive treatment in a book?
  c Is it a topic which is treated in a book but about which more recent information is needed?
  d Is it a topic which would be clarified by the discussions in one or more periodicals?

2 In what area does the problem belong?
  a History
  b Literature
  c Education
  d General

3 Which of the periodical indexes covers the literature of the area in question?

4 What years are involved, and which indexes cover those years?

5 Is an article from a general periodical, an article from a professional journal, or an article from each kind required?

Some useful indexes to periodical literature are listed below. The outstanding features of each index are given with the bibliographical entry.

Biography Index. New York: The H. W. Wilson Company, 1946– . (Quarterly; cumulated annual volumes are replaced by three-year permanent volumes.) Gives birth and death dates and occupation or **profession** of each person listed; includes an index by profession; indexes biographical material in periodicals covered by the H. W. Wilson Company indexes and in current books of individual biography; international in

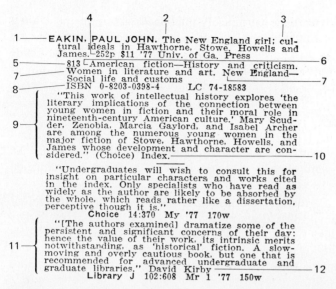

Figure 12 *Excerpt from Book Review Digest:* (1) Author of the book which is reviewed. (2) Title of book. (3) Subtitle of book. (4) Number of pages in book, price, year of publication, publisher. (5) Dewey Decimal Classification number. (6) Main subject dealt with in the book. (7) Other subjects treated in the book. (8) The book's identifying number—International Standard Book Number. (9) Quotation from the review which appeared in the journal *Choice*. (10) The book has an index. (11) Excerpt from the review which appeared in *Library Journal*, volume 102, page 608, March 1, 1977; this review has 150 words. (12) Review in *Library Journal* was written by David Kirby. (*Book Review Digest* Copyright © 1977 by The H. W. Wilson Company. Material reproduced by permission of the publisher.)

coverage, indicates nationality of persons who are not American; provides cumulative indexes which add to the ease of use.

Book Review Digest. New York: The H. W. Wilson Company, 1905– . (Monthly, except February and July; annual cumulations.) Indexes reviews of current books appearing in over seventy periodicals; gives author, title, pages, price, publisher, and descriptive note about each book included; gives citation for each review and may give excerpt. (See Figure 12.)

Book Review Index. Detroit: Gale Research Company, 1965– . (Bimonthly.) Indexes reviews appearing in more than 300 periodicals which include both adult and children's book reviewing media; excerpts are not given, only the source of the review. Suspended publication 1969–1971; resumed publication in 1972; and in 1973 began appearing bimonthly.

Catholic Periodical and Literature Index. New York: Catholic Library Association, 1930– . (Bimonthly.) An author and subject index to a selected list of Catholic periodicals published mainly in the United States, Canada, England, and Ireland; notes articles written from the Catholic point of view elsewhere. In July 1968, incorporated the *Guide to Catholic Literature;* includes an author-title-subject bibliography of books by Catholics or of interest to Catholics; formerly the *Catholic Periodical Index.*

Nineteenth Century Readers' Guide to Periodical Literature, 1890–1899. New York: The H. W. Wilson Company, 1944. 2 vols. Author and subject index to fifty-one leading periodicals published in the 1890s; records authorship of many articles which were originally published anonymously.

Poole's Index to Periodical Literature, 1802–1907. Boston: Houghton, Mifflin Company, 1891. (Reprinted 1938 by Peter Smith, New York.) Indexes by subject only about 470 English and American periodicals chiefly of a general nature; fiction, poems, and plays are indexed by first important word of title; includes book reviews; was the first of the periodical indexes.

Readers' Guide to Periodical Literature. New York: The H. W. Wilson Company, 1900– . (Semimonthly from September to June, monthly during July and August; two-year cumulations.) Indexes more than 180 periodicals of a general nature; follows closely the publication date of the periodicals with semimonthly issues; gives author and title of article, name, volume, and date of periodical, number of pages; illustrations, bibliography, maps; book reviews are in a separate section of the index.

Abridged Readers' Guide to Periodical Literature. New York: The H. W. Wilson Company, 1935– . (Monthly except June to August.) For schools and small public libraries; indexes by author and subject fifty-six periodicals of general interest; includes book reviews.

NEWSPAPERS

Newspapers developed from the seventeenth-century broadside, which was a single large page printed on one side only. These early newspapers were issued weekly or biweekly and were sometimes called "news-pamphlets" or "news-books."

"Corantos" was the name given to the periodical news-pamphlets issued between 1621 and 1641 to provide news of `foreign countries. The "diurnalls," or news-books, gave the domestic news during the years from 1641 to 1645.

The biweekly *Oxford Gazette* was the first newspaper in the modern sense to be published in England. It appeared in November 1665. A year later it was renamed the *London Gazette;*[6] it is still issued twice a week—not as a newspaper, however, but as a record of official matters.

The first newspaper published in America appeared in Boston in 1690 and was called *Publick Occurrences, Both Foreign and Domestick*; there was only one issue. The first newspaper to be published for a continuous period was the *Boston News-Letter*, which appeared in April 1704. The first daily newspaper in America was the *Pennsylvania Packet and General Advertiser*, established in Philadelphia in 1784. *The New York Times*, founded in 1851, was, from the very beginning, one of the world's outstanding newspapers. In the twentieth century there have been such developments as chains of newspapers, tabloids, and syndicated news services.

In addition to news events, the modern newspaper provides other features, such as illustrations; book reviews; articles on education, art, music, drama, and recreation; literary contributions; and biographical features.

The function of newspapers now, as in the past, is to keep the reader up to date on events. They are valuable sources of information on questions of the day and on trends of opinion in the past. They provide a contemporary history of any given modern period.

NEWSPAPER INDEXES

There is no general index to newspapers comparable to the periodical indexes, but since all newspapers publish news items at about the same time, the date of the event will serve as the needed clue. A chronology, like that in the *Americana Annual*, or an index to one newspaper, such as *The New York Times Index*, will serve as an index to all newspaper items of general interest, wherever published. This is not true, of course, in the case of strictly local-interest items.

New York Times Index. New York: New York Times, 1913– . (Semimonthly; annual cumulation.) Gives exact reference to date, page, and column; summaries of articles may answer question without reference to the paper itself.

The Newspaper Index. Wooster, Ohio: Bell & Howell, 1972– . (Monthly.) Indexes by subject and names in the news four major newspapers: *The Chicago Tribune, The Los Angeles Times, The New Orleans Times-*

---

[6]The word "gazette" probably came from *gazzetta*, the Italian name for a small Venetian coin which was the price charged (in the sixteenth century) for a copy of a newssheet or for permission to read it (*The Oxford English Dictionary*, IV, 88–89).

Picayune, and *The Washington Post*; covers national, regional, state, and local news; is available also in four separate indexes.

Times (London). *Index to the Times*, 1906– . London: London Times, 1907– . (Bimonthly since 1957.) Indexes the final edition of the *Times*; gives day of the month, page, column; includes book reviews.

LITERATURE IN COLLECTIONS

The practice of gathering extracts from the works of several writers into a collection is not a recent one. The name usually given to such a collection is "anthology," a word of Greek derivation which means "flower-gathering" and indicates that only the best pieces of literature are included.

The *Greek Anthology*, a collection of about 4,500 poems, inscriptions, and other kinds of writings by more than 300 writers, dates from about 60 B.C. The earliest English anthology dates from A.D. 975.

The original use of "anthology" to mean a volume containing only the "flower" of literature has been extended to mean any collection of extracts from the writings of various authors—often on one subject or of one kind, such as a collection of poems, short stories, essays, plays, speeches, or quotations.

Volumes of collected writings, including those called "readings," constitute an important part of any well-chosen library collection. Some of these collected works are analyzed in the card catalog (see pages 59, 60). Most of them contain so many selections that it is not possible to include all of them in the card catalog.

INDEXES TO LITERATURE IN COLLECTIONS

The student will find that it is a tedious, and perhaps impossible, task to locate a particular essay, speech, or quotation, or a selection on a particular subject, by examining the index of every anthology. The reference tool designed to facilitate this kind of search is the index to literature in collections.

Indexes to literature in collections follow the general pattern of indexes to periodicals and newspapers, but they cover books only. There are indexes to general literature in collections—that is, essays, articles, and speeches covering a variety of subjects. An example of this kind of index is the *Essay and General Literature Index* (Figure 13). There are indexes to collections of poetry, stories, and plays. Examples are *Granger's Index to Poetry*, the *Short Story Index*, and the *Play Index*. Indexing is by author, subject, and

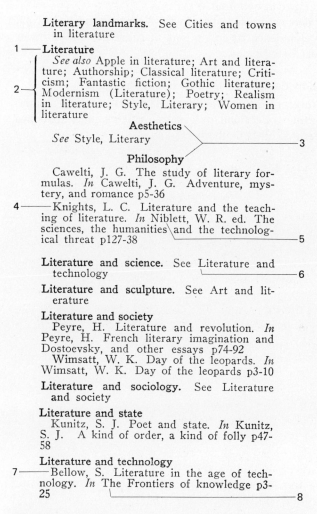

Literary landmarks. See Cities and towns in literature

1 —— Literature
See also Apple in literature; Art and literature; Authorship; Classical literature; Criticism; Fantastic fiction; Gothic literature;
2 Modernism (Literature); Poetry; Realism in literature; Style, Literary; Women in literature

Aesthetics
See Style, Literary
—————— 3

Philosophy
Cawelti, J. G. The study of literary formulas. *In* Cawelti, J. G. Adventure, mystery, and romance p5-36
4 ——— Knights, L. C. Literature and the teaching of literature. *In* Niblett, W. R. ed. The sciences, the humanities and the technological threat p127-38
—————— 5

Literature and science. See Literature and technology
—————— 6

Literature and sculpture. See Art and literature

Literature and society
Peyre, H. Literature and revolution. *In* Peyre, H. French literary imagination and Dostoevsky, and other essays p74-92
Wimsatt, W. K. Day of the leopards. *In* Wimsatt, W. K. Day of the leopards p3-10

Literature and sociology. See Literature and society

Literature and state
Kunitz, S. J. Poet and state. *In* Kunitz, S. J. A kind of order, a kind of folly p47-58

Literature and technology
7 ——— Bellow, S. Literature in the age of technology. *In* The Frontiers of knowledge p3-25
—————— 8

Figure 13 Excerpt from *Essay and General Literature Index:* (1) Subject heading. (2) *See also* references for additional material on the subject. (3) Subheadings under "Literature," i.e., "Literature—Aesthetics," "Literature—Philosophy." (4) Author of the essay "Literature and the Teaching of Literature." (5) Editor of the collection which includes this essay on pages 127–138. (6) *See* reference from "Literature and Science." (7) Essay on the subject "Literature and Technology." (8) Title of the collection in which the essay by S. Bellow is located on pages 3–25. (*Essay and General Literature Index* Copyright © 1976 by The H. W. Wilson Company. Material reproduced by permission of the publisher.)

title, and the location reference includes the name of the compiler of the anthology, the title of the anthology, and the page or pages on which the essay, poem, story, or play can be found.

Indexes to poetry, short stories, and plays are discussed in Chapter 22, Literature. Examples of indexes to collections of literature which cover several subject areas are listed below.

Biography Index. New York: The H. W. Wilson Company, 1946– . Indexes current books of individual and collective biography.

Essay and General Literature Index. New York: The H. W. Wilson Company, 1934– . Indexes collections of essays, articles, and speeches relating to the several subject fields.

CHAPTER TEN
BIOGRAPHICAL DICTIONARIES

The word "biography," from the Greek *bios*, "life," and *graphein*, "to write," is that form of history which is applied to individuals rather than to nations or civilizations. It is the purpose of biography[1] to tell accurately the history of an individual from birth to death in a manner that will reveal various aspects of character, personality, and philosophy.

Since ancient times, people have been interested in the lives of others, either from a desire to eulogize them, to learn from them, or to imitate them, or just from simple curiosity.

Toward the end of the first century after Christ, Plutarch wrote his *Parallel Lives*, the life histories of forty-six Greeks and Romans. The word "biography," however, did not appear in the English language until 1683, when John Dryden described this work of Plutarch's as the "history of particular men's lives." This meaning of "biography"—the history of the life of an individual—has become established as a literary form.

Other literary forms contribute to biography but must be distinguished from it. They are:

1   Autobiography, the narration of a person's life by himself or herself
2   Memoirs, the history of a person's times as seen by the individual who writes them

---

[1]Biography is a subject area; biographical dictionaries, which cover persons in many fields and are general in that sense, are included in general reference materials.

3 Diary, a day-by-day account of the happenings and events in a person's life, recorded by that person

4 Letters, written communications of a personal nature (as distinguished from belles lettres, meaning literature), which may be intimate narratives, records of events, or expressions of the writer's thoughts and philosophy

Biography may draw from these and other sources to present all the significant characteristics of the subject.

The outstanding example of individual biography in English—or in any language—is James Boswell's *Life of Samuel Johnson*, written in the eighteenth century. Since that time biography has become an increasingly important form of literature and occupies a prominent place in all library collections. The student who seeks material on a country, a civilization, or a period of history will do well to investigate the lives of outstanding persons who were a part of that country, civilization, or period of history.

Biography as a literary form differs in purpose, style, and content from simple biographical information about an individual.

In the nineteenth century, there appeared in most European countries publications called "dictionaries of national biography," presenting biographical information about all important national figures. These collections of biographical articles were the forerunners of the modern biographical dictionary, a work which combines biography (factual information about the life of an individual) and dictionary (alphabetical arrangement).

The biographical dictionary, with biographical sketches arranged alphabetically by surname, does not qualify as true biography, since it does not present all aspects of an individual's life. However, the *Dictionary of National Biography* and the *Dictionary of American Biography* are outstanding for their scholarly and objective treatment of the persons included.

Biographical dictionaries are among the most frequently used books in the academic library (or in any library). Questions about notable people and about people in the news—their lives, interests, education, background, affiliations, position, and even their addresses—come from faculty and students alike.

There are numerous sources of biographical information concerning individuals; these include encyclopedias, encyclopedia annuals, and dictionaries. However, the reference books which were written for the specific purpose of quickly and conveniently providing the kinds of biographical information mentioned above are:

1 Biographical indexes, which point out books, periodicals, and other sources in which the information can be found

2 Biographical dictionaries, which contain the information sought

KINDS OF BIOGRAPHICAL DICTIONARIES[2]

Biographical dictionaries can be divided into three classes according to the nationality, the profession, and the dates of the persons included:

1 Universal—not limited to any state, country, or profession
   a Persons no longer living
   b Living persons
2 National or regional—limited in coverage to particular countries or regions but including persons from all of the professions and occupations
   a Persons no longer living
   b Living persons
3 Professional or occupational—limited to persons in a specific profession or occupation
   a Universal
      (1) Persons no longer living
      (2) Living persons
   b National or regional
      (1) Persons no longer living
      (2) Living persons

CHOOSING A BIOGRAPHICAL DICTIONARY

To determine which biographical dictionary will provide information on a particular person, it is helpful to establish, if possible, the following facts about that person:

1 Dates of birth and death, if not living
2 Nationality
3 Profession or occupation

Sources which will aid in establishing these facts are:

1 Card catalog. If the individual has written a book, and if this book is listed in the card catalog, dates of birth and death may be given following the person's name on the catalog card. The subject matter of the book or books by and about this person may indicate field or work, and the place of publication may provide a clue to nationality.

[2]Some biographical dictionaries are called directories, e.g., *Directory of American Scholars* (see p. 159). They provide the same kinds of information that are found in biographical dictionaries.

2 *Cumulative Book Index.* If the card catalog does not include any books by or about the person in question, the *Cumulative Book Index*, which is a world list of books in the English language, will list the books he or she has written in English.

3 *Biography Index.* This index to biographical articles appearing in books and magazines (excluding biographical dictionaries) gives the dates and the profession of all persons included. If the individual is not an American, nationality is given also.

4 Periodical indexes. Any periodical articles by or about the person on whom the student seeks information should be listed in one of the indexes to periodical literature. The periodicals in which the articles appear often include a brief statement about the author. The dates of publication of these articles may provide a clue to the time when the individual might have been included in a biographical dictionary or was in the current news. The subject matter of the articles will indicate field of interest, and the place of publication may suggest nationality. Indexes to periodical literature also list obituaries, which often provide full biographical information.

5 A book by the person in question. The title page may list the author's position, such as Professor of History at McGill University, or Professor of English, Duke University, immediately following his or her name. The location of the university may be a clue to the nationality of the person teaching there. The position held indicates profession.

The advantage gained by establishing the dates, the nationality, and the profession of a person before consulting any biographical dictionary will more than make up for the time spent in locating this information. For example, if the subject is an important contemporary American politician, the following biographical dictionaries will be eliminated from consideration immediately:

Dictionary of American Biography
Dictionary of National Biography
Appleton's Cyclopaedia of American Biography

Among the biographical dictionaries which are possible sources of information about a living American politician are:

Who's Who in America
Current Biography
International Who's Who

It is necessary to point out that in some cases none of the sources mentioned above—card catalog, periodical indexes, *Cumulative Book Index*, *Biography Index*, or books by the individual—will provide dates, nationality, or profession. In such cases, locating biographical material about the individual becomes a tedious process of trial and error. Even when dates, nationality, and profession have been established, it is not always possible to find the subject in the biographical dictionary or dictionaries designed to cover the person's profession, nationality, and time of prominence. Information in the several biographical dictionaries is provided, for the most part, at the request of the publisher by the individuals included. The fact that a person is not included may mean that he or she failed to furnish the biographical information requested and that the publisher was unable to secure it from other sources. In such cases, it may be necessary to identify individuals by piecing together bits of information from the jackets of their books, from a few titles of periodical articles by or about them, and from the fact that they edit, or contribute to, professional journals.

USING A BIOGRAPHICAL DICTIONARY

Before using any biographical dictionary the first time, it is helpful to read the preliminary pages to determine (1) whether the alphabetical arrangement is letter-by-letter or word-by-word; (2) what special features are included; and (3) what abbreviations and symbols are used. The method of selecting names to be included should be noted, as a test of the objectivity of the work.

SUMMARY

A biography of an individual provides information not only about the person but also about the events which occurred during the time he or she lived. Biographical dictionaries generally do not go into that much detail, but there are some which do: *Dictionary of American Biography, Dictionary of National Biography, Dictionary of Canadian Biography*, etc.

Since achievement is a criterion for being included in a biographical dictionary, this kind of source will at least identify persons who are or were important at one time or another. There are biographical dictionaries which cover persons in a given region, and persons of a given race, profession, or religion as well as persons who lived during a certain period. It saves much time if you can establish the nationality, profession, and dates of the person before beginning to try to locate him or her in a biographical dictionary.

REPRESENTATIVE BIOGRAPHICAL DICTIONARIES[3]

UNIVERSAL BIOGRAPHY
Persons No Longer Living

Chambers's Biographical Dictionary. Rev. ed. Edited by J. O. Thorne. New York: St. Martin's Press, 1968. Covers the "great of all nations and all times" (subtitle); gives pronunciation; has some 150,000 entries.

James, Edward T. (ed.). *Notable American Women 1607–1950. A Biographical Dictionary.* Cambridge, Mass.: Belknap Press of Harvard University Press, 1971. 3 vols. Sponsored by Radcliffe College; covers 300 years of women's history in America; modeled after *Dictionary of American Biography;* includes women who have achieved distinction in their own right; includes bibliographies; articles are written by a person with "special knowledge of the subject or her field" (Preface).

The McGraw-Hill Encyclopedia of World Biography. New York: McGraw-Hill Book Company, 1972. 12 vols. Includes persons not living and living persons; articles include basic biographical facts and commentary on the person's background and character, evaluation of his or her role in history, a portrait whenever possible; Vol. XII contains historical maps, index, and study guides.

New Century Cyclopedia of Names. New York: Appleton-Century-Crofts, Inc., 1954. 3 vols. Identifies proper names of importance today: persons, places, events, literary characters, plays, operas, mythological and legendary names; provides a chronological table of world history.

Webster's Biographical Dictionary. Springfield, Mass.: G. & C. Merriam Company, 1972. Lists names of 40,000 noteworthy persons with pronunciation and concise biographies; is not limited by period, race, religion, or occupation; includes table of heads of state and other high officials, historical and contemporary.

Living Persons

Current Biography. New York: The H. W. Wilson Company, 1940– . (Monthly except December.) *Current Biography Yearbook*, 1946– . Aims to cover all important contemporary figures in all fields; includes pronunciation for unusual names, a photograph of the biographee, and a bibliography of the sources used. Yearbooks contain indexes by names and professions and a cumulated five-year index.

Dictionary of International Biography. 14th ed. Cambridge: International Biographical Centre, 1978. 2vols. First published in 1963; aims to be a

---

[3]See Chapters 16 to 23 for biographical dictionaries in the subject fields.

record of contemporary achievement; reports personal information, professional positions, publications, honors; covers many countries and many walks of life.

Encyclopedia of American Biography. Edited by John A. Garraty. New York: Harper & Row, Publishers, Incorporated, 1974. Presents about 1,000 biographical accounts of persons living and not living; selection is based on their significance, achievement, and fame. Each sketch consists of a summary of the essential biographical data, followed by an interpretative essay evaluating the person's career; includes minorities and women who may have been omitted from other sources.

International Who's Who. London: Europa Publications, Ltd., 1935– . (Annual.) Includes sketches of important people in the world today.

The New York Times Biographical Service: A Compilation of Current Biographical Information of General Interest. New York: New York Times, 1970– . (Monthly.) Gives profiles of people in the news; contains from twenty to fifty articles each week reprinted from the *Times*; represents all sections of the country; some articles are obituaries; some are news items; others are interviews. Loose-leaf format.

Webster's American Biographies. Edited by Charles Van Doren and Robert McHenry. Springfield, Mass.: G. & C. Merriam Company, 1975. Covers some 3,000 persons, living and not living, who have made a significant contribution to American life; special attention is given to groups often neglected: Indians, Western pioneers, women; geographical and careers and professions indexes are provided.

NATIONAL OR REGIONAL BIOGRAPHY
Persons No Longer Living

Appleton's Cyclopaedia of American Biography. Rev. ed. New York: D. Appleton and Company, Inc., 1887–1900. 7 vols. Includes all important persons identified with American history from its earliest beginnings; has lengthy articles and many portraits.

The Conspectus of American Biography. Compiled by the Editorial Staff of *The National Cyclopedia of American Biography.* 3d ed. Clifton, N.J.: James T. White & Company, 1973. "A tabulated record of American History," includes sections on government, wars, military, foreign service, religion, art, science, etc.

Dictionary of American Biography. Published under the auspices of the American Council of Learned Societies. New York: Charles Scribner's Sons, 1928–1944. 21 vols. Provides scholarly, signed articles on persons who influenced their time, with bibliographic references for further information on the person. Vol. 21 is the first supplement. *Supplement*

2, to December 31, 1940; *Supplement 3*, 1941–1945; *Supplement 4*, 1946–1950; *Supplement 5*, 1951–1955.

Concise Dictionary of American Biography. 2d ed. Edited by Joseph G. E. Hopkins. New York: Charles Scribner's Sons, 1977. Provides the essential facts for each biographee in the larger work and in the supplements to January 1950; useful for quick reference.

Dictionary of Canadian Biography/Dictionnaire Biographique du Canada. Toronto: University of Toronto Press, 1966– . (In progress.) Vol. I: 1000–1700; Vol. II: 1701–1740; Vol. III: 1741–1770; Vol. IX: 1861–1870; Vol. X: 1871–1880. Follows the scholarly tradition of the *Dictionary of National Biography;* is arranged by period, each volume covering a given range of years; includes persons born and residing in Canada and persons from other countries who have made contributions to Canadian life. Is expected to have some twenty volumes.

Dictionary of National Biography. Edited by Leslie Stephen and Sidney Lee. London: Oxford University Press, 1922. 22 vols. *Supplements*, 1901–1911, 1912–1921, 1922–1930, 1931–1940, 1941–1950, 1951–1960, 1961–1970. Provides full, accurate biographies of all notable inhabitants of Great Britain and the colonies (exclusive of living persons) from the earliest historical period to the present time; includes bibliographical references.

The Compact Edition of the Dictionary of National Biography, 1975. 2 vols. Offers the complete text of the twenty-two volumes and the supplements reproduced micrographically; it must be read with a reading glass, which is provided.

Concise Dictionary of National Biography. Oxford: Oxford University Press, 1952, 1961. 2 vols. Pt. I: to 1900; Pt. II: 1900–1950. Provides abstracts of the articles in the original set down to 1950.

The National Cyclopedia of American Biography. Clifton, N.J.: James T. White & Company Publishers, 1888– . 65 vols. Based on original materials; provides detailed biographical articles about noteworthy Americans from the beginning of this nation to the present; includes every field of activity and every period of history; covers men and women who are distinguished locally as well as nationally; in two series (the Permanent Series covers deceased persons, the Current Series living Americans); index volume includes names of all subjects in all volumes and thousands of topical entries.

Who Was Who. London: A. & C. Black, Ltd., 1929–1972. 6 vols. Companion volume to *Who's Who;* contains biographies of persons in *Who's Who* who have died, with the date of the death added. These volumes cover the period 1897–1970.

Who Was Who in America. Chicago: Marquis—Who's Who, Inc., 1942–1976. 6 vols. Gives biographies of persons in *Who's Who in America* who have died, with date of death added.

Who Was Who in America: Historical Volume 1607–1896. Chicago: Marquis—Who's Who, Inc., 1963. Supplements *Who Was Who in America.* Treats Americans and other outstanding figures in the early development of America.

Living Persons

The National Cyclopedia of American Biography. Includes living persons in the Current Series.

Who's Who. London: A. & C. Black, Ltd., 1849– . (Annual.) The first "who's who"; includes persons of distinction in all fields; covers Great Britain and the Commonwealth nations.

Who's Who among Black Americans. Northbrook, Ill.: Who's Who Among Black Americans, Inc., 1976. Gives biographical sketches of more than 10,000 living notable black American men and women in many fields, selected on the basis of significant achievement; has geographical and occupation indexes.

Who's Who in America. Chicago: Marquis—Who's Who, Inc., 1899– . (Biennial.) Includes persons of special prominence in every line of work and those who are selected arbitrarily because of their position in government, religion, education, industry, and other fields. Since 1972–1973 is in two volumes.

Who's Who in the World. 3d ed. Chicago: Marquis—Who's Who, Inc., 1977. Aims to identify important personalities of the world; contains 25,000 names from some 150 countries of persons who are "shaping today's world and tomorrow's future"; entries are chosen by members of the Marquis staff.

Other useful biographies of the "who's who" type, which include eminent living persons from all professions, are:

American Catholic Who's Who
Who's Who in France
Who's Who in Germany
Who's Who in Israel
Who's Who of American Women

In addition to those listed above, there are biographical dictionaries by section of a country and by profession.

Professional and occupational biographical dictionaries are discussed in the chapters which treat each subject field.

INDEXES TO BIOGRAPHY[4]

In addition to the biographical dictionaries which provide the desired information, there are indexes which point out biographies in books and in periodical literature. Indexes to periodical literature, indexes to newspapers, and indexes to collected works include biographical articles. The following indexes cover only biographical material. They point out where biographical articles or books can be found and give the titles and pages of books or the volumes, dates, and pages of periodicals.

Biographical Dictionaries Master Index. Detroit: Gale Research Company, 1975– . 3 vols. (Biennial.) "A guide to more than 800,000 listings in over fifty current who's who's and other works of collective biography" (subtitle); includes persons in all fields; is international in scope; entry includes biographee's name and birth date and code for the biographical dictionary in which a sketch can be found.

Biography Index. New York: The H. W. Wilson Company, 1947– . (Quarterly; annual cumulations which are replaced by three-year permanent volumes.) Locates biographical material of all types in current books in the English language and in some 2,400 periodicals indexed in Wilson publications; includes obituaries of national interest appearing in these periodicals and in *The New York Times;* gives dates of birth and death, profession, and nationality of persons other than Americans; provides an index by profession and occupation.

Hyamson, Albert M. (ed.). *A Dictionary of Universal Biography of All Ages and All Peoples.* 2d ed. New York: E. P. Dutton & Company, Inc., 1951. An index to individuals who are included in twenty-four biographical dictionaries of various countries; gives dates, nationality, and profession for each name and indicates the biographical source by a symbol.

Ireland, Norma Olin. *Index to Women.* (Useful Reference Series No. 97.) Boston: F. W. Faxon Company, Inc., 1970. An index to information about outstanding women of the world from ancient to modern times which has appeared in books, periodicals, and serials; indexes more than 930 collections covering some 10,000 women; date, nationality, and profession are given for each woman, and a portrait is included when available.

[4]See also Chapter 9, Indexes.

CHAPTER ELEVEN

ATLASES
AND GAZETTEERS

Before they could write, and perhaps before they could speak, primitive people left landmarks (cairns) to show where they had been. The oldest known map is a Babylonian clay tablet dating from about 2300 B.C. There are many other clay tablets which show geographical locations.

The Greeks, using their knowledge of science, philosophy, mathematics, geography, and astronomy, succeeded in developing mapmaking (cartography) to a point not again attained until the sixteenth century. Greek geographers from the fifth century B.C. believed that the earth is a sphere. About A.D. 150, Claudius Ptolemy of Alexandria, perhaps the greatest single contributor in history to cartography and geography, compiled his eight-volume *Geographia*, the first scientific and comprehensive treatment of cartography. It contained, in addition to the text, twenty-eight maps and a list of all the principal places then known. The *Geographia* disappeared during the Middle Ages and was not found until the fifteenth century. Its rediscovery[2] helped make possible the voyages of Columbus, Magellan, Vasco da Gama, John Cabot, and others, thus hastening the era of discovery and exploration. In turn, the discoveries of these explorers greatly increased the demand for maps.

[1] Atlases and gazetteers belong in the subject field of geography. They are included here because of their general reference value.

[2] The *Geographia* had been preserved by the Arabs.

Important contributors to mapmaking during this period were Mercator, famous for his celestial and terrestrial globes and for his system of projection, and Ortelius, credited with the publication of the first modern atlas in 1570. Both were members of the Dutch school of cartography.

ATLASES

A map is a representation, usually flat, of the earth's surface or a part of it or of the celestial sphere or a part of it.[3] An atlas is a collection of maps, usually bound together in one volume. The word "atlas" was first used in this sense by Mercator, from the figure of the mythological Atlas, which was often used as the frontispiece of early collections of maps. It has come to mean any volume containing not only maps, but also plates, engravings, charts, and tables, with or without descriptive text. It is sometimes used as the name of a volume in which subjects are presented in tabular form.

While it is generally recognized that atlases are essential in studying history,[4] geography, and other branches of the social sciences, it is becoming increasingly apparent that many atlases are valuable also as general reference sources because of the descriptive materials they contain in addition to maps. Today, maps are necessary companions to the daily newspaper and radio and television news commentary, verifying names, places, and events in the news and presenting them in proper geographical relationship to other names, places, and events.

There are many sources of maps. Most of the general encyclopedias include maps either in a separate volume or as illustrative material within the text; encyclopedia annuals include up-to-date maps; many handbooks, almanacs, newspapers, and periodicals also contain maps. However, the atlas is the reference source designed primarily to provide maps.

Atlases vary in quality, and they also vary according to the country of publication. For example, an atlas of the world which is published in America will include more or larger maps of America than one published in France. The latter will include larger maps of France.

CHOOSING AN ATLAS
To be able to choose an atlas to answer a given question, it is necessary to know certain things about each atlas.

---

[3]*Webster's New Collegiate Dictionary* (Springfield, Mass.: G. & C. Merriam Company, 1960), p. 513.

[4]A historical atlas is made up of maps which delineate past events or periods of history; it is not a collection of old maps.

1 Scope
   a Is it worldwide in coverage, or is it limited to one or more regions?
   b Does it include all kinds of maps, or only maps of a specific nature?
   c Does it provide descriptive material about the various geographical locations?
2 Place of publication as an indication of emphasis
3 Date of publication as an indication of up-to-dateness
4 Kind of index
   a Is there one comprehensive index for the entire volume, or are there separate indexes for each map or section of maps?
   b Is the index a separate volume, or is it a part of the atlas?
   c Does it indicate pronunciation?
   d Is the reference to the location on a given map clear and definite?
5 Quality and content of the maps
   a Is the scale indicated clearly?
   b Are the symbols distinct and easily read?
   c Are the projections in keeping with the purpose of the map?
   d Is the lettering clear and legible?
   e Is the coloring varied and well differentiated?
   f Is the legend clearly explained?
   g Are the names of countries given in the language of each country or in translation?

GAZETTEERS

A gazetteer gives information about geographical places; it does not define them. In addition to geographic location, it gives historical, statistical, cultural, and other relevant facts about these places. It may also indicate pronunciation. Because they provide a variety of factual material about places, gazetteers are important reference sources. Recent editions describe a place as it is now; old editions give historical information about it. The economic growth or decline of a town or city, as indicated by data on population, number of industries, schools, and so on, will often be shown by the brief facts given in gazetteers over a period of years.

In using a gazetteer, it is important to note the copyright date as an indication of the recency of the material; the system of pronunciation and the abbreviations used; the arrangement of the material; and any additional material, such as maps and tables, which may be included in appendixes.

USEFUL ATLASES AND GAZETTEERS[5]

ATLASES

Bartholomew, John W. (ed.). *The Times Atlas of the World.* Vol. I: *The World, Australasia & East Asia.* Vol. II: *South-west Asia & Russia.* Vol. III: *Northern Europe.* Vol. IV: *Southern Europe & Africa,* Vol. V: *The Americas.* Midcentury Edition. London: The Times Publishing Company, Ltd., 1955–1959. Each volume has its own index-gazetteer; provides inset maps of many cities; is outstanding for the beauty and accuracy of maps. *The Times Index Gazetteer of the World* (1965) lists in one volume the place names separately indexed in the five volumes of the Midcentury Edition.

The Times Atlas of the World: Comprehensive Edition. Edited by John W. Bartholomew. 5th ed. New York: Quadrangle/New York Times Book Company, 1975. Gives physical-political maps for regions, nations, and localities of the earth; has thematic maps for world physiography, oceanography, climatology, vegetation, population; includes air routes and city maps, geographical glossaries, and a 200,000-item gazetteer.

Hammond Medallion World Atlas. Maplewood, N.J.: C. S. Hammond & Company, 1977. Places all the information about a continent, country, state, or province on consecutive pages; maps of various kinds plus all other relevant political, economic, and geographical data placed together. Other atlases which are comparable in arrangement are *Hammond Ambassador World Atlas* (1977), *Hammond Citation World Atlas* (1977), and *Hammond International World Atlas* (1977).

The International Atlas. Rev. 2d ed. Chicago: Rand McNally & Company, 1974. Maps are designed to show geographical and economic regions rather than individual countries or states; place names are shown in English and in the local language; has a glossary of selected terms on maps in English, French, German, and Spanish.

The National Atlas of the United States of America. Washington, D.C.: U.S. Department of the Interior, Geological Survey, 1970. The official national atlas of the United States, it has 765 maps and an index which identifies more than 41,000 place names; includes many thematic maps which present the physical, economic, social, and historical features of the country; includes six plastic overlays correlated with the thematic and special maps; divided between "General Reference Maps" and "Special Reference Maps."

National Geographic Atlas of the World. 4th ed. Melville Bell Grosvenor, editor in chief. Washington, D.C.: National Geographic Society, 1975.

---

[5]See also pp. 254–257 for additional materials in the field of geography.

Maps and text are arranged by geographical regions, with separate section on oceans; short essay precedes each section; has tables, glossary, and index to more than 139,000 entries.

The New Oxford Atlas. 3d ed. Prepared by the Cartographic Department of the Oxford University Press. London: Oxford University Press, 1978. Includes general reference, thematic, and relief maps; covers oceans, temperature, climate, rainfall, land use, vegetation, and population data (1974 census).

Oxford World Atlas. Saul B. Cohen, Geographic Editor. Prepared by the Cartographic Department of the Clarendon Press. London: Oxford University Press, 1973. Presents political, geophysical, demographic, and economic data in maps; many factors are shown in the same map; includes climate, ocean features, population distribution, mineral resources; has gazetteer.

Rand McNally Cosmopolitan World Atlas. (Enlarged "Planet Earth" ed.) Chicago: Rand McNally & Company, 1978. Shows the earth as part of the vast universe; includes photographs of the earth as seen from space; includes oceanographic maps, political maps, metropolitan area maps, and individual maps for each state and Canadian province; gives United States and world population tables.

GAZETTEERS

Columbia-Lippincott Gazetteer of the World. Edited by Leon E. Seltzer with the Geographical Research Staff of Columbia University Press and with the cooperation of the American Geographical Society. With 1961 *Supplement.* New York: Columbia University Press, 1962. Gives information about history, population, trade, industry, cultural institutions, and agricultural and natural resources.

Webster's New Geographical Dictionary. Springfield, Mass.: G. & C. Merriam Company, 1972. Provides geographical, economic, and historical information about places; gives pronunciation; includes maps; 1970 census figures are used for the United States; lists 450 geographical terms from other languages translated into English.

CHAPTER TWELVE

YEARBOOKS AND HANDBOOKS[1]

Every library has a number of books for quick reference which provide brief information on a multitude of subjects. Among these "ready-reference" works are yearbooks and handbooks.

A yearbook is a publication which is issued annually for the purpose of giving current information in narrative, statistical, or directory form. There are several types of yearbooks:

1 Encyclopedia annuals, issued by the major encyclopedia publishers as a means of keeping the encyclopedia up to date, are comprehensive in coverage and give a summary of all the major events of the preceding year.

2 Yearbooks, which treat several subject areas, include social, political, educational, cultural, and other information.

3 Almanacs, which were originally calendars of months and days with special dates and anniversaries, forecasts of the weather, and astronomical calculations, are now collections of miscellaneous facts and statistics.

4 Directories, which list persons or organizations in alphabetical or classified arrangement, include addresses and affiliations for individuals and officers and other data for organizations. Not all directories are issued annually.

[1]See also yearbooks and handbooks in each of the subject fields.

A handbook (literally, a small book which can be held in the hand) is a volume which treats broad subjects in brief fashion. It may include odd bits of information about a variety of topics. Among the most useful types of handbooks are:

How to Books

1 Manuals, which give instruction on, or serve as guides to, occupations, hobbies, art forms, trades, etc.
2 Miscellanies, which include bits of unusual and hard-to-find information on many subjects.

Compendium
3 Companions, which explain and interpret various aspects of a subject
4 Digests, which present in condensed form information that is classified and arranged under proper headings or titles; examples are digests of laws, digests of articles from periodicals, or digests of the plots of novels, short stories, dramas, or poems.[2]

SELECTION AND USE OF A YEARBOOK OR HANDBOOK

Each yearbook and handbook is designed to provide certain kinds of information for the purpose of answering specific kinds of questions. Therefore, before attempting to choose a yearbook or a handbook, the student must examine the question to be answered:

1 Does it require statistical information?
2 Is it a directory-type question?
3 Is it a "trend" question?
4 Does it come under the heading of miscellany?

In order to use a yearbook or a handbook quickly and satisfactorily, it is necessary to understand:

1 Organization and arrangement of material
  a Is it organized into chapters or into broad general subjects, and does it have a detailed table of contents, a comprehensive index, or both?
  b Is it broken down into small topics, arranged alphabetically?
  c Does it have tables only, or does it give both text and tables?
2 Kinds of material included
  a Is it statistical? If it is, does it give the source for the statistics presented?
  b Does it give instructions and directions?
  c Is it a collection of miscellaneous information?

[2]See also p. 238.

3 Scope

   a Does it cover all countries and all subjects?

   b Is it limited to one country and to a selected number of subjects?

4 Period covered

   a Is it one year? Two years?

   b If it is a handbook, is it revised often?

5 Special aids to the reader

   a Does it provide bibliographical references for further reading?

   b Does it provide cross references?

   c Is the illustrative material—charts, tables, maps, pictures— appropriate and adequate?

6 Kinds of questions it will answer

   a Will it answer factual and statistical questions?

   b Will it provide "trend" and background information?

REPRESENTATIVE YEARBOOKS AND HANDBOOKS

YEARBOOKS

Encyclopedia Annuals

Americana Annual. New York: Americana Corporation, 1923– . Covers events of the previous year; features a brief chronological listing of events.

Britannica Book of the Year. Chicago: Encyclopaedia Britannica, Inc., 1938– . Gives a calendar of events, many short articles under specific titles, statistics, and bibliography.

Collier's Year Book. New York: P. F. Collier & Son Corporation, 1938– . Surveys the events of the year; is especially strong in sports and chronology.

Other Yearbooks

Europa Year Book, 1946– . London: Europa Publications, Ltd., 1946– . 2 vols. Vol. I is devoted to international organizations, including the United Nations and European communities; gives information on foundations, organization, activities, financial structure; includes U.S.S.R., Cyprus, and Turkey. Vol. II covers Africa, the Americas, Asia, and Australasia; gives for each country information on political conditions, statistics, religion, communications media, and education.

The Statesman's Yearbook. London: Macmillan & Co., Ltd., 1864– . Covers government, area, population, education, religion, social welfare, money, industry, and other statistical and historical information about the countries of the world.

U.S. Bureau of the Census. *Statistical Abstract of the United States.* Washington, D.C.: Government Printing Office, 1878– . Summarizes statistics of political, industrial, economic, and social institutions and organizations in the United States; provides bibliography.

ALMANACS

Canadian Almanac and Directory. Toronto: Copp Clark Company, 1848– . (Annual.) Gives statistical and other information for Canada on miscellaneous subjects, including geography, history, education, law, sports, and religion.

Information Please Almanac, Atlas & Yearbook. New York: Information Please Publishing Company, Inc., 1947– . Has a topical arrangement and subject index; covers "people & places, facts & figures, news & views, past & present (subtitle); emphasizes sports.

New York Times Encyclopedic Almanac. Edited by Seymour Kurtz. New York: The New York Times, 1969– . Summarizes the events of the preceding year; covers both current and historical topics under twenty-two broad subject headings.

Whitaker, Joseph. *Almanack.* London: J. Whitaker & Sons, 1868– . (Annual.) Gives complete statistical information regarding government finances, population, and commerce for the various nations in the world, with emphasis on Great Britain and the United States; contains material relating to astronomical and other phenomena; includes maps.

— *The World Almanac and Book of Facts.* New York: Newspaper Enterprise Association, Inc., 1868– . (Annual.) Gives comprehensive coverage of factual material of all kinds; index is in the front of the book.

DIRECTORIES

Encyclopedia of Associations. 12th ed. Detroit: Gale Research Company, 1978. 3 vols. Covers national organizations of the United States (Vol. I), with a geographic and executive index (Vol. II), and a list of new associations and projects (Vol. III); gives information on 15,000 national, nonprofit membership organizations grouped by categories according to their principal interest; includes foreign groups of interest in America and local and regional associations in the United States. *3 volumes*

The Foundation Directory. 6th ed. New York: Foundation Center, 1977. Lists more than 2,500 foundations which are included on the basis of size of assets, total annual giving, or both; gives information on their fields of interest and their personnel.

McGraw-Hill Directory and Almanac of Canada. Toronto: McGraw-Hill Company of Canada, Limited, 1966– . (Annual.) Covers all of Canada; each provincial government is treated separately; gives information relating to history, geography, educational, social, and cultural characteristics.

Thomas' Register of American Manufacturers. New York: Thomas Publishing Company, 1905– . (Annual.) Lists major manufacturers geographically; arranged by product; has an index to manufacturers, trade names, and specific products.

U.S. Congress. *Official Congressional Directory for the Use of the United States Congress,* 1809– . Washington, D.C.: U.S. Government Printing Office, 1809– . Includes a variety of information concerning members of Congress, committees, other bodies of the government, independent agencies, diplomatic representatives, and members of the press.

Young, Margaret L., and others (eds.). *Directory of Special Libraries and Information Centers.* 4th ed. Detroit: Gale Research Company, 1977. 3 vols. Lists in Vol. I some 14,000 special libraries and information centers in the United States and Canada with facts about sponsorship, location, specialization, staff, size and nature of collection, and services; Vol. II is a geographic-personnel index; Vol. III is a loose-leaf supplement.

HANDBOOKS

Dreyfuss, Henry. *Symbol Sourcebook: An Authoritative Guide to International Graphic Symbols.* New York: McGraw-Hill Book Company, 1972. Covers more than 6,000 symbols used internationally in business, industry, the sciences, and all fields; arranged by broad subject.

Gregory, Ruth W. (ed.). *Anniversaries and Holidays.* 3d ed. Chicago: American Library Association, 1975. International in scope; identifies fixed holidays and special days and men and women who are honored by nations or professions; some holidays are centuries old, some as new as 1974.

Hutchinson, Lois Irene. *Standard Handbook for Secretaries.* 8th ed. New York: McGraw-Hill Book Company, 1977. Covers English spelling; how to write letters; addresses; postal information; minutes of meetings; report writing.

Kane, Joseph Nathan. *Famous First Facts.* 3d ed. New York: The H. W. Wilson Company, 1964. Covers first happenings, events, discoveries, and inventions in the United States; has index by years, days of the month, personal names, and geographical location.

Myers, Robert J. *Celebrations: the Complete Book of American Holidays.* Prepared with the editors of Hallmark Cards. Garden City, N.Y.: Doubleday, 1972. Arranged according to the calendar; covers religious, regional, ethnic, and federal legal holidays; has bibliography of sources and illustrations.

The Oxford Companion to Ships & the Sea. Edited by Peter Kemp. London: Oxford University Press, 1976. Covers a wide range of topics: terms related to the sea, names and kinds of ships, seafaring history, authors and artists of the sea, pirates, fictional and mythological characters; has photographs, line drawings, and diagrams.

Payton, Geoffrey (comp.). *Webster's Dictionary of Proper Names.* Springfield, Mass.: G. & C. Merriam Company, 1970. Identifies over 10,000 contemporary and historical place names, nicknames, and names from the arts, science, movies, sports, and other areas; includes names unique to America; grouped in sixty-seven categories.

Post, Elizabeth L. *The New Emily Post's Etiquette.* New York: Funk & Wagnalls Company, 1975. Revises *Emily Post's Etiquette* according to the more informal ways of life in the 1970s.

Robert, Henry M. *Robert's Rules of Order Newly Revised.* New and enlarged ed. revised by Sarah Corbin Robert with the assistance of Henry M. Robert III and others. Glenview, Ill.: Scott, Foresman and Company, 1970. Rewritten in a simpler, clearer style than the original; is the guide for parliamentary procedure; provides some new material.

Smith, Whitney. *Flags through the Ages and across the World.* New York: McGraw-Hill Book Company, 1975. A guide to the history of all kinds of flags; includes national flags of ethnic minority groups, political parties, airlines, steamship lines, and sports groups; has many illustrations.

United States Government Organization Manual. Washington, D.C.: Government Printing Office, 1935– . (Annual.) The "official organization handbook of the federal government"; gives essential information regarding the executive, legislative, and judicial branches and the authority, organization, and functions of the agencies in these branches.

CHAPTER THIRTEEN
BIBLIOGRAPHIES

The word "bibliography," deriving from two Greek words, *biblion*, "book," and *graphein*, "to write," was used in postclassical Greece in the sense of "the writing of books." The scribes who copied books were the first bibliographers. This meaning was in use as late as 1761, as is indicated by the definition of the word "bibliographer" in Fenning's *English Dictionary* of that date as "one who copies books."

The transition from the meaning of writing *of* books to that of writing *about* books dates from the eighteenth century; the latter meaning is in use today.

In the sense of "writing about books," the term "bibliography" has several uses:

1   It is the systematic description of groups of books, manuscripts, and other publications as to authorship, title, edition, and imprint, and their enumeration and arrangement into lists for purposes of information.[1]
2   It is the name given to a list of books, manuscripts, and other publications, systematically described and arranged, which have some relationship to each other. Thus, there are several kinds of bibliographies.
   a   General—not limited to one author, subject, country, or period of time

[1]See Chapter 24.

    b   Author—listing the works by and about one author
    c   Subject—restricted to one subject or to one subject field
    d   National or regional—including material relating to one country or to one region
    e   Trade—directed to the book trade and supplying information needed in buying and selling books

3   It is the science of books, that branch of learning concerned with the historical and technical examination of written works, in which books and manuscripts are examined to discover or verify their origin, dates, number and order of pages, authorship, and textual material.

A bibliography may be complete, including *all* works of a particular kind, or it may be selective, containing only a part of the works. It may be descriptive, having only a brief descriptive note (annotation); it may be evaluative, that is, with critical comment; or it may be both descriptive and evaluative. There are bibliographies of forms other than books, such as periodicals, newspapers, and nonbook materials, and bibliographies of types of material, such as book reviews, biographical materials, and bibliographies.

Bibliographies may be found in individual books, in periodical articles, and in encyclopedias and other reference books, or they may be separate books. There are bibliographies both of a general nature and in the subject fields to aid the researcher in the quest for material.

The printed catalogs of individual and of national libraries are forms of bibliography. They are photographic reproductions of the cards in the card catalog of the libraries they represent. Some printed catalogs are union catalogs, that is, lists of the combined holdings of several or many libraries. Union catalogs and lists indicate by means of symbols on the cards the libraries which hold a given title and enable researchers to know where they can borrow a copy if their library does not have it or secure a photocopy of a desired piece of material. There are union catalogs (lists) of books, periodical publications, nonbook materials, and combinations of these.

Bibliographies are useful sources in any search on a subject.

1   They locate material on the subject in question.

2   They provide a means of verifying such items as author's name, complete title of work, place of publication, publisher, date of publication, edition, and number of pages.

3   If they are annotated, they indicate the scope of the subject and the manner in which it is treated; if the annotation is critical and evaluative, it comments upon the usefulness of the publication.

4 They point out material, including parts of books, which cannot be analyzed in the card catalog.

5 They group works according to form, location, and period.

Bibliographies in the subject fields are discussed in Chapters 16 to 23.

REPRESENTATIVE BIBLIOGRAPHIES

GENERAL BIBLIOGRAPHIES

Besterman, Theodore. *A World Bibliography of Bibliographies*. 4th ed. revised and greatly enlarged. Lausanne: Societas Bibliographica, 1965. 5 vols. International in scope; includes bibliographical catalogs, calendars, abstracts, and digests.

The Bibliographic Index. New York: The H. W. Wilson Company, 1938– (Semiannual; annual and larger cumulations.) A subject list of bibliographies of fifty or more citations; includes those published as books and pamphlets and those which appear in books, pamphlets, and periodical articles, both in English and in foreign languages.

UNION CATALOGS

The National Union Catalog, Pre-1956 Imprints. London: Mansell, 1968– . (In progress.) To be completed in 610 volumes. A comprehensive, cumulative author list which includes the following works: *A Catalog of Books Represented by Library of Congress Printed Cards Issued to July 31, 1942*; *Supplement*, August 1, 1942–December 31, 1947; *The Library of Congress Author Catalog*, 1948–1952; *The National Union Catalog, 1952–1955 Imprints*; and *The National Union Catalog, A Cumulative Author List, 1953–1957*. When complete, will have more than 12 million entries, including books, pamphlets, atlases, maps, music, periodicals, and other publications cataloged by the Library of Congress and several hundred cooperating libraries in the United States and Canada over the past century; arranged by main entry.

The National Union Catalog: A Cumulative Author List, 1956– . Washington, D.C.: Library of Congress, 1958– . (Monthly with quarterly and annual cumulations.) Lists the holdings of the Library of Congress and cooperating libraries in the National Union Catalog arrangement; locations for most titles are given.

Library of Congress Catalogs: Subject Catalog 1950– , Washington, D.C.: Library of Congress, 1955– . (Three quarterly issues with annual and quinquennial cumulations.) A subject catalog of 1945 and later works represented by Library of Congress printed cards; includes books cataloged by members of the National Union Catalog arrangement; after 1956 a location in at least one library is given. Formerly *Library of Congress Catalog. Books: Subjects.*

BIBLIOGRAPHIES OF PERIODICAL PUBLICATIONS

Ayer Directory of Publications. Philadelphia: N. W. Ayer & Son, Inc., 1880– . (Annual.) Provides information about newspapers and periodicals printed in the United States and its possessions, Canada, Bermuda, Panama, and the Philippines; includes information about the states, provinces, towns, and cities in which they are published; arranged geographically.

Farber, Evan Ira. *Classified List of Periodicals for the College Library.* 5th ed., revised and enlarged, with the assistance of Thomas G. Kirk, Jr., and James R. Kennedy, Jr. (Useful Reference Series No. 99.) Westwood, Mass.: The F. W. Faxon Company, Inc., 1972. An annotated list of periodicals that began publication before 1969; is an aid in selecting journals for college libraries; provides titles for general and recreational reading and some titles for research; arranged by subject and alphabetically by title within the subject.

Katz, Bill, and Richards, Berry. *Magazines for Libraries.* 3d ed. New York: R. R. Bowker Company, 1978. Arranged by subject; lists more than 6,500 titles with descriptive and critical annotations of the important features of the magazine including editorial point of view; an aid in selecting magazines for public, college, and school libraries; is useful for the student and nonspecialist; includes some popular titles; gives publication details.

The Standard Periodical Directory. 5th ed. New York: Oxbridge Communications, Inc., 1977. Lists 62,500 periodical publications in 230 subject classifications including consumer and special interest magazines, newsletters, house organs, directories, government publications, and bulletins.

Ulrich's International Periodicals Directory. 17th ed. New York: R. R. Bowker Company, 1977. Revised biennially. Arranged by subject; lists world periodicals in each field, giving detailed information regarding contents, sponsorship, frequency, and language of text; includes some 60,000 periodicals; lists publications on microform and gives abstracting and indexing information. Supplemented by *Ulrich's Quarterly.*

Union List of Serials in Libraries of the United States and Canada. 3d ed. Edited by Edna Brown Titus. New York: The H. W. Wilson Company, 1965. 5 vols. Lists more than 150,000 serial titles in 956 libraries—periodicals, proceedings, annual reports—which began publication before December 31, 1949; arranged by title; indicates by symbols the libraries which have copies of each title; is supplemented by *New Serial Titles, A Union List of Serials Commencing Publication after December 31, 1949.* Washington, D.C.: Library of Congress, 1953– . (Monthly with annual cumulations; beginning 1969, eight monthly issues, four quarterly issues, and annual and five- or ten-year cumulations.)

SELECTIVE AND EVALUATIVE BIBLIOGRAPHIES

The Booklist. Chicago: American Library Association, 1905– . (Semimonthly; monthly in August.) Combined with *Subscription Books Bulletin* in September 1956. Gives reviews of reference books prepared by the ALA Reference and Subscription Books Committee at the end of each issue under the heading "Reference and Subscription Reviews"; offers a selective list of currently published books, arranged by broad classes; each issue has special sections such as lists of fiction, books for children and young people, United States government publications, pamphlets, filmstrips, recordings, periodicals for school libraries, and books for special groups.

Reader's Adviser: A Layman's Guide to Literature. 12th ed. New York: R. R. Bowker Company, 1974–1977. 3 vols. Lists and annotates the best books in nearly every field of human knowledge from antiquity to the present. Vol. I: *The Best in American and British Fiction, Poetry, Essays, Literary Biography, Bibliography, and Reference.* Edited by Sarah L. Prakken, 1974. Vol. II: *The Best in American and British Drama and World Literature in English Translation.* Edited by F. J. Sypher, 1974. Vol. III: *The Best in the Reference Literature of the World.* Edited by Jack A. Clarke, 1977.

Sheehy, Eugene P. (Comp.). *Guide to Reference Books.* 9th ed. Chicago: American Library Association, 1976. Follows the general arrangement of the 8th edition by Constance M. Winchell (1967); titles are grouped under large headings; subdivided by specific kind of work, subject, country, or all three; annotations are evaluative; emphasis is on sources for scholarly research, but some popular titles are included.

"The Standard Catalog Series." New York: The H. W. Wilson Company. Includes *Children's Catalog,* 13th ed., 1977; *The Junior High School Library Catalog,* 3d ed., 1975; *The Senior High School Library Catalog,* 11th ed., 1977; *Public Library Catalog,* 6th ed., 1973; and *Fiction Catalog,* 9th ed., 1977. Each catalog provides annotated lists of books for the type of library or material covered; each is kept up to date by annual supplements.

Walford, A. J. (ed.). *Guide to Reference Material.* 3d ed. London: Library Association, 1973–1977. 3 vols. Vol. I: *Science and Technology,* 1973; Vol. II: *Social and Historical Sciences, Philosophy and Religion,* 1975. Lists significant reference books and bibliographies published in recent years; international in scope; emphasizes British publications. Vol. III: *Generalities, Languages, the Arts and Literature*, 1977, gives the same coverage to those areas.

Wynar, Bohdan S. (ed.). *American Reference Books Annual*. Littleton, Colo.: Libraries Unlimited, 1970– . (Annual.) Provides a record of the reference books published and distributed in the United States during the preceding year; gives signed, critical reviews; *ARBA* covers every subject area of general and specific interest.

TRADE BIBLIOGRAPHIES

American Book Publishing Record. New York: R. R. Bowker Company, 1960– . (Monthly; annual cumulation.) Presents a complete record of American book publication in the four (sometimes five) calendar weeks preceding its date of issue; is a listing by subject of the titles in the *Weekly Record*, formerly a section of *Publishers Weekly*, now a separate publication; arranged by subject according to the Dewey Decimal Classification, gives Dewey number, Library of Congress subject headings, LC card number, and LC number; has separate sections for adult and juvenile fiction.

Books in Print. New York: R. R. Bowker Company, 1948– . (Annual.) 4 vols. Lists available books by author and title; gives publisher, series, edition, date of publication, price; the 1977–1978 set lists some 480,000 books of all kinds in print in the United States from some 5,300 publishers. *Authors Index*, 2 vols., *Titles Index*, 2 vols. *Books in Print Supplement*, published in the spring, updates the basic volume.

Cumulative Book Index. New York: The H. W. Wilson Company, 1898– . (Monthly except August; frequently cumulated monthly issues; bound semiannual and larger cumulations.) "A world list of books in the English language" (subtitle); lists all books included by author, title, and subject; gives author, title, price, publisher, date of publication for each entry; continues the *U.S. Catalog*.

Forthcoming Books. New York: R. R. Bowker Company, 1966– . (Bimonthly.) Provides author and title indexes to all books scheduled for publication in the coming five-month period. *Subject Guide to Forthcoming Books* (1967–) is a bimonthly companion to *Forthcoming Books*, listing the coming books under subject.

Paperbound Books in Print. New York: R. R. Bowker Company, 1955– . 2 vols. (Available January and September.) Lists by author, title, and subject new titles in paperback and titles still in print.

Publishers Trade List Annual. New York: R. R. Bowker Company, 1873– . 6 vols. An annual compilation of publishers' catalogs; provides a list of most of the books currently in print in America; not all publishers are included.

Subject Guide to Books in Print. New York: R. R. Bowker Company, 1957– . 2 vols. (Annual.) Lists, according to the subject headings established by the Library of Congress, more than 400,000 nonfiction books under some 62,000 subject headings; gives author, title, publisher, current price, and year of publication.

U.S. Catalog. 4th ed. New York: The H. W. Wilson Company, 1928. Lists books in English in print on January 1, 1928, by author, title, and subject; gives author, title, edition, publisher, price, and generally date, paging, and illustrations; continued currently by *Cumulative Book Index.*

Weekly Record. New York: R. R. Bowker Company, 1974– . (Weekly.) Formerly a section in *Publishers Weekly* but now a separate publication; lists by author or main entry new books published in the United States the previous week. Every four weeks the titles are cumulated, arranged by subject, and published as the *American Book Publishing Record.*

CHAPTER FOURTEEN

NONBOOK INFORMATION SOURCES AND GOVERNMENT PUBLICATIONS

In addition to books, magazines, and newspapers, which have been discussed in the preceding chapters, the library provides other kinds of information sources for the student who is seeking the answer to a question, aid in solving or clarifying a problem, or illustrative material in any of the several subject fields. Since these materials are not always listed in the main catalog, it is important that users of the library know what they are, how they are organized and arranged, and the rules which govern their use. (Figure 14 shows some catalog cards for nonbook materials.)

Among these sources are (1) pamphlets and clippings; (2) audiovisual materials; (3) microfilms, microcards, microprint, and other microforms; (4) automated information sources; and (5) government publications.

NONBOOK SOURCES

PAMPHLETS AND CLIPPINGS

A pamphlet is a publication which deals with only one subject and consists of a few pages stitched together and enclosed in paper covers. Pamphlets may be issued singly or in a series such as the "Headline Books" of the Foreign Policy Association. Pamphlets cover topics of current importance in

Filmstrip
020
Us85

Using library resources for a research paper (*Filmstrip*)
McGraw-Hill Book Co., 1966. Made by William P. Gott-
lieb Co.
39 fr. color. 35 mm. (The College library series)
Eastman color.
Correlated with Guide to the use of books and libraries, by Jean
Key Gates.

Microfilm
330.1
C94p   Cropsey, Joseph.

Polity and economy; an interpretation of the principles of
Adam Smith. Ann Arbor, University Microfilms [1952]
([University Microfilms, Ann Arbor, Mich.] Publication no. 3879)
Microfilm copy of typescript. Positive.

Film
940.1   The medieval knights (Motion Picture) Encyclo-
M48   paedia Britannica Films, 1956.
         22 min., sd., color, 16mm.

Music
785.71
Am52w   **Amram, David.**

The wind and the rain; viola and piano. New York, C. F.
Peters [°1964]
score (9 p.) and part. 30 cm. (Edition Peters, no. 6692)
"Based on the second movement of the Shakespearean concerto for
small orchestra."
Duration: 7 min.

Phonodisc
629.45   PROJECT MERCURY
Am5i   **America's** men in space [the story of Project Mercury.
         Phonodisc] CMS Records CMS 71,000. [1964]
         2 s. 12 in. 33⅓ rpm. microgroove. stereophonic.

         Documentary, with narration by John H. [i. e. A.] Powers and Fred
         Hanney of Mercury Control, N. A. S. A.
         Historical notes by Willy Ley on slipcase.

         1. Project Mercury. I. Powers, John H. II. Hanney, Fred.
         III. Title: The story of Project Mercury.

                                                    R 64-1579

         Library of Congress   [1]

Figure 14 Sample catalog cards for nonbook materials.

any subject field and appear more frequently in areas of thought and activity
which are constantly changing.

When they are first published, pamphlets are excellent sources of recent information or opinion on a subject. Parts of books may appear first as pamphlets, and writings which have never been published in book form are often found in pamphlet form.

When pamphlets become out of date as current information, they serve as valuable historical sources because they indicate the trend of interest and opinion at a particular time.

Pamphlets are organized for use in several ways:

1 Some are classified, cataloged, and shelved in the general collection.
2 Some are listed in the card catalog but arranged in a filing cabinet.
3 Others may be filed in a cabinet designated as the "pamphlet file," arranged alphabetically by subject or numerically if part of a series. In this case, there is usually a separate catalog or listing of the available pamphlets on or near the filing cabinet.

Clippings which have been taken from newspapers, magazines, brochures, and other sources are useful for current events and for providing information on subjects too brief to be treated in pamphlets or books.

Clippings may be mounted on cardboard or placed in folders. In general, they are kept in a filing cabinet called the "vertical file" and are arranged alphabetically by subject. As a rule, they are not listed in the main catalog.

AUDIOVISUAL MATERIALS

Included in the broad field of audiovisual materials are pictures (clipped from newspapers and magazines), postcards, reproductions of art masterpieces, slides, filmstrips, motion-picture films, charts, graphs, maps, models, phonograph records, tape and wire recordings, sheet music, transparencies, programmed books, kits, cassettes, videotapes, and the equipment needed for their use.

There are audiovisual materials in all subject fields. They are essential in art and music appreciation courses and in language courses; they will enhance the study of drama, literature, and history; they are useful in all the social sciences and in the pure and applied sciences.

Originally, audiovisual materials were used for recreational purposes and to supplement textbook teaching, and they are still used for these purposes. But in some courses, and for some purposes, the audiovisual medium is the course, as in a course on films or television.

Audiovisual materials are no longer considered extra or additional; they are now a significant part of all areas of learning. The student seeking information on a given subject or the answer to a given question may find that a film, filmstrip, slide, videotape, transparency, or other nonbook form will provide the information needed more satisfactorily than a printed source. In any search for material on a subject, nonbook forms should be included.

Many academic libraries have production facilities, including dark-rooms, where teachers and students can make their own audiovisual materials. Students can use these facilities to make slides, films, prints, tapes, transparencies, or other audiovisual materials to illustrate, clarify, and support oral and written reports.

Audiovisual materials may be listed in the general catalog, or they may be kept in separate files in special rooms or areas, with a catalog or listing for each kind of material. In general, these types of materials are kept together according to kind (films, filmstrips, tapes, and so on) and are arranged on shelves or in files according to subject classification.[1] Thus a library may have a map file, a picture file, a room where films, slides, filmstrips and other audiovisual materials are kept and projected, and booths for listening to phonograph and tape recordings.

Audiovisual materials are entered in the catalog, as other materials are, under author, title, subject, and under other appropriate headings, such as illustrator, producer, and so on. They are described on the catalog card by author, title, imprint, and subject matter, and by their peculiar features, such as form, running time, whether sound or silent, color or black and white, and size (see Figure 14).

Regulations governing the use of audiovisual materials and equipment vary greatly. In some libraries, certain kinds of materials are circulated while others must be used in specified areas or rooms of the library. Other regulations govern the use of production facilities.

MICROFORMS

The book—the printed page—is still the easiest and most convenient means of disseminating written documents, but printed materials have been increasing at such a rapid rate that libraries as well as businesses, industry, and government have had to find ways of housing them satisfactorily and making them conveniently accessible to those who need them. One of the means they have used is microforms.

"Microform" is the name given to any microphotographically produced printed matter. A number of forms and production methods have been developed. Kinds of microforms include microfilm, microprint, microcards, and microfiche (Figure 15).

Microfilm may be 16-mm or 35-mm roll or cartridge film. It is one of the principal forms for reproducing information. Developed as a means of saving space by microcopying back issues of newspapers and magazines, it is used also to reproduce books, reports, government publications, dissertations, and other kinds of printed material.

[1]The Dewey Decimal Classification System or the Library of Congress Classification System may be used or new classification systems may be devised for each kind of material. In some cases, materials may be numbered in the order they were received and shelved by that number.

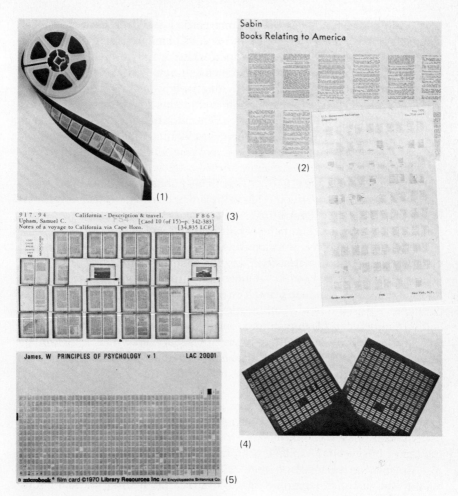

Figure 15 Microforms: (1) microfilm; (2) microprint; (3) microcard; (4) microfiche; (5) microbook fiche. (Photographed and reproduced by permission of the publishers: 1, University Microfilms; 2, Readex Microprint; 3, Lost Cause Press; 4, NCR Corporation; 5, Library Resources, Inc.)

Microprint is a microphotograph of printed material reproduced in printed form on 6- by 9-inch cards or sheets, containing up to 100 pages of text. Images are placed on the sheet in rows.

A microcard is a microscopic photographic reproduction of printed material on standard-size 3- by 5-inch library catalog cards. A microcard contains up to eighty pages of printed material, and images are placed on the card in rows. Microfilm might be compared to the negative of a picture taken by a camera, microcard and microprint to the final snapshot. Increasingly, the microcard is giving way to microfiche.

A microfiche is a 4- by 6-inch film card. Each fiche carries reduced images that are placed on the card in rows, as in microprint and microcard. Microfiche film may be either black and white or full color. The reduction ratio—low, medium, or high—determines the number of pages on a fiche. The conventional fiche contains up to ninety-eight pages of text.

A microbook fiche is a photographic reproduction of materials at very great reductions on a small transparent film card. In a microbook fiche, each page is reduced photographically from 55 to 90 times depending on the page size. Up to 1,000 page images can be reproduced on a single fiche. Microbook cards fit in the standard library catalog drawer.

A recent use of fiche (1976) is Text/fiche, published by the University of Chicago Press. Text/fiche combines print and fiche and is used chiefly for art books that have many illustrations: the text and captions are in printed form and the illustrations are in fiche—color or black and white.

Originally conceived of as a means of reducing in size and storing great quantities of printed material in a very compact and inexpensive form, microforms are now used for numerous purposes; e.g.: (1) to preserve information which has been printed on poor-quality, perishable paper;[2] (2) to duplicate material quickly and inexpensively; (3) to protect valuable information against loss; (4) to restore out-of-print books to in-print status; (5) to enable libraries in the United States to secure materials from foreign libraries; (6) to store very small images for production of full-size copy on demand; and (7) to store and retrieve bits of data from large data bases.

Among the kinds of materials which are available in microfilm, microcard, microprint, or microfiche are: periodicals, newspapers, reports of research, out-of-print books, rare books, new books, government publications, theses, dissertations, manuscripts, library card catalogs, records and reports of business and industry, archival materials, and telephone books.

All microforms must be read with the aid of a device which will enlarge the microphotographic image. Microcards, microprint, and microfiche are read left to right, beginning with the top line. Many devices have been designed ranging from hand viewers to large tabletop models. They are not always easy to use, and many devices do not produce an easily read image on the screen.

A reader-printer is available in many libraries. The reader-printer prints the image which is produced on the reading machine screen on a sheet of paper in print that is easily read without the aid of any device. In a sense, the reader-printer returns the microform to its original state.

Once considered as aids in advanced research, microforms are useful to

[2]It is estimated that most books published in the first half of this century will not be usable by the end of the century and that materials totaling some 3 billion pages will require preservative measures. *Ninth Annual Report for the Year Ending June 30, 1965* (Washington, D.C.: Council on Library Resources, Inc., 1965), pp. 23, 30.

any person who is looking for information on a subject. Because of the many kinds of material—on almost every subject—which are issued in one or another of the microforms, the student must learn about them and how and when to use them.

In some libraries, catalog cards for microforms are filed in the main catalog with a form or location included in the call number (see Figure 14). Microforms are shelved in a separate area, usually in card catalog drawers or in other file drawers.

Some libraries have a special room, called "Microforms," "Microtext Reading Room," or the like, in which microforms are housed and reading machines are located. Light is controlled to provide better contrast for images on the reading machine screens. A catalog or list of microforms is placed in or near this room.

AUTOMATED INFORMATION SOURCES[3]

Some academic libraries have terminals (cathode-ray tubes or CRTs; see Figure 16) which are on-line[4] to one or more data bases and which are used in computer searches. At the present time (1978) in most academic libraries, computer-assisted reference or automated reference service means that the computer searches a standard subject index or abstracting service, but the index or abstracting service is on magnetic tape or disks rather than in printed form. For example, *Psychological Abstracts*, *Chemical Abstracts*, and *Index Medicus* are printed volumes, but they are also data bases. They can be searched in the printed form manually, or the data bases can be searched by computer if the library has computer access to them. The information is the same: the format is different. The search by computer is much quicker.

At present, the result of a computer search is generally a list of citations which appears on the screen of the CRT. From the list of references, the searcher selects the ones which appear to be useful. Some computers are also printers and can print out the citations.

Few data bases provide the documents cited in the computer search, and the user must find the book, journal, or report and read the item cited. In using ERIC, one of the best-known data bases (see p. 185), the student will usually find all but journal articles in the ERIC microfiche collection. Some data base distributors and some commercial firms offer documents on microfiche or reprints of articles. If the library does not have the item cited

---

[3]For a discussion of reference service and the computer, see William A. Katz, *Introduction to Reference Work*, 3d ed. (McGraw-Hill Series in Library Education). Vol. II: *Reference Services and Reference Processes* (New York:McGraw-Hill Book Company, 1978), pp. 123–175.

[4]"On-line" means "in direct access to a data base"; when a CRT is "off-line," requests for searches are submitted to a processing center which makes the search.

Figure 16 Computer terminal (cathode-ray tube). (Photograph reproduced by permission of System Development Corporation.)

in the computer search, it may be possible to borrow it from another library on interlibrary loan.

There is a charge for computer use ranging from about $25 to $120 per on-line hour. The cost for a single search varies depending on the data base searched, the number of terms used, the number of citations obtained, and the time required to make the search.

The New York Times Information Bank contains the index and abstracts printed in *The New York Times* since 1969. The two largest distributors of data base services are Lockheed Information Service, which offers an information retrieval service called DIALOG, and Systems Development Corporation, which has a group of data bases referred to as ORBIT.

Each data bank has a thesaurus—a detailed list of subject headings (descriptors)—which must be used in making a search of that data base, just as the card catalog subject headings must be used in searching the card catalog (see pp. 57–59).

In general, at present, the reference librarian conducts the computer search, but in some libraries students carry out their own searches.

DETERMINING THE USEFULNESS OF NONBOOK INFORMATION SOURCES
These questions can be asked in evaluating any nonbook source:

1 Are those who produced the material specialists in their fields?
2 Is the usefulness of the subject matter presented affected by time, and, if so, is this source out of date?
3 Does it attempt to cover more than it is possible to cover in a source of this length?
4 Is the quality of reproduction acceptable, or does it detract from the content?
5 Is the material presented clearly?
6 Is the material presented without bias?
7 What purposes will it serve:
   a Will it answer a question completely?
   b Will it supplement another source?
   c Will it illustrate and clarify a topic?
   d Will it give current information if it is needed?
8 What subject areas are emphasized?
9 Does its usefulness justify the cost, if any?

REFERENCE SOURCES ON NONBOOK MATERIALS
General

Audiovisual Market Place: A Multimedia Guide. New York: R. R. Bowker Company, 1969– . (Biennial.) Provides information on materials, equipment, sources, persons, organizations, manufacturers, and services in the audiovisual field.

Educational Media Year Book 1978. 5th ed. Edited by James W. Brown. New York: R. R. Bowker Company, 1978. Gives an annual review of important developments in educational media, including libraries, training, reference sources, and organizations.

Learning Directory, 1970–1971: Instructional Materials Index. New York: Westinghouse Learning Corporation, 1970. 7 vols. Lists, by subject, 200,000 items including both print and nonprint media. All types of material on a subject are listed together. Includes films, filmstrips, tapes, transparencies, 8-mm loops, disks, and books. *Supplement 1972/73.*

Previews: Audiovisual Software Reviews. New York: R. R. Bowker Company, 1972– . (Monthly, September–May.) Presents evaluative reviews for all media.

Rufsvold, Margaret I., and Guss, Carolyn. *Guides to Educational Media.* 4th ed. Chicago: American Library Association, 1977. Identifies and describes published catalogs devoted to nonprint educational media; does not include trade catalogs.

Equipment

Audio-Visual Equipment Directory. Fairfax, Va.: National Audio-Visual Association, 1953– . (Annual.) Serves as a guide to current models of audiovisual equipment.

Rosenberg, Kenyon C., and Doskey, John S. *Media Equipment: A Guide and Dictionary.* Littleton, Colo.: Libraries Unlimited, 1976. Defines terms related to media equipment; includes criteria for media.

Films

Educators Guide to Free Films. Randolph, Wis.: Educators Progress Service, 1941– . Lists and gives pertinent information on the nature, purposes, sources, and uses of films.

8mm Film Directory. New York: Educational Film Library Association, 1969/70. Lists all forms of 8-mm films, silent and sound, arranged by subject with description; includes information on 8-mm projectors.

Film Evaluation Guide. New York: Educational Film Library Association, 1965. *Supplement*, 1968, 1972. Describes and evaluates; give synopses and uses; indicates grade level.

National Audiovisual Center. *A Reference List of Audiovisual Materials Produced by the United States Government 1978.* Washington, D.C.: National Archives and Records Service, General Services Administration, 1978. Lists more than 6,000 audiovisual materials produced by federal agencies, available for sale, rental, or free loan; covers a wide range of subjects; is arranged by subject and title.

National Information Center for Educational Media.[5] *Index to 8mm Cartridges.* Los Angeles: National Information Center for Educational Media, 1977. Gives brief summary of contents, audience level, description, availability; has subject index.

———. *Index to 16mm Educational Films.* 6th ed. Los Angeles: National Information Center for Educational Media, 1977. 4 vols. Indicates audience level of each film, availability, and physical description; gives brief summary of contents; is arranged alphabetically by title and has a subject index.

U.S. Library of Congress. *Library of Congress Catalog: Motion Pictures and Filmstrips.* Washington, D.C.: Government Printing Office, 1953–1972.

[5]National Information Center for Educational Media (NICEM) catalogs and stores in computerized form current and comprehensive data on all types of nonbook educational media.

Gives a reproduction of the catalog cards for motion pictures and filmstrips in the library's collection. Continued by *Film and Other Materials for Projection*, 1973– . (Quarterly.)

Filmstrips

Educators Guide to Free Filmstrips. Randolph, Wis.: Educators Progress Service, 1949– . Lists, describes filmstrips and gives sources. Since 1975 in 2 vols.

National Information Center for Educational Media. *Index to 35mm Educational Filmstrips.* 6th ed. Los Angeles: National Information Center for Educational Media, 1977. 3 vols. Produced by computer from the Master Data Bank at the University of Southern California (Los Angeles); gives bibliographical and other data on 35-mm filmstrips in all subject areas.

Microforms

Diaz, Albert James (ed.). *Guide to Microforms in Print*, 1961– . Washington, D.C.: Microcard Editions, 1961– . (Annual.) Lists microforms available from United States publishers; does not include dissertations and theses.

––––––. *Subject Guide to Microforms in Print.* 1961/1963– . Washington, D.C.: Microcard Editions, 1962– . (Biennial). A companion to *Guide to Microforms in Print;* covers all forms of microreproductions; gives bibliographical and ordering information.

Walsh, John J. (ed.). *Guide to Microforms in Print Incorporating International Microforms in Print 1978.* Westport, Conn.: Microform Review, Inc., 1978. A cumulative annual listing of microform titles including books, journals, newspapers, government publications, archival material, collections, and other materials currently available from micropublishers throughout the world; arranged alphabetically by author and title; includes a directory of publishers.

Music

Roach, Helen. *Spoken Records.* 3d ed. Metuchen, N.J.: Scarecrow Press, 1970. Gives a critical evaluation of commercially produced recordings selected for their literary or historical merit, interest, or entertainment value; includes all types of recordings.

U.S. Library of Congress. *Library of Congress Catalog: Music and Phonorecords.* Washington, D.C.: Government Printing Office, 1953–1972. (Annual.) A reproduction of cards in catalogs of the Library of Congress; is arranged alphabetically; has a subject index. Continued by *Music, Books on Music, and Sound Recordings.* 1973– . (Semiannual.)

Tapes

Educators Guide to Free Tapes, Scripts, and Transcriptions. Randolph, Wis.: Educators Progress Service, 1955– . Describes and gives pertinent information about the sources and uses of these materials.

National Information Center for Educational Media. *Index to Educational Audio Tapes.* 4th ed. Los Angeles: National Information Center for Educational Media, 1977. Gives a brief summary of contents of each tape, audience level, availability, and description; has subject index.

————. *Index to Educational Video Tapes.* 4th ed. Los Angeles: National Information Center for Educational Media, 1977. Contains brief summary of the content, gives audience level, availability, description; has subject index.

Transparencies

National Information Center for Educational Media. *Index to Educational Overhead Transparencies.* 5th ed. Los Angeles: National Information Center for Educational Media, 1977. 2 vols. Gives summary, description, availability, audience; has subject index.

Examples of Professional Journals[6]

AV Communication Review. Washington, D.C.: Association for Educational Communications and Technology, National Education Association, 1953– . (Quarterly.) Emphasizes the theoretical aspects of AV; has technical articles on the use of materials in learning; gives book reviews and abstracts of research.

American Record Guide. New York: American Record Guide, 1934– . (Monthly.) Incorporates the *American Tape Guide* (formerly *The American Music Lover*); reviews recordings and tapes; covers classical records and jazz recordings; gives reviews of music and drama.

Audiovisual Instruction. Washington, D.C.: Association for Educational Communications and Technology, National Education Association, 1956– . (Monthly, September–May.) Official journal of the association; each issue is devoted to one theme; has practical information about equipment and techniques; includes news items; carries an index to reviews of audiovisual materials in other publications (*Multi Media Review Index* supplement).

---

[6]In addition to the journals in the audiovisual fields, there are journals which carry reviews of nonbook materials as regular features, for example, *Booklist* and *Saturday Review.* Professional journals in specific subject fields, such as art, music, social sciences, and so on, frequently include evaluations of nonbook materials. Additional aids in locating information about audiovisual materials are the periodical indexes; see listings under such subject headings as "Audiovisual Aids," "Audiovisual Equipment," "Audiovisual Instruction."

Educational Screen and Audio-Visual Guide. Chicago: Trade Periodicals, Inc., 1922– . (Monthly.) Occasionally devoted to one subject; gives information about new materials and new developments in preparation and utilization of media.

The Film Journal. Hollins College, Va.: Hollins College, 1971– . (Quarterly.) Gives book reviews, reports of film festivals, critical studies of actors and directors, personal interviews; is illustrated.

GOVERNMENT PUBLICATIONS

A government publication is a publication issued (or purchased) at public expense by authority of Congress or any other government office or institution—national, state, or local—for distribution to government officials or to the public. Documents which contain the records of government in their original form are placed in government archives. In published form, they are made available to libraries, organizations, and individuals.

Some kinds of government publications are issued at all levels of government—national, state, and municipal—but the chief source of government publications is the federal government. It is said that the United States government is the largest single publisher in the world. Each year the departments, offices, and agencies of the federal government prepare and issue tens of thousands of publications.

During the early years of our nation's history, printing was done by printers selected by Congress under a contract system. The publications of these contract printers were often poorly made and inadequately indexed, and sometimes they were not even identifiable as government publications. In 1846, Congress created a Joint Committee on Printing, composed of three members from each house, to bring about reforms in printing practices. In 1852, a Superintendent of Public Printing was appointed to supervise the work of the printers who were selected under the contract system. The establishment of a national printing plant was authorized by Congress in 1860, and the United States government began doing its own printing in 1861.

The United States Government Printing Office is an independent body in the legislative branch of the government. The Public Printer, who is appointed by the President with the approval of the Senate, is responsible for its management. The Congressional Joint Committee on Printing has jurisdiction over the Government Printing Office in matters pertaining to the materials used in printing, wages of employees, and the efficient operation of the Office; it controls the arrangement and style of the *Congressional Record* and the *Congressional Directory*. The Superintendent of Documents (an office created in the Government Printing Office in 1895) is responsible for centralized distribution of government publications.

GENERAL INFORMATION SOURCES

The Superintendent of Documents sells government publications to individuals, organizations, and institutions; distributes them to depository[7] libraries; compiles and distributes catalogs and lists; and provides information, upon request, about government publications.

Individuals may obtain certain government publications free, when available, from members of Congress or from the issuing agency, or they may purchase them from the Superintendent of Documents. Free price lists are issued by certain agencies and lists of selected publications are available, free of charge, from the Superintendent of Documents. The Government Printing Office has bookstores in twenty cities around the United States. Each bookstore has a complete microfiche catalog of all titles and subscriptions offered for sale.

PURPOSE AND KINDS OF GOVERNMENT PUBLICATIONS

Government publications grow out of the peculiar function of the governmental agencies which issue them and are a public record of the operation and activities of the government. They provide a means of keeping the public informed, so that each citizen can understand and make use of the services the government provides and can carry out more intelligently the duties of citizenship.

The contents of government publications are as varied as the departments, agencies, and bureaus which issue them, and they cover every subject area. They include annual reports, transcripts of congressional hearings, statistical analyses, manuals of instruction, recordings of proceedings, bibliographies, directories, speeches, rules and regulations, results of research, and travel information.

They are printed or processed (that is, duplicated by some means—mimeograph or other process), and they appear in almost every form: loose-leaf, unbound and bound books, pamphlets, leaflets, newspapers, periodicals, maps, charts, multivolume reports, abstracts, motion pictures, filmstrips, posters, and catalogs of art reproductions; some are examples of fine printing.

[7]The distribution free of charge of federal government publications to designated libraries was authorized by act of Congress, February 5, 1859. The law provided for one depository library for each congressional district in the United States and for two depositories at large for each state. All state libraries and the libraries of land-grant colleges and universities were named federal depositories. Government publications in depository libraries are permanent and are available to the public, at least for reference use. The Depository Library Act of 1962 (Public Law 87-579) increased the total number of depository libraries to 792 and made available to them practically all government publications, including those not printed at the United States Government Printing Office. There are now more than 1,200 Federal Depository Libraries, and more are added monthly.

USEFULNESS OF GOVERNMENT PUBLICATIONS

Government publications provide primary source material in many areas, especially in statistics, in government operations, and in certain areas of the sciences, such as the results of scientific and medical research or patent and copyright applications. They provide information of many kinds which is not available from any other source. They are useful in most areas of study but are particularly useful in the study of history, the social sciences, education, personnel management, and the physical and biological sciences. Prepared by specialists who are in reality writing about their particular activities, they can be considered authoritative in the subjects they cover. They are up to date in that they present the latest information available to the agency which issues them. Many government publications provide bibliographies which are useful for further study and research. In general, the publications are concise and readable.

ORGANIZATION AND ARRANGEMENT OF GOVERNMENT PUBLICATIONS IN LIBRARIES

Library users are often confused by the great number of government publications and do not know how to select or locate them. There are several ways in which libraries organize and arrange them.

1 They may be classified, cataloged, and shelved like other library materials. This is usually the case if the library receives only a few titles. If government publications are treated like other library materials, they will be assigned a number from the classification system in use in the library and will be arranged on the shelves according to the call number. In this case, the reader will locate them by using the card catalog, just as any other kind of library material is located.

2 They may be classified and cataloged like other library materials but kept in a special file or section of shelves. If this is the case, the words "Gov. Doc." are usually added to the call number.

3 They may be classified as "Government Documents" (or "Government Publications") and arranged alphabetically or numerically on shelves or in filing cabinets. Where this system is used, a listing, index, or catalog is kept nearby.

4 Some government publications in a given library may be classified and cataloged like other library materials, and others in the same library may be treated as government publications and kept in a separate place. The physical location will be included in the call number.

5 They may be treated as a separate collection, as they are in depository libraries, and arranged by the classification number of the issuing agency.

GENERAL INFORMATION SOURCES

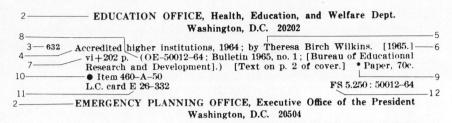

1 — **Entries 1–1569**

2 ——————— EDUCATION OFFICE, Health, Education, and Welfare Dept.
Washington, D.C. 20202

8 —————————————————————————————— 5

3 — 632 Accredited higher institutions, 1964; by Theresa Birch Wilkins. [1965.] — 6
4 — vi+202 p. (OE–50012–64; Bulletin 1965, no. 1; [Bureau of Educational
7 — Research and Development].) [Text on p. 2 of cover.] * Paper, 70c.
10 — ● Item 460–A–50 —————————————————— 9
11 — L.C. card E 26–332 FS 5.250 : 50012–64 — 12

2 ——————— EMERGENCY PLANNING OFFICE, Executive Office of the President
Washington, D.C. 20504

657 Application of statistics to resource management program, paper by Joseph
D. Coker, chief, National Resource Evaluation Center, prepared for
American Statistical Association annual meeting, Dec. 27–30, 1964, Chi-
cago, Ill. [1965.] [2]+13 leaves, 2 pl. 4° ‡ PrEx 4.18/4 : R 31/2

Index

MONTHLY CATALOG JANUARY 1966

NOTE.—*Entries appear in this Index under subjects or titles. Bulletins, circulars, etc.,
having no specific subjects are entered under the issuing office only. Index citations are to
entry numbers in the catalog.*

13 — Colleges and universities :
14 — accredited higher institutions, 1964. 632 — 15
debate topic, 1965–66, selected excerpts
and references, 466
English major undergraduate requirements. curriculum patterns, 637
facilities, survey, 636
higher education act of 1965—

Figure 17 Excerpts from *United States Government Publications: Monthly Catalog*,
title page, pp. 40, 42, 111. (1) Items in each issue are listed sequentially. (2)
Arrangement of the *Monthly Catalog* is alphabetical by government department,
bureau, office, or agency which issues the publication; indexed by subject or title. (3)
Location of reference in the *Catalog*. (4) Title of publication. (5) Author of publication.
(6) Date of publication; information in brackets does not appear on the title page of the
publication. (7) Number of pages. (8) Office of Education classification by the
Superintendent of Documents; also a series listing, i.e., this is no. 1 in the 1965 series
of bulletins issued by the Office of Education. (9) Paperback; asterisk means that it is
for sale by the Superintendent of Documents. (10) This symbol means that the
publication is sent to depository libraries. (11) Library of Congress catalog card
number. (12) Superintendent of Documents classification number (FS was the class
number for the Department of Health, Education, and Welfare—formerly the Federal
Security Agency—until 1970, when it was changed to HE); also the location symbol
used in libraries (see p. 145). (13) Subject heading. (14) A publication on this subject;
see (4) above. (15) Item no. 632 in the *Catalog* (not a page reference). The format of the
Monthly Catalog was changed in 1974; see Figure 18.

In general, the printed bibliographies or lists published by the Superintendent of Documents serve as an index to government publications when
they are treated as a separate collection, as in a depository library. Instead
of looking in the card catalog for a government publication, the students will
consult a printed bibliography, such as the *Monthly Catalog* (Figures 17 and

1———— ENTRIES 77-1 to 77-1386

2————————**LABOR STATISTICS BUREAU**
Labor Dept.
Washington, DC 20210

3———— **77-754**

L 2.2:J 57/5/976 ————————————4

5————United States. Bureau of Labor Statistics.

6———————— Jobs for which a college education is usually required. —

7————————[Washington] : U.S. Dept. of Labor, Bureau of Labor
Statistics, 1976.————————————————8

9————————[18] p. : ill. ; 28 cm.

10———————— Cover title.

11———————— Item 769

12————————pbk.

13———————— 1. Universities and colleges. 2. Occupations. 3. United
States — Occupations. I. Title.

14———— OCLC 2595002

Subject Index

Monthly Catalog   January 1977

15————————————— **Universities and colleges.**

16————————————— Jobs for which a college education is
usually required., 77-754 ————————————17

Figure 18 Excerpts from *Monthly Catalog of United States Government Publications*,
January 1977, title page, pp. 123, I-816. (1) Items in each issue are listed sequential-
ly. (2) Arrangement of the *Monthly Catalog* is alphabetical by government bureau,
office, or agency which issues the publication. (3) Location in the *Catalog*. (4) Labor
Statistics Bureau classification by the Superintendent of Documents. (5) Author. (6)
Title. (7) Place of publication and publisher. (8) Date of publication. (9) Collation. (10)
Note about physical makeup. (11) Depository information. (12) Item is in paperback.
(13) Subject headings (what the publication is about). (14) The number assigned by
OCLC to identify this record in the data base. (15) Heading in the subject index. (16)
Publication on this subject. (17) Item number in *Catalog;* not the page—see (3). The
Monthly Catalog changed to this format in 1974.

18), in much the same manner as they would a periodical index. The printed
bibliography will give the information needed to locate the item on the shelf.
The location symbol is a combination of letters of the alphabet, which
designate the governmental agency which issued the publication, plus
Arabic numerals, which designate the individual office and the kind of
publication (leaflet, bulletin, report, etc.), and letters and Arabic numerals
which make up the number for that specific publication.

For example, the Defense Department is designated D, from the first distinctive letter in the title; the Secretary of Defense is designated D. 1, and all annual reports are given the symbol .1. Thus the symbol for the annual report of the Secretary of Defense is D 1.1.

Every item in the printed symbol is important, and every reference to the publication is important: the series, the type (whether leaflet, bulletin, circular, or monograph), and the year. It is necessary to copy all of them when locating a given publication in a library which uses this kind of organization (as well as when ordering a publication from the Superintendent of Documents).

Examples of Superintendent of Documents classification numbers and the order in which they would appear on the shelf are:

D 1.2:	D 1.6/2:	D 1.16/3:	D 1.42:	D 7.2:
B 85/977-81	C 49	8	10	P 44/976

The printed bibliographies may provide descriptive and evaluative annotations for the publications listed and are useful in determining the kind of government publication to select for a particular problem.

REFERENCE SOURCES
In addition to the printed bibliographies and lists, there are reference works to aid the researcher in choosing government publications for particular purposes. Listed below are (1) printed bibliographies and lists of government publications and (2) reference sources which are helpful in finding and using them.

Bibliographies and Lists
U.S. Library of Congress. Exchange and Gifts Division. *Monthly Checklist of State Publications*. Washington, D.C.: Government Printing Office, 1910– . Arranged alphabetically by state; lists publications received by the Library of Congress; gives full bibliographic information and, in some cases, contents.

U.S. Superintendent of Documents. *Monthly Catalog of United States Government Publications*. Washington, D.C.: Government Printing Office, 1895– . Arranged by Superintendent of Documents Classification; provides complete bibliographical information about each document (author, title, issuing agency, date, etc.—see Figures 17 and 18.) Includes sales information.

——. *Selected U.S. Government Publications*. Washington, D. C.: Government Printing Office, 1928– . Since 1972 issued monthly (except January/February and November/December). Each issue lists and describes about 150 new or still popular publications for sale by the

Superintendent of Documents; arranged by subject; each entry gives information for ordering and price.

Useful Reference Sources

American Statistics Index. Washington, D.C.: Congressional Information Service, 1973– . (Annual, monthly, and quarterly supplements.) "A comprehensive guide and index to the statistical publications of the U.S. government" (subtitle); aims to provide access to all statistics produced by Federal agencies. In two parts: *Index* section and *Abstract* section; is indexed by subject and names; a microfiche service provides most of the documents indexed.

Andriot, John L. *Guide to U.S. Government Publications.* McLean, Va.: Documents Index, 1976–1978. 4 vols. (Published at six-month intervals and then each volume is revised.) An annotated guide to the important series and periodicals currently being published by the various United States government agencies; gives a complete listing of Superintendent of Documents Classification numbers from the time it was devised.

Congressional Information Service. *Index to Publications of the United States Congress.* Washington, D.C.: Congressional Information Service, 1970– . (Monthly, with quarterly cumulation; annual cumulation in two volumes is the *CIS/Annual.*) Aims to provide access to all publications of the U.S. Congress except the *Congressional Record*; includes hearings, committee prints, reports, and other Congressional publications. In two parts: the *Index* section gives access by subject, author, and title; the *Abstract* section gives full titles of the document and an abstract of most items indexed. Indexed items are available on microfiche.

Government Reference Books 68/69: A Biennial Guide to U.S. Government Publications. Littleton, Colo.: Libraries Unlimited, 1970– . (Biennial.) Provides an annotated list of directories, bibliographies, indexes, dictionaries, catalogs, biographical dictionaries, handbooks, statistical works, and almanacs arranged by subject.

Leidy, W. Philip. *A Popular Guide to Government Publications.* 4th ed. New York: Columbia University Press, 1978. Presents a compilation of government publications, popular in nature, which were issued mainly from 1967 to 1975 arranged by broad subjects; titles are annotated; includes topics of current concern such as pollution and mental health.

Morehead, Joe. *Introduction to United States Public Documents* (Library Science Text Series) Littleton, Colo.: Libraries Unlimited, 1975. Gives an overview of the function, nature, and use of United States public documents; includes a discussion of the Government Printing Office, the Superintendent of Documents, and the depository library system; includes only publications of the federal government.

Palic, Vladimir M. *Government Publications: A Guide to Bibliographic Tools.* 4th ed. Washington, D.C.: Library of Congress, 1976. Lists bibliographic aids in the field of government publications issued by the federal government, the states, foreign countries, and international governmental organizations; gives information about each United States agency.

Popular Names of U.S. Government Reports: A Catalog. 3d ed. Washington, D.C.: Library of Congress, 1976. Lists selected reports of the federal government by both the popular name and the official title; is arranged alphabetically by popular name; has annotations and a subject index.

Schmeckebier, Laurence F., and Eastin, Roy B. *Government Publications and Their Use.* 2d rev. ed. Washington, D.C.: The Brookings Institution, 1969. Designed to provide an understanding of government publishing practices past and present and to describe how publications may be obtained; indicates sources of information about publications; includes information about laws, presidential papers, reports, maps, periodicals, microforms, foreign affairs, court decisions; gives a list of depository libraries.

PART FOUR
INFORMATION SOURCES IN THE SUBJECT FIELDS

CHAPTER FIFTEEN
SUBJECT
REFERENCE SOURCES

$\mathbf{A}$ general reference source, which has many subject specialists on its editorial staff, provides much information on the different subject fields; however, since the aim of the general reference source is to give wide and unrestricted coverage, specialized treatment on any one subject is necessarily limited.

For those persons who require more than general treatment of a specific subject, there are specialized reference sources in every subject area.

A subject reference book[1] can be defined as a publication in which items of information about one particular subject—literature, history, music, sports, education—are brought together from many sources and arranged so that individual items can be found quickly and easily.

Subject reference books introduce the student (or nonspecialist) to the subject matter of the different branches of knowledge.

1 They supplement general reference books by giving more specific information and by including specialized information omitted from the general reference sources.
2 They provide specialized definitions and explanations for the words and phrases in a given field which are not found in general word dictionaries.
3 They trace the growth of important ideas in a subject area.

[1]Nonbook sources are discussed in Chapter 14.

4 They provide an introduction to the development of the literature of the subject.

5 They give authoritative information on major questions and issues in a specialized area.

6 They explain and clarify concepts.

7 They locate, describe, and evaluate the literature of the field.

8 They provide facts which indicate trends, and they summarize the events of a given year in a given subject field.

Subject reference books are adapted to the peculiar characteristics of the subject under consideration. For example, in music there are dictionaries of musical themes and musical scores; in art, catalogs of reproductions and auctions; and in science, handbooks of tables and formulas.

KINDS AND PURPOSES OF SUBJECT REFERENCE SOURCES

The kinds of reference material in each subject field are the same as those in the general area, and they serve similar purposes on a more restricted scale. Not all the reference materials listed provide all types of information indicated.

1 Bibliographies and guides
   a Point out the literature of the field in question
   b Indicate works which may not be in the library and therefore serve as aids to further search
   c Provide descriptive and evaluative information which the catalog card cannot include and point out materials in the library which are not listed in the card catalog, such as periodical articles, parts of books, and so on
   d Arrange works according to form: dictionaries, histories, encyclopedias, handbooks, indexes, and books of criticism (if the subject field is literature), and give instructions regarding their use
2 Indexes
   a Indicate where periodical articles on a subject can be found
   b Indicate collections in which plays, short stories, essays, and poems can be found
   c Analyze books and parts of books
3 Dictionaries
   a Provide specialized definitions and explanations of terminology and concepts

    b Help to establish terminology

    c Serve as a guide to current as well as historical usage of words and phrases

    d Give short, concise answers to questions

    e May give chronology

    f May give biographical information

    g May give pronunciation

4 Encyclopedias

    a Give a "summary treatment" of the different phases and aspects of a subject

    b Explain historical backgrounds, trends, and the influence of events outside the subject area, such as the influence of social conditions on the literature of a period

    c Trace the development of ideas in a subject field

5 Handbooks and manuals

    a Identify references, allusions, dates, quotations, and characters in literature

    b Summarize literary plots

    c Provide statistics and useful bits of information

    d Give instructions in specialized areas

6 Yearbooks and annuals

    a Summarize events of the past year, including research projects undertaken and completed

    b Provide a source for hard-to-locate items of information

7 Collections (anthologies)

    a Bring together in one place selections or quotations from essays, poetry, drama, short stories, periodicals, and other forms of literature

    b Serve as source materials for courses in literature, history, education, psychology, and other subject fields

8 Atlases and gazetteers

    a Provide geographical information in any subject area in maps, text, or both

    b Give overall picture emphasizing location of industries, products, literature

9 Biographical dictionaries

    a Provide concise information about important persons in a subject field: authors, scholars, scientists, educators

    b May include bibliographies and evaluations of an author's work

10 Reference histories give factual information, trends, and main facts of development, covering

    a Chronology

  b Interpretation of events

  c Biographical data

  d Bibliographical information

11 Professional journals provide up-to-date articles, essays, book reviews, and other material relating specifically to the subject matter of a given branch of knowledge

12 Abstract journals contain abstracts of periodical and other literature. An abstract is a brief digest or summary which gives the essential points of an article, pamphlet, book, monograph, or report. An abstract journal is a collection of such abstracts (in a particular field) arranged by subject and within the subject alphabetically by author or main entry with subject and author indexes. Usually an abstract of a work gives the researcher enough information to decide whether or not the entire work should be read. Abstract journals give full biographical information regarding the works abstracted. Abstracts may be in the original language in which the work appeared, or they may be in translation.

The choice of a reference source in a subject field, as in a general area, depends upon the nature of the question to be answered: (1) the kind of information required, (2) the subject area of which it is a part, and (3) the factors affecting the question, such as time and location.

USING SUBJECT REFERENCE SOURCES[2]

Reference materials in the subject fields are located in the card catalog under author or editor, title, and subject. Subject headings consist of the subject, subdivided by kind of material: for example, American literature-Bibliographies; Education—Yearbooks, English language—Dictionaries; Literature—Dictionaries.

Efficient use of subject reference materials is dependent upon an understanding of (1) the purposes of each kind of subject reference source, (2) the organization and the arrangement of the material, and (3) the distinguishing features. Before using a subject reference book, one should examine the table of contents and the preliminary pages which explain the purpose, the plan and arrangement, and any special features.

Chapters 16–23 introduce the several subject areas and present representative reference sources in each area. The subject fields discussed are the major classes of knowledge as they are organized in the Dewey Decimal Classification System. They are presented in the order in which they appear

[2]See also pp. 68–70.

in the classification schedule. Not all the reference materials discussed in the preceding paragraphs are found in each subject field.

Since new reference sources and new editions of old ones are being published continually, it is necessary to consult the card catalog frequently in order to keep up to date on the reference materials in the library. The titles listed here are only suggestions, for they represent but a small portion of the thousands that are available. Each reader will supplement them and, in time, replace them with new publications.

CHAPTER SIXTEEN
PHILOSOPHY AND PSYCHOLOGY

The first subject class in the Dewey Decimal Classification System (100), as well as in the Library of Congress Classification System (B), is philosophy. When there was infinitely less to learn than there is today, philosophy comprised all learning except technical rules and the practical arts. In the medieval universities, it was the omnibus subject which covered the whole body of sciences and the liberal arts. Remnants of this comprehensive meaning are carried forward in the present in the highest academic degree, doctor of philosophy (Ph.D.), although increased specialization in the social sciences and humanities, as well as in the pure and applied sciences, has greatly narrowed the range of interest and inquiry of most "doctor of philosophy" students.

Derived from two Greek words, *philein*, "to love," and *sophia*, "wisdom," "philosophy" has historically been thought of both as the seeking of wisdom and the wisdom sought. In this day of rapidly advancing science and technology, of wide-sweeping change, and of increasingly complex domestic and world problems which overlap and intertwine and thus require the most mature thought and judgment of generalists as well as specialists, philosophy is more often thought of as the quest for wisdom than as the wisdom for which search is made. Consequently, philosophy is seen as a mode and method of thought, as a continual invitation to those of serious concern to ask reasoned questions of life and to examine and criticize rationally the ends and purposes which men and women establish and the methods they pursue in their efforts to achieve those purposes. Today, no area of investigation is denied to scientific research; correspondingly, no presupposition, premise, prejudice, assumption, belief, or disbelief—in short, no area of action and thought—is "protected" from the disciplined, probing, analytical approach of philosophy.

In this concept of philosophy as the quest for wisdom, the central emphasis is on *values* (morals and ethics) and on the rational ways (logic) by which value judgments can and should be developed and criticized. Philosophy tries to locate, to understand, and to clarify the nature and importance of the issues and values at stake in situations of uncertainty, confusion, dispute, competition, and conflict. Philosophers who are true to the principles and procedures inherent in the philosophical method of inquiry are concerned about mature, serious, constructive, and hard-won matters. On the basis of facts and knowledge which they draw from wide-ranging fields of recorded and observable experience, philosophers offer for critical examination their own concepts, ideas, and propositions, and they seek to analyze rationally the concepts, ideas, and propositions set forth by others.

Consequently, since there is no such thing in a free society as an "established" philosophy—an accepted, authoritative credo of belief and action—but only philosophers and their philosophies, the basic literature of philosophy is the writings of past and present philosophers and critical commentaries upon these writings.

REFERENCE SOURCES IN PHILOSOPHY
Bibliographies and Indexes[1]
The Philosopher's Index: An International Index to Philosophical Periodicals. Bowling Green, Ohio: Bowling Green University, 1967– . (Quarterly.) Indexes more than eighty American and a selected number of foreign philosophy journals; uses key-word-in-context approach for subject and author.

Walford, A. J. (ed.). *Guide to Reference Material.* Vol. II: *Social & Historical Sciences, Philosophy & Religion.* 3d ed., Chicago: American Library Association, 1975.

Dictionaries and Encyclopedias
Baldwin, James Mark (ed.). *Dictionary of Philosophy and Psychology.* New ed. New York: The Macmillan Company, 1925. 3 vols. (Reprinted by Peter Smith, 1946.) Out of date for modern developments, but still useful; covers the entire field.

Brugger, Walter (ed.). *Philosophical Dictionary.* (Walter Brugger: editor of the original German edition. Kenneth Baker: translator and editor of the American edition.) Spokane, Wash.: Gonzaga University Press, 1972. Translated from the German *Philosophisches Wörterbuch*; explains

[1]See also Chapter 9, Indexes and Chapter 13, Bibliographies.

philosophical terms; gives the history of philosophy from ancient times to the present; includes coverage of contemporary Anglo-American concerns.

Bullock, Alan, and Stallybrass, Oliver (eds.). *The Harper Dictionary of Modern Thought*. New York: Harper & Row, Publishers, Incorporated, 1977. Covers twentieth-century words and phrases; defines words in their intellectual, historical, and cultural context.

Edwards, Paul (ed.). *The Encyclopedia of Philosophy*. New York: The Macmillan Company and The Free Press, 1967. 8 vols. For specialists and nonspecialists; covers all of philosophy and related disciplines; treats topics at length and emphasizes individual thinkers; provides bibliographies and many cross references; contributors are from all parts of the world; Vol. 8 is the index. (Also available in four vols.)

Lacey, A. R. *A Dictionary of Philosophy*. Boston: Routledge & Kegan Paul, Ltd., 1976. Published in paperback by Charles Scribner's Sons, 1976. Intended for students and nonspecialists; covers only Western philosophy; defines terms; explains concepts; gives some biographies; entries are brief; some have bibliographies.

Urmson, J. O. (ed.). *The Concise Encyclopedia of Western Philosophy and Philosophers*. New York: Hawthorn Books, Inc., 1960. Provides analytical biographical articles on philosophy from Abelard to the late 1950s and gives discussions of specific topics; has bibliographies; includes portraits.

Wiener, Philip P. (ed.). *Dictionary of the History of Ideas: Studies of Selected Pivotal Ideas*. New York: Charles Scribner's Sons, 1973. 4 vols. *Index*, 1974. A collection of long, scholarly articles by an international group of experts; provides interdisciplinary coverage of many topics in the history of ideas, including philosophy, history, religion, science, mathematics, literature, the arts, the social sciences; bibliographies are provided.

Digests

Magill, Frank N., and McGreal, Ian P. *Masterpieces of World Philosophy in Summary Form*. New York: Salem Press, 1961. 2 vols. Vol. I: sixth century B.C. to A.D. 1800; Vol. II: from 1800. Gives a selection of essay-reviews of philosophical works, chronologically arranged.

Biographical Dictionaries[2]

Directory of American Philosophers. Bowling Green, Ohio: Philosophy Documentation Center, Bowling Green University, 1962–   . (Biennial.)

[2]See also Chapter 10, Biographical Dictionaries.

Companion volume to *International Directory of Philosophy and Philosophers;* gives a list of colleges and universities in the United States and Canada, with information about the philosophy department, if any; includes a list of societies, journals, and publishers of materials in this field.

Directory of American Scholars. 7th ed. Vol. IV: *Philosophy, Religion and Law.* Edited by the Jacques Cattell Press. New York: R. R. Bowker Company, 1978. Devoted to United States and Canadian scholars.

International Directory of Philosophy and Philosophers. 1st ed. Bowling Green, Ohio: Philosophy Documentation Center, 1966– . Published under the auspices of the International Institute of Philosophy with the aid of UNESCO; serves as a worldwide guide to philosophy; provides survey essays on the history and character of philosophy in the various parts of the world; lists organizations, institutes, research centers, members of college and university philosophy faculties, and associations and societies.

Examples of Professional Journals in Philosophy[3]

The Journal of Philosophy. New York: Journal of Philosophy, Inc., Columbia University, 1904– . (Fortnightly.) Provides historical articles on philosophers or systems; includes notes and news.

Journal of the History of Ideas. New York: The City College, City University of New York, 1940– . (Quarterly.) "Devoted to cultural and intellectual history" (subtitle); offers articles on the history of philosophy, literature, the arts, natural and social sciences, religion, political and social movements; emphasizes the influence of one figure or school on another; has lengthy book reviews.

Journal of the History of Philosophy. St. Louis, Mo.: Washington University, Department of Philosophy. 1963– . (Quarterly.) Includes articles on the history of Western philosophy; some are in foreign languages; has book reviews.

The Modern Schoolman. St. Louis, Mo.: St. Louis University, 1925– . (Quarterly.) Aims to promote original and scholarly contributions in all fields of philosophy; includes book reviews.

Philosophical Review. Ithaca, N.Y.: Cornell University, 1892– . (Quarterly.) Publishes papers regarding problems of interest to contemporary philosophers; discusses philosophers and their ideas; gives book reviews.

---

[3]See also *Ulrich's International Periodicals Directory*, 17th ed., and *Magazines for Libraries*, 3d ed., edited by Bill Katz and Berry Richards.

PSYCHOLOGY

Psychology, from the Greek words *psyche*, meaning "mind" or "soul," and *logos*, meaning "law," has historically been the science which treats of the mind in any of its aspects—function, organization and structure, and effect on behavior. Once a part of philosophy and still a close companion, psychology developed and became a separate branch of learning within the past century. Class B of the Library of Congress Classification and class 100 of the Dewey Decimal Classification include both philosophy and psychology.

In recent times, psychology has been thought of as the serious study of the organism as an individual whole, as the study of the organism and its activities rather than of physiological functions. For example, the study of the functions of the brain is thought of more as a physiological than a psychological theme. Thus the general theme of psychology is the study of the activities of the total organism (humans and lower animals) in its interrelations with its physical environment and with its social setting and influences.

Psychology is often referred to and identified in terms of a school or system; for example, behaviorist psychology or Gestalt psychology.

Perhaps the best and most comprehensive way in which to see modern psychology is through an acquaintance with some of its many subdivisions, which are determined by, and are named to describe, the kinds of problems studied. These kinds and fields of psychological study are so connected that one should not try to arrange them either chronologically or in order of their current importance. Some of the more important subdivisions of psychology are abnormal, analytic, animal, applied, experimental, genetic, motor, and physiological. Other subdivisions of psychology are child, adolescent, adult, educational, social, and industrial. Other fields of inquiry which draw heavily upon the basic concepts, principles, and findings of medicine, religion, education, physiology, and sociology are psychiatry, psychoanalysis, psychotherapy, and psychopathology.

REPRESENTATIVE REFERENCE SOURCES IN PSYCHOLOGY

Bibliographies[4]

Harvard University. *The Harvard List of Books in Psychology.* Compiled and annotated by the psychologists in Harvard University. 4th ed. Cambridge, Mass.: Harvard University Press, 1971. A guide to important titles in psychology; is arranged by types of psychology; gives some evaluations.

[4]See also Chapter 13, Bibliographies.

Indexes[5]

Index Medicus. (See p. 199.)

Council on Research in Bibliography. *Mental Health Book Review Index.* New York: Research Center for Mental Health, New York University, 1956–1972. Gives references to book reviews which appeared in some 200 journals, many of which are not listed elsewhere; worldwide in coverage; useful especially for large and specialized libraries.

Dictionaries and Encyclopedias

The Encyclopedia of Mental Health. Edited by Albert Deutsch. New York: Franklin Watts, 1963. 6 vols. Covers a wide range of topics; articles are written by experts; meets needs of educated nonprofessionals and students; has glossary, bibliography, and index.

English, Horace Bidwell, and English, Ava C. (eds.). *A Comprehensive Dictionary of Psychological and Psychoanalytical Terms.* New York: Longmans, Green & Co., Inc., 1958. Gives definitions of all terms that are used frequently in a specialized or technical sense; is not encyclopedic.

Eysenck, H. J. (ed.). *Encyclopedia of Psychology.* New York: Herder and Herder, 1972. 3 vols. International in coverage; treats all facets of psychology today; gives definitions of terms, historical overview, discussion of research and scientific controversies, descriptions of various schools of psychology and related disciplines; gives background and summary of leading international opinion on current issues; includes bibliographies.

Goldenson, Robert M. (ed.). *The Encyclopedia of Human Behavior: Psychology, Psychiatry, and Mental Health.* Garden City, N.Y.: Doubleday & Company, 1970. 2 vols. Aims to cover all major phases of these areas; presents essential information for students and nonprofessionals; gives definitions, illustrative cases, illustrations.

Warren, Howard C. (ed.). *Dictionary of Psychology.* Boston: Houghton Mifflin Company, 1934. Defines both English and foreign terminology; has extensive bibliographies.

Biographical Dictionaries and Directories[6]

American Men and Women of Science. 13th ed. Edited by Jaques Cattell Press. New York: R. R. Bowker Company, 1976. 7 vols.

American Psychological Association. *Biographical Directory.* Washington,

[5]See also Chapter 9, Indexes.
[6]See also Chapter 10, Biographical Dictionaries.

D.C.: American Psychological Association, 1970– . (Triennial.) Lists affiliated organizations; gives brief biographical information on members and background information on the association.

Yearbooks

Annual Review of Psychology. Palo Alto, Calif.: Annual Reviews, 1950– . Gives interpretative and evaluative reviews by psychologists of many topics in contemporary psychology.

Buros, Oscar Krisen. *The Eighth Mental Measurements Yearbook.* Highland Park, N.J.: Gryphon Press, 1978. 2 vols. Makes available bibliographies of recent critical reviews of tests published in English, bibliographies of references on the construction and use of tests and on books in the field.

Examples of Professional Journals in Psychology[7]

American Journal of Psychology. Urbana: University of Illinois Press, 1887– . (Quarterly.) Publishes reports of original research; emphasis is on experimental psychology; includes some short notes and discussions; gives book reviews.

Journal of General Psychology. Provincetown, Mass.: The Journal Press, 1928– . (Quarterly.) Covers experimental, physiological, and comparative psychology.

The Psychological Review. Lancaster, Pa.: American Psychological Association, Inc., 1894– . (Bimonthly.) Presents articles of theoretical significance to any area of scientific endeavor in psychology.

Psychology Today, the Magazine about Psychology, Society, and Human Behavior. Del Mar, Calif.: CMR, Inc., 1967– . (Monthly.) Presents current developments in American psychology for professionals and nonprofessionals; is broad in coverage.

Abstract Journals

Psychological Abstracts. 1927– . Lancaster, Pa.: American Psychological Association, 1927– . (Monthly.) Contains nonevaluative summaries of the world's literature in psychology and related disciplines; includes abstracts from more than 850 technical reports, journals, monographs, and other scientific documents; abstracts are arranged under sixteen major classification categories; has author and subject indexes. Records published since 1967 are on machine-readable tapes which are the basis for automated search known as Psychological Abstracts Information Services.

[7]See also *Ulrich's International Periodicals Directory,* 17th ed., and *Magazines for Libraries,* 3d ed., edited by Bill Katz and Berry Richards.

CHAPTER SEVENTEEN
RELIGION
AND MYTHOLOGY

T he second subject class in the Dewey Decimal System (200) is assigned to religion. This class embraces all religions, including pagan religions and mythology. In the Library of Congress Classification, religion is included in class B with philosophy and psychology.

RELIGION

There are many religions and many definitions of religion.

> . . . In essence religion is related to the beliefs concerning some ruling force or forces and the ways in which these forces are worshipped and obeyed.[1]

In extent and variety, religious literature is perhaps the largest subject class. As was noted in Chapter 1, the earliest records of every civilization are religious or moral works. Temple records constitute the first historical annals.

In addition to the basic scriptures of each religion, there are many kinds

[1]Lester Asheim, *The Humanities and the Library* Chicago: American Library Association, 1957), p. 3.

of religious literature, including historical studies, devotional and inspirational literature, church doctrines and works of interpretation, lives of the saints, digests of ecclesiastical law, church rituals, and informational literature.

The reference books in the field of religion, like all other reference books, are compilations of factual information and are planned to answer specific questions about religions and the literature of the various religions. Reference sources include bibliographies, dictionaries, encyclopedias, biographical dictionaries, concordances,[2] directories, yearbooks, digests, indexes, books of quotations, atlases, and professional journals.

REPRESENTATIVE REFERENCE SOURCES IN RELIGION

Bibliographies, Guides, and Indexes[3]

Adams, Charles J. (ed.). *A Reader's Guide to the Great Religions*. 2d ed. New York: The Free Press, 1977. A collection of bibliographic essays by authorities on the literature, history, and beliefs of the world's great religions; includes religions of the ancient world, Mexico, and South America; provides guidance on what to read.

American Theological Library Association. *Index to Religious Periodical Literature* 1949–1952– . Chicago: American Theological Library Association, 1953– . (Annual until 1962; biennial 1962– .) Indexes by author and subject more than 150 religious periodicals from the United States and foreign countries; includes an author index of book reviews which appear in the periodicals indexed; many articles have abstracts.

Religious and Theological Abstracts. Youngstown, Ohio: Theological Publishers, 1958– . (Quarterly.) Gives brief abstracts in English of articles appearing in a selected group of religious periodicals in various languages; includes Jewish, Christian, and Muslim publications.

Walford, A. J. (ed.). *Guide to Reference Material*. Vol. II: *Social & Historical Sciences, Philosophy & Religion*. 3d ed. London: Library Association, 1975.

Concordances

Cruden, Alexander (comp.). *A Complete Concordance to the Holy Scriptures of the Old and New Testaments*. New ed. Westwood, N.J.: Fleming H. Revell Company, n.d. Includes a concordance to the Apocrypha.

---

[2]A concordance lists, in alphabetical order and in context, the principal or key words in a book or in the works of an author.

[3]See also Chapter 9, Indexes, and Chapter 13, Bibliographies.

Nelson's Complete Concordance of the Revised Standard Version of the Bible. Compiled under the supervision of John W. Ellison. New York: Thomas Nelson & Sons, 1957. Gives context and location of each key word.

Strong, James, *Exhaustive Concordance of the Bible.* New York: Hunt, 1894. First printed in 1894; gives every word of the text of the King James Version and a comparative concordance of the Authorized and Revised Standard Versions.

Thompson, Newton Wayland, and Stock, Raymond (comps.). *Complete Concordance to the Bible (Douay Version).* St. Louis: B. Herder Book Company, 1945. Indexes the actual words of the Douay Roman Catholic version of the Bible.

Dictionaries

Brandon, S. G. F. (ed.). *A Dictionary of Comparative Religion.* New York: Charles Scribner's Sons, 1970. Articles cover a wide variety of topics relating to the world's religions from prehistoric times to the present; aims to "treat the religions in proportion to their significance in the history of human culture" (Preface).

Cross, F. L. (ed.). *The Oxford Dictionary of the Christian Church.* 2d ed. Edited by F. L. Cross and E. A. Livingstone. London: Oxford University Press, 1974. Covers historical developments, doctrine, and definitions of terms; includes biographies and provides bibliographies; gives attention to new developments in the churches, new movements, and new personalities.

Gehman, Henry Snyder (ed.). *The New Westminster Dictionary of the Bible.* Philadelphia: Westminster Press, 1970. Gives a brief outline of the books of the Bible, definitions, biographies, places, pronunciation of proper names; has maps, charts, and illustrations; quotations are from the Revised Standard Version of the Bible.

Hastings, James. *Dictionary of the Bible.* Revised ed. by Frederick C. Grant and H. H. Rowley. New York: Charles Scribner's Sons, 1963. Offers all definitions in line with modern knowledge and scholarship (1963); many new articles; is not an abridgment of the five-volume work; references are to the Revised Standard Version of the Bible.

The Interpreter's Dictionary of the Bible. Nashville: Abingdon Press, 1962. 4 vols. "An illustrated encyclopedia identifying and explaining all proper names and significant terms and subjects in the Holy Scriptures, including the Apocrypha, with attention to archaeological discoveries and researches into the life and faith of ancient times" (subtitle). Serves the needs of students, scholars, teachers, preachers, and general readers. Supplementary volume, 1976.

Julian, John (ed.). *A Dictionary of Hymnology.* Revised ed. with new supplement. London: John Murray, 1915. Sets forth the origin and history of Christian hymns of all ages and nations.

Kauffman, Donald T. *The Dictionary of Religious Terms.* Westwood, N.J.: Fleming H. Revell Company, 1967. Gives very brief definitions or explanations of terms in religion, art, architecture, music, literature, church history, and related areas ranging from the major faiths to the smallest religious groups and from ancient to modern times.

Macquarrie, John (ed.). *Dictionary of Christian Ethics.* Philadelphia: Westminster Press, 1967. Not a manual on Christian morality, but a subject-matter guide to Christian ethics; represents many points of view; treats basic ethical concepts, Biblical and theological ethics; has articles by Christian and Jewish scholars.

Mathews, Shailer, and Smith, Gerald B. (eds.). *A Dictionary of Religion and Ethics.* New York: The Macmillan Company, 1923. Defines and discusses the terminology of religion and ethics; gives biographies of persons not living.

Miller, Madeleine S., and Miller, J. Lane. *Harper's Bible Dictionary.* 8th ed. New York: Harper & Row Publishers, Incorporated, 1973. Covers archaeology, geography, persons, places, and new developments in theology and religion; some pronunciation is given; is illustrated.

Parrinder, Geoffrey. *A Dictionary of Non-Christian Religions.* Philadelphia: The Westminster Press, 1971. Explains terminology, concepts, gods, and religious systems of all non-Christian religions; covers primitive and classical as well as contemporary religions; emphasis is on Hinduism, Buddhism, and Islam; provides drawings and photographs.

Wigoder, Geoffrey (ed.). *Encyclopedic Dictionary of Judaica.* New York: Leon Amiel Publisher, 1974. Provides contemporary information on Jewish life, culture, history, customs, literature, persons of importance, and places that are important in Jewish life and history.

Encyclopedias

Bodensieck, Julius H. (ed.). *The Encyclopedia of the Lutheran Church.* Minneapolis: Augsburg Publishing House, 1965. 3 vols. Prepared for the general public as well as for theologians, the clergy, teachers, and students, with contributors from all parts of the world; this standard reference work on the Lutheran Church gives the scope, history, and influence of the church; does not include biographies of living persons.

Encyclopaedia Judaica. New York: The Macmillan Company, 1972. 16 vols. Presents all aspects of Jewish life and knowledge up to the present time; gives bibliographies for further reading; includes biographical articles. *Yearbook,* 1973– .

Hastings, James (ed.). *Encyclopaedia of Religion and Ethics.* New York: Charles Scribner's Sons, 1908–1927. 12 vols. and index. Contains articles on all religions, all of the great ethical systems and movements, religious beliefs and customs, philosophical ideas, moral practices, and important persons and places.

The New Catholic Encyclopedia. Prepared by an editorial staff at the Catholic University of America. New York: McGraw-Hill Book Company, 1967. 15 vols. "An international work of reference on the teachings, history, organization, and activities of the Catholic Church and on all institutions, religions, philosophies, and scientific and cultural developments affecting the Catholic Church from the beginning to the present" (subtitle). Vol. XVI: *Supplement 1967–1974.* Edited by David Eggenberger, 1974.

The New Schaff-Herzog Encyclopedia of Religious Knowledge. Based on 3d ed. Grand Rapids, Mich.: Baker Book House, 1951. 13 vols. Covers Biblical, historical, doctrinal, and practical theology from the earliest times to the present; includes biography.

Roth, Cecil, and Wigoder, Geoffrey (eds.). *The New Standard Jewish Encyclopedia.* New rev. ed. Garden City, N.Y.: Doubleday & Company, 1970. Aims to be a work of contemporary reference but also covers every phase of Jewish life from the beginning—history, traditions, culture, biography, customs; emphasizes Jewish life in America; includes events of significance since World War II.

Books of Quotations
Mead, Frank Spencer (ed. and comp.). *The Encyclopedia of Religious Quotations.* Westwood, N.J.: Fleming H. Revell Company, 1965. Contains quotations about religion and related topics from both religious and secular sources.

Stevenson, Burton Egbert. *The Home Book of Bible Quotations.* New York: Harper & Row, Publishers, 1949. Based on the King James Version of the Bible; has a key-word concordance index arranged by subject.

Woods, Ralph L. (comp. and ed.). *The World's Treasury of Religious Quotations.* New York: Hawthorn Books, 1966. Offers a great variety of quotations of religious thought from religious and secular sources, modern and ancient; is nondenominational; does not include poetry and has only two verses from the Bible.

Digests
Magill, Frank N. (ed.). *Masterpieces of Catholic Literature in Summary Form.* New York: Harper & Row, Publishers, 1965. Presents, in the form of essay-reviews, a selection of Roman Catholic literature from

earliest times to the present; includes books in the fields of philosophy, theology, and history.

———. *Masterpieces of Christian Literature in Summary Form.* New York: Harper & Row, Publishers, 1963. 2 vols. A selection of literature in essay-review form from the Protestant viewpoint.

Atlases

AlFaruqi, Isma'il R., and Sopher, David E. (eds.). *Historical Atlas of the Religions of the World.* New York: The Macmillan Company, 1974. Historical and geographical approach to the world's religions; covers major religions or groups of religions—past and present—including American Indian religions, African religions, and such universal religions as Buddhism, Christianity, and Islam. Maps, bibliographies, and chronologies are provided; covers origin and distribution; locates shrines and temples.

The Macmillan Bible Atlas. Revised edition by Yohanan Aharoni and Michael Avi-Yonan. New York: The Macmillan Company, 1977. Uses maps and text to cover all aspects of Bible history.

May, Herbert Gordon, and others (eds.). *Oxford Bible Atlas.* 2d ed. London: Oxford University Press, 1974. Covers physical geography, historical changes, and geographical name changes; maps are accompanied by explanatory text; includes articles on historical background of the region; gives archaeological data; has a gazetteer.

Yearbooks

Each denomination has its own yearbook which provides information regarding its organization, membership, officers, local officials, development, publications, and annual achievements; it may include articles on doctrine and questions regarding theology. Examples are *American Jewish Yearbook, Official Catholic Directory,* and *The Episcopal Church Annual.* The titles listed below cover all denominations.

Mead, Frank Spencer. *Handbook of Denominations in the United States.* 5th ed. Nashville: Abingdon Press, 1970. Provides factual information on the history, organization, doctrines, and status of more than 250 religious bodies; includes statistical information, a glossary of terms, and bibliographies.

Yearbook of American and Canadian Churches. Prepared and edited in the Office of Research, Evaluation, and Planning of the National Council of the Churches of Christ in the U.S.A. Nashville, Tenn.: Abingdon Press, 1973– . (Annual.) Supersedes *Yearbook of American Churches;* attempts to provide information on most of the established religious groups in the United States and Canada; gives brief historical description of the religious body, names and addresses of officers, organizations, periodicals, and statistics.

Biographical Dictionaries[4]

Bowden, Henry Warner (ed.). *Dictionary of American Religious Biography.* Westport, Conn.: Greenwood Press, 1977. Presents 425 biographies of men and women (no longer living) who influenced American religious life; covers more than three centuries and includes religious leaders, reformers, philosophers, and members of minority groups; emphasis is on ordained clergy, but laypersons are represented; gives essential biographical information and an evaluation of the person's contribution to religious history, a brief list of works by the biographee, and bibliographical references.

Directory of American Scholars. 6th ed. Vol. IV: *Philosophy, Religion and Law,* 1974. Covers persons active in the field of religion.

Professional Journals in Religion

Each denomination has its own journals. See *Ulrich's International Periodicals Directory,* 17th ed., and *Magazines for Libraries,* 3d ed., edited by Bill Katz and Berry Richards, for a comprehensive listing. The following titles are examples of general-coverage journals in the field of religion.

Church History. Oreland, Pa.; American Society of Church History, 1932– . (Quarterly.) Nondenominational; considers all aspects of church history; gives information on religion in America and abroad; includes book reviews.

Harvard Theological Review. Cambridge, Mass.; Harvard University Press, 1908– . (Quarterly.) Nondenominational; covers Bible studies, history and philosophy of religion, and theology.

History of Religions: An International Journal for Comparative Historical Studies. Chicago: University of Chicago Press, 1961– . (Quarterly.) Devoted to the study of historical religious phenomena; one primary aim is the integration of results of the several disciplines of the science of religion.

MYTHOLOGY

"Mythology" is a collective word, usually thought of by social anthropologists as including the stories and tales (myths) which describe the origin, nature, and adventures of the gods and goddesses of a people. In other

[4]See also Chapter 10, Biographical Dictionaries.

words, myths are concerned with the supernatural and are especially associated with religious feasts, festivals, rites, and beliefs. For this reason, mythology is often classified by social scientists as a part of primitive religion. Both mythology and religion have their beginnings beyond recorded history.

REPRESENTATIVE REFERENCE BOOKS IN MYTHOLOGY

Indexes[5]
Art Index. (See p. 212.)

Encyclopedias and Handbooks
Everyman's Dictionary of Non-Classical Mythology. 3d ed. compiled by Egerton Sykes. (Everyman's Reference Library.) London: J. M. Dent & Sons, Ltd., 1962. Identifies allusions, terms, myths, and mythological terms and names from the earliest times.

Frazer, Sir James (ed.). *The Golden Bough: A Study in Magic and Religion.* 3d ed. revised. New York: St. Martin's Press, Inc., 1955. 12 vols. A comprehensive collection of information about primitive religions; traces many myths and rites to their prehistoric beginnings.

Gray, Louis Herbert (ed.). *The Mythology of All Races, Greek and Roman.* 26th ed. Boston: Marshall Jones Company, 1958. 13 vols. Includes text and illustrations.

Grimal, Pierre (ed.). *Larousse World Mythology.* New York: G. P. Putnam's Sons, 1965. Translated from two French works, *Mythologies de la Méditerranee au Gange* and *Mythologies des Steppes, des Iles et des Forêts.* Includes mythology of every region in the world; has outstanding illustrations, many in color; a reference work for students of art, literature, history, theology, etc.

Larousse Encyclopedia of Mythology. Rev. ed. New York: G. P. Putnam's Sons, 1968. Covers world mythology; is divided by nationalities.

Tripp, Edward (ed.). *Crowell's Handbook of Classical Mythology.* New York: Thomas Y. Crowell Company, 1970. Designed as a companion to reading, tells major myths of Greece and Rome in readable story form; includes personal and place names.

[5]See also Chapter 9, Indexes.

CHAPTER EIGHTEEN
THE SOCIAL SCIENCES AND EDUCATION

The social sciences[1] comprise those branches of knowledge which have to do with the activities of the individual as a member of society. Included in the social sciences class of the Dewey Decimal System (300) are sociology, statistics, political science, economics, law, government, social welfare, education,[2] commerce, and customs and folklore.[3] These areas are part of Library of Congress classes H, J, K, and L.

There are numerous reference sources devoted to the subject matter of the several social sciences. They include bibliographies, guides, indexes, dictionaries, encyclopedias, handbooks, yearbooks, biographical dictionaries, atlases, and professional journals.

BIBLIOGRAPHIES AND GUIDES[4]

American Behavioral Scientist. *The ABS Guide to Recent Publications in the Social and Behavioral Sciences.* New York: American Behavioral

[1]The social sciences are not to be confused with "social studies," which are portions of the subject matter of the social sciences suitable for study in elementary and secondary schools and are developed into courses of study which place emphasis on social aims.

[2]Education as a subject field is discussed on pp. 180–181.

[3]For a full discussion of the social sciences, see Edwin R. A. Seligman, "What Are the Social Sciences?" *Encyclopaedia of the Social Sciences,* I (1930), 3–7.

[4]See also Chapter 13, Bibliographies.

Scientist, 1965. Lists and annotates a selection of books, pamphlets, and articles from material cited in the "New Studies Section" of the *American Behavioral Scientist* from 1957 to 1964. Supplemented by *Recent Publications in the Social and Behavioral Sciences*, 1966– . (Annual.)

Brock, Clifton. *The Literature of Political Science*. New York: R. R. Bowker Company, 1969. A guide to the literature of the field; includes reference books, periodicals, and abstract journals; points out the most useful materials and explains their use.

Coman, Edwin T. *Sources of Business Information*. Revised ed. Berkeley: University of California Press, 1964. A guide to the literature of business, with annotated lists of reference sources and general books and periodicals; limited to American and Canadian publications; gives simple research methods. Includes a lengthy listing of books in section called "Basic Bookshelf."

Daniells, Lorna M. *Business Information Sources*. Berkeley: University of California Press, 1976. Annotates a selected list of business books and business information sources with emphasis on recent material (through 1976); contains a basic book list of multipurpose works for the business-person or student; discusses broad subjects such as computers, marketing, etc., and sources related to them.

Fisher, Mary L. *The Negro in America: A Bibliography*. 2d ed., revised and enlarged. Cambridge, Mass.: Harvard University Press, 1970. Lists titles on numerous subjects such as black theater, dance and the arts, music, the Negro in literature and the arts; includes books, journals, pamphlets, and government documents; gives references to language and idiom, black studies, etc.

Goodman, Leonard K. *Current Career and Occupational Literature: 1973–1977*. New York: The H. W. Wilson Company. 1978. Lists and annotates books and pamphlets; arranged alphabetically by occupation.

Handbook of Latin American Studies. Gainesville: University of Florida Press, 1936– . (Annual.) Various publishers. A critical bibliography of Latin American research, provides an annual record of important publications in the various disciplines; beginning with Vol. 26 (1964), the handbook is divided into two parts, Vol. 26 (Humanities) and Vol. 27 (Social Sciences), published in alternate years.

Hoselitz, Bert F. *A Reader's Guide to the Social Sciences*. Rev. ed. New York: The Free Press, 1970. Discusses each area, such as sociology, anthropology, psychology, economics, geography; gives a selective list of titles for each area including general references, textbooks, bibliographies, and journals.

Porter, Dorothy B. (comp.). *The Negro in the United States: A Selected Bibliography.* Washington, D.C.: Library of Congress, 1970. A selected bibliography of materials by or about Negroes in the United States; arranged alphabetically by author under twenty-three broad subject headings; designed to meet current needs of students, teachers, researchers, and others for introductory guidance to the study of the Negro in the United States.

Walford, A. J. (ed.). *Guide to Reference Materials:* Vol. II: *Social and Historical Sciences, Philosophy & Religion.* 3d ed. London: Library Association, 1975.

Wasserman, Paul, and Bernero, Jacqueline (eds.). *Statistics Sources.* 5th ed. revised. Detroit: Gale Research Company, 1977. "A subject guide to data on industrial, business, social, educational, financial, and other topics for the United States and internationally" (subtitle); serves as a sourcebook to aid the user in locating current statistical data; has a bibliography of statistical sources.

White, Carl M., and Associates (eds.). *Sources of Information in the Social Sciences: A Guide to the Literature.* 2d ed. revised. Chicago: American Library Association, 1973. Treats the literature of history, geography, economics, business administration, sociology, anthropology, psychology, education, political science, and geography; chapters on each of these areas are prepared by specialists.

INDEXES[5]

Business Periodicals Index. New York: The H. W. Wilson Company, 1958– . (Monthly except July.) One of the two indexes which succeeded the *Industrial Arts Index* in January, 1958; indexes by subject periodicals in business and related fields.

Index to Legal Periodicals. New York: The H. W. Wilson Company for the American Association of Law Libraries, 1908– . (Monthly except September.) Indexes by author and subject more than 325 legal periodicals; other materials indexed are yearbooks and annual reviews in a given field.

Industrial Arts Index. 1913–1957. Includes periodical articles on business and finance.

International Index. New York: The H. W. Wilson Company, 1907–1965. A guide to periodical literature in the social sciences and humanities; includes periodicals published in the United States, Great Britain, and Canada; succeeded by *Social Sciences and Humanities Index.*

[5]See also Chapter 9, Indexes.

Public Affairs Information Service. *Bulletin.* New York: Public Affairs Information Service, 1915– . (Twice monthly.) "A selective subject list of the latest books, pamphlets, government publications, reports of public and private agencies and periodical articles relating to economic and social conditions, public administration and international relations published in English throughout the world" (subtitle). The PAIS data base is the machine-readable version of the hard copy PAIS *Bulletin,* beginning with 1976.

Social Sciences Index. New York: The H. W. Wilson Company, 1974– . (Quarterly, annual cumulations.) Indexes by author and subject 263 periodicals in the social sciences area; book reviews are indexed in a separate section.

Social Sciences and Humanities Index. New York: The H. W. Wilson Company, 1965–1974. (Quarterly.) Succeeded the *International Index;* is an author and subject index to 202 periodicals in the social sciences and the humanities; includes periodicals of general scholarly interest, English and foreign. Succeeded by two indexes: *Social Sciences Index* and *Humanities Index* in 1974.

DICTIONARIES

Abrams, Charles. *The Language of Cities: A Glossary of Terms.* New York: The Viking Press, 1971. Identifies and defines terms and concepts related to housing, city planning, land economics, real estate, public administration, architecture, social welfare, transportation, public law, government, race, and other aspects of urban life.

Black's Law Dictionary. Rev. 4th ed. New York: Charles Scribner's Sons, 1976. Defines terms and concepts; includes a guide to pronunciation, rules for admission to the bar, code of professional ethics, abbreviations.

Gould, Julius, and Kolb, William L. (eds.). *A Dictionary of the Social Sciences.* Compiled under the auspices of UNESCO. New York: Free Press of Glencoe, 1964. Defines and describes in essay form the key concepts most widely employed in the various social science disciplines with illustrative quotations from the literature; definitions are signed. Gives all major definitions of a term, including common usages as well as "accepted scientific usages." Omits highly technical terms.

Greenwald, Douglas, and others (eds.). *McGraw-Hill Dictionary of Modern Economics.* 2d ed. New York: McGraw-Hill Book Company, 1973. Written for the nonspecialist; defines 1,300 selected contemporary terms in economics; has some charts and tables; lists references to additional sources; identifies some 200 organizations and agencies connected with economics.

Laqueur, Walter (ed.). *A Dictionary of Politics.* Rev. ed. New York: The Free Press, 1974. Presents concise, up-to-date information about facts, changes in terminology, and historical background of contemporary politics; traces developments since 1933; includes some biographical sketches; for each country, covers area, politics, current government, and recent history.

Plano, Jack C., and Greenberg, Milton. *The American Political Dictionary.* 4th ed. New York: Holt, Rinehart and Winston, Inc., 1976. Provides an overview of important concepts, terms, court cases.

———. and Olton, Roy. *The International Relations Dictionary.* New York: Holt, Rinehart and Winston, 1969. Designed as a guide to the basic vocabulary of international relations and foreign policy; defines terms from the areas covered; arranged by twelve topical chapters, including American foreign policy, diplomacy, wars, military policy; a detailed index provides access to the individual terms discussed in the larger subject areas.

Sloan, Harold S., and Zurcher, Arnold J. (eds.). *Dictionary of Economics.* 5th ed. New York: Barnes & Noble, Inc., 1970. Represents the entire field of economics, traditional as well as modern thought; includes terminology relating to methods and concepts, economic history and theory, international trade, public finance, taxation, money, and such special areas as social welfare, business cycles, etc.

Smith, Edward C., and Zurcher, Arnold J. (eds.). *Dictionary of American Politics.* 2d ed. New York: Barnes & Noble, 1968. Defines terms in general use in the field of American politics and state, county, and city government; describes laws and cases; identifies agencies.

Theodorson, George A., and Theodorson, Achilles G. *A Modern Dictionary of Sociology.* New York: Thomas Y. Crowell Company, 1969. Gives concise definitions of terms; includes related fields of psychology, social psychology, anthropology, and statistics.

ENCYCLOPEDIAS

International Encyclopedia of the Social Sciences. New York: Macmillan and The Free Press, 1967. 17 vols. Complements, does not supplant, the *Encyclopaedia of the Social Sciences;* aims to "reflect and encourage the rapid development of the social sciences throughout the world" (Preface); represents the social sciences of the 1960s; emphasis is on the analytical and comparative aspects of each topic; includes some biographical articles, including living persons; selected bibliographies follow articles; Vol. 17 is the index.

Seligman, Edwin R. A., and Johnson, Alvin (eds.). *Encyclopaedia of the Social Sciences.* New York: The Macmillan Company, 1930–1935. 15

vols. Provides articles on all of the social sciences, bringing out the relationships of each science to all other relevant sciences.

Worldmark Encyclopedia of the Nations. 5th ed. revised. New York: Worldmark Press and Harper & Row, 1976. 5 vols. Gives factual information in uniform format relating to topography, language, religion, and certain socioeconomic categories on countries which belong to the United Nations; Vol. I is devoted to the United Nations; remaining volumes devoted to Africa, Americas, Asia and Australasia, and Europe.

HANDBOOKS[6]

Africa Contemporary Record, 1968–69– . Edited by Colin Legum. London: Rex Collings, 1969– . (Annual.) An annual survey and documents; divided into three parts—Part One: Essays on Current Issues; Part Two: A Country-by-country Review (Legal, Political, Social, Military, Economic); Part Three: Documents.

Barone, Michael, and others. *The Almanac of American Politics 1978.* New York: E. P. Dutton & Co., Inc., 1977. Covers "the Senators, the Representatives, the Governors, their records, states, and districts" (subtitle).

Bergman, Peter M. (comp.), with the assistance of Mort N. Bergman and others. *The Chronological History of the Negro in America* (A Bergman Book). New York: Harper & Row, Publishers, 1969. Covers the period 1492–1968; arranged chronologically; each yearly entry gives information on statistics, people, publications, court decisions, political events, etc.

Colombo, John Robert. *Colombo's Canadian References.* London: Oxford University Press, 1976. Presents Canada in some 6,000 articles on every aspect of Canadian life, past and current; includes culture, communication, education, geography, history, resources, business, politics, technology.

Davidson, Sidney (ed.). *Handbook of Modern Accounting.* New York: McGraw-Hill Book Company, 1970. Covers accounting as a whole— traditional problems and procedures and new techniques arising from computer applications.

The Ebony Handbook. Chicago: Johnson Publishing Company, 1974. Gives factual and statistical information on the present-day status of blacks in the United States; includes biographical information.

Klein, Barry (ed.). *Reference Encyclopedia of the American Indian.* 3d. ed. Rye, N.Y.: Todd Publications, 1978. 2 vols. Gives many sources on government agencies, tribal councils, schools, museums; Volume II

[1]See also Chapter 12, Yearbooks and Handbooks.

contains biographical information with emphasis on professional achievements.

Ploski, Harry A., and Marr, Warren (comps. and eds.). *The Negro Almanac: A Reference Work on the Afro American.* 3d rev. ed. New York: The Bellwether Company, 1976. Covers black American history, biography, and statistics; contains biographical sketches of persons past and present; gives statistical information in charts and graphs, photographs, drawings, and reproductions of art; includes information on private and federal sources of aid for black Americans and other minorities.

Political Handbook of the World: 1977. Published for the Center for Social Analysis of the State University of New York at Binghamton and the Council on Foreign Relations. New York: McGraw-Hill Book Company, 1977– . Published annually since 1927 by various publishers; gives current information on the independent nations of the world regarding government, social, educational, and political conditions; covers religions, geography, and borders; has section on the United Nations.

Smythe, Mabel M. (ed.). *The Black American Reference Book.* Englewood Cliffs, N.J.: Prentice-Hall, Inc., 1976. In thirty-four lengthy essays by prominent authors, treats virtually every aspect of the black experience, historical, social, educational, religious, artistic, literary; points out black influence on American culture.

Wint, Guy (ed.). *Asia: A Handbook.* New York: Frederick A. Praeger, 1966. Provides basic factual information and surveys and discusses the politics, economics, society, and culture of the countries of Asia.

YEARBOOKS[7]

The Annual Register of World Events: A Review of the Year. 1758– . London: Longmans, Green & Co. Discusses events of the year by geographic region: the United Kingdom, the Commonwealth, the Americas, Europe, the Middle East; treats subjects such as politics, science, religion, technology, the arts, literature; reprints important documents; has chronology section; provides some maps.

The Book of the States. Lexington, Ky.: Council of State Governments, 1935– . (Biennial.) Provides an authoritative source of information on the structure, working methods, financial and functional activities of state governments; gives a comprehensive listing of elected state officials and members of the legislatures; tables give information for each state; kept up to date by supplements.

Britain: An Official Handbook. London: Her Majesty's Stationery Office. (Annual.) Revised each year, gives a factual account of the administra-

[7]See also Chapter 12, Yearbooks and Handbooks.

tion and the national economy of the United Kingdom; describes activities of many of the national institutions both official and unofficial.

Demographic Yearbook. New York: United Nations, 1949– . (Annual.) Surveys statistics of more than 250 countries and territories on population trends, marriages, births, deaths, and life expectancy. English/French.

Economic Almanac. New York: National Industrial Conference Board, 1940– . (Biennial.) Provides useful facts about business, labor, and government in the United States and in other countries.

Facts on File: A Weekly Digest of World Events with Cumulative Index. New York: Facts on File, Inc., October 30, 1940– . (Weekly with annual bound volumes.) Digests from a number of metropolitan newspapers the important news of the day; the *News Dictionary.* (1965– . [Annual.]) gives a selection of the news arranged alphabetically by subject, person, and country.

The Far East and Australasia. 9th ed. London: Europa Publications, Ltd., 1977. Covers the region as a whole, then subdivisions of the region, giving social, physical, and economic surveys of each area, including government, political parties, education, religion, finance, trade, etc.

Keesing's Contemporary Archives: Weekly Diary of Important World Events with Index Continually Kept Up-to-date. London: Keesing's Publications, Ltd., 1931– . Reports statistics and data selected, condensed, summarized, and indexed from newspapers, periodicals, official publications of the United Kingdom, British Commonwealth, and from foreign countries and recognized foreign news agencies; includes texts of speeches and documents.

Municipal Year Book. Chicago: International City Managers' Association, 1934– . (Annual.) Gives information concerning governmental units, personnel, finance, and activities of United States and Canadian cities; has a directory of chief officers of Canadian cities over 10,000 population and of mayors and clerks of United States cities over 2,500.

South American Handbook. London: Trade and Travel Publications, 1924– . (Annual.) Covers South and Central America, Mexico, and the West Indies; presents information about government, transportation, communication, natural resources.

Statistical Yearbook/Annuaire Statistique. Paris: United Nations Educational, Scientific, and Cultural Organization, 1948– . (Annual.) Gives political, scientific, educational, and cultural data for over 200 countries; includes information about book production and mass media.

Women's Rights Almanac, 1974– . Edited by Nancy Gager. Bethesda, Md.: Elizabeth Cady Stanton Publishing Company, 1974– . (Annual.) Reports on the status of the women's rights movement; gives a survey of demographic information state by state and for the District of Columbia and United States Territories; gives information on elected women officials, women's organizations, federal legislation affecting women; discussions of issues relating to women.

Yearbook of the United Nations. New York: United Nations, Department of Public Information, 1947– . (Annual.) Provides a comprehensive account of the activities of the United Nations and its related intergovernmental agencies.

The Yearbook of World Affairs. Published under the auspices of the London Institute of World Affairs. New York: Frederick A. Praeger, Inc., 1947– . Gives long articles on subjects in the social sciences.

ATLASES

Oxford Economic Atlas of the World. Prepared by the Cartographic Department of the Clarendon Press. 4th ed. London: Oxford University Press, 1972. Provides maps which show world distribution patterns for all the important industries, resources, and commodities; includes topographic maps, urban land-use maps of selected cities throughout the world, thematic maps of a wide range of political, economic, physical, and geographical subjects; includes gazetteer of some 8,000 names and a section of statistical information. Detailed information about specific areas is provided in companion volumes, e.g., *Oxford Regional Economic Atlas of the United States and Canada* (2d ed., 1975).

BIOGRAPHICAL DICTIONARIES[8]

American Men and Women of Science: Social and Behavioral Sciences. 13th ed. Edited by Jaques Cattell Press. New York: R. R. Bowker Company, 1978. Gives brief biographical sketches of some 24,000 scientists actively engaged in teaching or research in economics, political science, psychology, and sociology.

Who's Who in American Politics. 6th ed. New York: R. R. Bowker Company, 1977. Covers important political figures and public servants in the United States on the national, state, and local levels from the President of the United States to local political figures about whom information is not easily available; includes a geographical index to all biographees.

EXAMPLES OF PROFESSIONAL JOURNALS IN THE SOCIAL SCIENCES[9]

American Academy of Political and Social Science. *Annals.* Philadelphia: American Academy of Political and Social Science, 1890– . (Bimonth-

[8]See also Chapter 10, Biographical Dictionaries.

[9]See also *Ulrich's International Periodicals Directory,* 17th ed., and *Magazines for Libraries,* 3d ed., edited by Bill Katz and Berry Richards.

ly.) Each issue is devoted to a selected topic of current social or political interest; articles present different aspects of the subject.

American Behavioral Scientist. Beverly Hills, Calif.: Sage Publications, Inc., 1957– . (Bimonthly.) Devoted to the methods and techniques of social research, each issue has articles by specialists; the "New Studies" section is an annotated listing of new publications including books, pamphlets, and articles on sociology, psychology, and other behavioral sciences.

American Economic Review. Evanston, Ill.: American Economic Association, 1911– . (Five times a year.) Reviews new books; has articles on such topics as wages, employment, marketing, inflation, unemployment; provides bibliographical references.

American Journal of Economics and Sociology. Lancaster, Pa.: American Journal of Economics and Sociology, Inc., 1941– . (Quarterly.)Reports original research; covers social aspects of economic institutions and economic aspects of social and political institutions.

American Political Science Review. Washington, D.C.: American Political Science Association, 1906– . (Quarterly.) Stresses theoretical rather than practical aspects of political science; has book reviews.

Journal of Economic History. New York: Economic History Association, New York University, 1941– . (Quarterly.) The journal of the Economic History Association; presents articles on economic history and related aspects of history or economics, taxation, investments, business, and industry.

Journal of Human Relations. Wilberforce, Ohio: Central State University, 1952– . (Quarterly.) Provides an interdisciplinary approach to human relations with articles from literature, education, social sciences, philosophy, etc.

Political Science Quarterly. New York: Academy of Political Science, Columbia University, 1886– . (Quarterly.) Covers the broad field of political science; has long articles and many book reviews.

Sociological Quarterly. Edwardsville, Ill.: Southern Illinois University, 1960– . (Quarterly.) Emphasizes trends in social thought, ideas, and contributions of individual sociologists; is the journal of the Midwest Sociological Society.

EDUCATION

The word "education" has several meanings, and it is necessary to make clear its meaning as a *subject field* before beginning a study of reference materials in this area. A brief statement of two of the several meanings of "education" will help to clarify its meaning as a branch of knowledge.

In the broad sense, education is the sum total of all of the ways, both formal and informal, by which a person develops attitudes, abilities, and behavior patterns and acquires knowledge.

In another and less broad sense, education is the social process by which people are placed under the influence of an organized and controlled environment, such as a school, in the hope that they will attain more rapidly and effectively their fullest possible development as individuals and will learn how to live as competent citizens in their society. Elementary school, high school, and college are some of the stages in this controlled process.

Education as a subject field—that is, as a branch of knowledge—is the science which has to do with the principles and practices of teaching and learning. It is also the name given to that curriculum, in institutions of higher education, which consists of professional courses for the preparation of teachers, supervisors, and administrators. Included in these courses are philosophy and history of education (that is, education as a social process), psychology as applied to learning and teaching, curriculum, methods of teaching (how to teach), administration, and supervision.

The following reference sources are designed to answer, in the language of the educator, some of the numerous and specialized questions in this subject field.

REPRESENTATIVE REFERENCE SOURCES IN EDUCATION
Bibliographies, Guides, and Indexes[10]

Burke, Arvid, J., and Burke, Mary A. *Documentation in Education.* New York: Teachers College Press, Columbia University, 1967. The 5th edition of *How to Locate Educational Information and Data;* emphasizes the literature of the field of education but is also useful for the social sciences; includes chapters on information storage and retrieval, sources of information, bibliographic methods, catalogs, indexes, government documents, and new media in education. Retains some of the features of the previous editions.

The Education Index. New York: The H. W. Wilson Company, 1929– . (Monthly, except July and August.) Indexes by author and subject some 228 educational periodicals, as well as books, pamphlets, monographs, yearbooks, bulletins, and reports published in the English language; covers all aspects of education. Book review citations are in a separate section of the index.

Public Affairs Information Service. *Bulletin.* New York: Public Affairs Information Service, 1915– . (Twice a month.) Lists books, pamphlets, government publications, reports, and periodical articles relating to education.

[10]See also Chapter 9, Indexes, and Chapter 13, bibliographies.

Richmond, W. Kenneth. *The Literature of Education: A Critical Bibliography 1945–1970*. London: Methuen & Co., Ltd., 1972. Gives an introductory discussion of each area, then a listing of works in that area, including reference books, general works, and specialized works; some have annotations; includes philosophy of education, educational theory, curriculum study, educational psychology, history of education, sociology of education, educational administration, comparative education, economics of education, and educational technology.

Dictionaries and Encyclopedias

Blishen, Edward (ed.). *Encyclopedia of Education*. New York: Philosophical Library, 1970. Covers education and related topics including laws, societies, educational practice, universities, colleges, journals; is primarily British.

Ebel, Robert L. (ed.). *Encyclopedia of Educational Research*. 4th ed. New York: The Macmillan Company, 1969. Gives the status of research in all aspects of education and includes articles on methods of research and the characteristics of particular groups, such as the gifted and the retarded; is not an encyclopedia but a guide to the literature of educational research.

The Encyclopedia of Education. New York: The Macmillan Company and The Free Press, 1971. 10 vols. Intended for all persons concerned with education; gives an overview of education covering history, theory, research, philosophy, and structure of education; emphasizes American education.

Good, Carter Victor (ed.). *Dictionary of Education*. 3d ed. New York: McGraw-Hill Book Company, 1973. Defines and explains more than 30,000 professional terms in education and related fields.

Hopke, William E. (ed.). *The Encyclopedia of Careers and Vocational Guidance*. 3d ed. 2 vols. Garden City, N.Y.: Doubleday & Company, 1975. Gives information about specific careers and provides guidance in career planning; comprehensive coverage of each occupational field.

Directories

Cass, James, and Birnbaum, Max. *Comparative Guide to American Colleges*. 8th ed. New York: Harper & Row, Publishers, Incorporated, 1977. Gives admission requirements, curricula, costs, scholarships, regulations; arranged alphabetically by name of the institution.

———. *Comparative Guide to Two-Year Colleges and Career Programs*. New York: Harper & Row, Publishers, Incorporated, 1976. Lists alphabetically by state public community colleges, private junior colleges, and other institutions which offer a two-year degree; gives information about admission, costs, degrees, curricula, training programs.

The College Blue Book. 16th ed. New York: Macmillan Information, a Division of Macmillan Publishing Company, Inc., 1977. 5 vols. Gives narrative description of more than 3,000 colleges; includes costs, accreditation, enrollment figures, faculty, administration, degrees, curricula, and facilities; covers vocational schools, grants, fellowships, and scholarships.

Furniss, W. Todd (ed.). *American Universities and Colleges*, 11th ed. Washington, D.C.: American Council on Education, 1973. Gives detailed information about 1,400 four-year accredited institutions of higher education in the United States; lists more than 2,600 professional schools accredited by the council's professional associations.

Gleazer, Edmund J., and Cooke, Jane Follett (eds.). *American Junior Colleges*. 8th ed. Washington, D.C.: American Council on Education, 1971. Provides information on 800 public and private junior colleges in the United States, the Canal Zone, the District of Columbia, and Puerto Rico; offers latest facts on staff, fees, curriculums, history, library facilities, location, admission and graduation requirements; has discussion of the junior college movement and trend; institutions are included on the basis of recognition by accrediting agencies.

International Handbook of Universities and Other Institutions of Higher Education. 5th ed. Paris: The International Association of Universities, 1971. (Distributed by the American Council on Education, Washington, D.C.) Describes, in English, some 140 institutions of higher education in 104 countries outside the United States and British Commonwealth; gives brief entries for technical colleges and other professional schools.

Quick, Robert (ed.). *A Guide to Graduate Study: Programs Leading to the Ph.D. Degree*. 4th ed. Washington, D.C.: American Council on Education, 1969. Lists complete offerings of 250 institutions in hundreds of separate fields of graduate study; includes requirements, fees, special facilities for study and research.

Handbooks and Yearbooks

Commonwealth Universities Yearbook. 1914– . London: Association of Commonwealth Universities, 1914. Presents the essential facts about the history, facilities, organization, staff, and admission requirements of universities in the Commonwealth; arranged by countries.

International Yearbook of Education. Geneva: International Bureau of Education, and Paris: UNESCO, 1948–1969. Gives country-by-country developments in administration, curriculum, teaching staff; compares educational developments; discusses trends; covers countries which belong to the United Nations.

Requirements for Certification of Teachers, Counselors, Librarians, and Administrators for Elementary Schools, Secondary Schools, Junior Colleges. Chicago: The University of Chicago Press, 1935– . (Annual.) Arranged by state, then by level and positions; gives certification requirements, recommendations of regional and other accrediting associations, information concerning applications.

Standard Education Almanac. Los Angeles: Academic Media, 1968– . (Annual.) Aims to be an up-to-date source of educational facts and statistics; provides information on most aspects of education from kindergarten through graduate school.

UNESCO. *Study Abroad.* Vol. 1, 1948– . New York: International Documents Service, Columbia University Press, 1948– . (Biennial.) Gives information on eligibility, fields of study, financial assistance, applications; covers all levels of education.

U.S. Office of Education. Division of Educational Statistics. *Digest of Educational Statistics.* Washington, D.C.: Government Printing Office, 1962– . (Annual.) Offers compilation of current statistics on schools, teachers, enrollments, finances, etc.; makes use of tabular comparisons.

————. *Education Directory.* Washington, D.C.: Government Printing Office, 1912– . (Annual.) Issued in three parts: public school systems, higher education, and education associations; provides statistical and general information concerning organizations and officials.

World of Learning. London: Europa Publications, Ltd., 1947– . (Annual.) 2 vols.Arranged alphabetically by country; gives information about educational, cultural, and scientific organizations all over the world.

Biographical Dictionaries[11]

Leaders in Education. 5th ed. Compiled by the Jaques Cattell Press. New York: R. R. Bowker Company, 1974. Gives biographical information about more than 14,000 men and women in education in the United States and Canada; includes administrators, teachers, and authors.

Examples of Professional Journals in Education[12]

Community and Junior College Journal. Washington, D.C.: American Association of Community and Junior Colleges, 1930– . (Monthly.) Covers all aspects of the junior college.

---

[11]See also Chapter 10, Biographical Dictionaries.

[12]See also *Ulrich's International Periodicals Directory*, 17th ed., and *Magazines for Libraries*, 3d ed., edited by Bill Katz and Berry Richards.

Educational Leadership. Washington, D.C.: Association for Supervision and Curriculum Development, 1943– . (Monthly, October through May.) Emphasizes curriculum; reports research data to the membership.

Journal of Higher Education. Columbus: Ohio State University Press, 1930– . (Monthly.) A general magazine devoted to issues of interest to higher education; includes book reviews.

Phi Delta Kappan. Bloomington, Ind.: Phi Delta Kappa, Inc., 1918– . (Monthly, September–June.) Aims to promote leadership in education at all levels.

Today's Education. Washington, D.C.: National Education Association, 1913– . (Bimonthly.) Formerly *NEA Journal;* is the official journal of the National Education Association; provides articles of general interest and reports new developments in education; covers all aspects of education.

Abstract Journals

Current Index to Journals in Education. New York: Macmillan Information, a Division of Macmillan Publishing Company, Inc., 1969– . (Monthly.) Covers the periodical literature as a counterpart to *Resources in Education* (formerly *Research in Education*); gives complete citation to the journal in which the article appears; brief annotations (not abstracts) are included when the titles and descriptors do not cover the content of the article; covers more than 700 periodicals.

Resources in Education, Vol. I, No. 1, November 1966– . Washington, D.C.: United States Department of Health, Education, and Welfare/National Institute of Education, 1967– . (Monthly.) *Research in Education* until 1975. A monthly abstract journal announcing recent report literature related to the field of education, it is made up of résumés and indexes. The résumés highlight the significant parts of the document and are numbered sequentially in the Document Section by ED number. The ED prefix identifies Educational Resources Information Center (ERIC)[13] selected documents of educational significance. The contents

---

[13]The Educational Resources Information Center (ERIC), a nationwide information network for acquiring, abstracting, indexing, storing, and disseminating significant research reports and projects in the field of education, was established in June 1964 to disseminate educational research results, research-related materials, and other resource information. Special centers or clearing houses acquire, evaluate, abstract, and index these report materials and the abstracts in *Resources in Education* (formerly *Research in Education*). Reports are available in microfiche or hard copy from the ERIC Document Reproduction Service, which is part of ERIC's information storage and retrieval system. (ERIC files can be searched by computer.) Many large libraries have part or all of the ERIC microfiche collection. It is usually housed in the area where microfilm and other microforms are kept. Each microfiche is filed in a drawer by its identifying ED number, which is given in the entry in *Resources in Education*. Microfiche must be read with a reader.

of each issue are indexed by subject, author, and sponsoring institution. The document résumés (abstracts) give the name of the sponsoring agency of the research project, date, report number, EDRS price, descriptors (subject headings which describe it), brief abstract, educational documents number which is the means of locating it in the ERIC file, availability, and price in microfiche and hard copy.

The source for all subject headings used in the ERIC collection and in indexing *Current Index to Journals in Education* and *Resources in Education* is *The Thesaurus of ERIC Descriptors*, 7th ed. (New York: Macmillan Information, A Division of Macmillan Publishing Company, Inc., 1977), which lists descriptors and synonyms and near synonyms.

CHAPTER NINETEEN
LANGUAGE (PHILOLOGY)

$\mathbf{P}$hilology (by derivation, "love of learning" and "love of speech and discourse") is that branch of learning concerned with human speech and what it reveals about humans. The 400 class in the Dewey Decimal Classification is devoted to language; class P of the Library of Congress classification includes language and linguistics.

Language as a subject was first studied because it was important in reading and in understanding literature, and emphasis was placed upon the study of Greek, Latin, and Hebrew, since most of the early writing was done in those languages. When the study of language, as such, emerged as a branch of learning during the nineteenth century, it was called "linguistics."

Linguistics, the scientific study of human speech, includes an investigation of the sound, form, and meaning of language and of the relations of one language to another.

The study of language as a branch of knowledge includes:

1   Morphology, the study of the historical development of speech patterns
2   Syntax, the study of the use and forms of the language and of the parts of speech and their various forms
3   Etymology, the study of the origin of words
4   Semantics, the historical and psychological study of meaning and change of meaning of words

In the study of language and linguistics, dictionaries[1] are the major aids, both the general word dictionaries of a language and dictionaries which provide more than a mere listing of the words of a language and their several meanings. The latter include:

1 Dictionaries based on the historical development of words
2 Etymological dictionaries
3 Dictionaries of usage
4 Dictionaries of slang, dialect, and colloquialisms
5 Dictionaries of synonyms and antonyms

In addition to these kinds of dictionaries, there are specialized dictionaries which treat abbreviations, acronyms, eponyms, foreign words and phrases, and pronunciation.

Other types of reference books useful in the study of language are bibliographies, indexes, general histories of language, and biographical dictionaries.

USEFUL REFERENCE SOURCES IN LANGUAGE[2]

BIBLIOGRAPHIES AND INDEXES[3]

Collison, Robert Lewis. *Dictionaries of Foreign Languages.* 2d ed. New York: Hafner Publishing Company, 1971. "A bibliographical guide to both general and technical dictionaries with historical and explanatory notes and references" (subtitle); includes dictionaries of the chief foreign languages; discusses specific dictionaries.

Modern Humanities Research Association. *Annual Bibliography of English Language and Literature.* Cambridge: Cambridge University Press, 1921– . (Annual.) Includes books, periodical literature, pamphlets, and references to book reviews; the language section is arranged by subject.

Modern Language Association of America. *MLA International Bibliography of Books and Articles on the Modern Languages and Literatures.* 1921– . (Annual; since 1969 in multi-volume format separate from the parent journal, *PMLA.*) Offers a classified list of books, articles, and monographs; includes American and foreign authors; arranged by language. From 1921 to 1955 the title was *MLA American Bibliography.*

[1]This chapter is concerned with specialized dictionaries of language. See Chapter 7 for a discussion of general word dictionaries.

[2]See also Chapter 7, Dictionaries.

[3]See also Chapter 9, Indexes, and Chapter 13, Bibliographies.

DICTIONARY OF LANGUAGE AS A SUBJECT FIELD

Pei, Mario. *Glossary of Linguistic Terminology.* New York: Columbia University Press, 1966. Includes the historical, descriptive, and geolinguistic terminology, American and European, that has gained acceptance in the field.

DICTIONARIES OF CERTAIN ASPECTS OF LANGUAGE

Abbreviations and Acronyms

Crowley, Ellen T. (ed.). *Acronyms, Initialisms, and Abbreviations Dictionary.* 6th ed. Detroit: Gale Research Company, 1978. 3 vols. Some 130,000 entries in Vol. 1 range from the time of ancient Rome to the present day; all areas of knowledge are represented; humorous and slang acronyms are included. Vol. 2 is the annual supplement and is called *New Acronyms, Initialisms, and Abbreviations.* Vol. 3 is entitled *Reverse Acronyms, Initialisms, and Abbreviations Dictionary.*

De Sola, Ralph (ed.). *Abbreviations Dictionary.* New International Fifth Edition. New York: Elsevier, 1978. Defines and explains abbreviations, acronyms, anonyms, and eponyms, contractions, geographical equivalents, historical and mythological characters, initials and nicknames, signs and symbols, slang, and short forms in all areas.

Etymology[4]

Klein, Ernest. *A Comprehensive Etymological Dictionary of the English Language.* New York: American Elsevier, 1966–1967. 2 vols. Treats the origin of words and the development of their meanings, thus illustrating the history of civilization and culture; includes many scientific and technical terms and personal and mythological names.

Onions, Charles Talbut, and others, (eds.). *The Oxford Dictionary of English Etymology.* New York: Oxford University Press, 1966. Based on the *Oxford English Dictionary,* but brought up to date by recent research; includes some words of United States origin and some proper names; notable for its breadth of coverage, scholarship, and ease of use.

Partridge, Eric (ed.). *Origins.* 4th ed. New York: The Macmillan Company, 1966. Emphasizes civilization rather than science; includes the most common words in modern English.

Foreign Words and Phrases

Bliss, Alan Joseph (ed.). *A Dictionary of Foreign Words and Phrases in Current English.* New York: E. P. Dutton & Co., 1966. Aims to explain the majority of foreign words and phrases encountered in current

---

[4]In etymological dictionaries, definitions as such are not given. The meaning of the word is determined through the etymology.

English, both written and spoken; gives original language and when word came into use; has appendix in which entries are arranged by century and by country; does not give pronunciation.

Guinagh, Kevin (comp.). *Dictionary of Foreign Phrases and Abbreviations.* 2d ed. New York: The H. W. Wilson Company, 1972. Aims to help students and nonspecialists understand foreign expressions, proverbs, mottoes, etc., which they frequently hear or read; covers phrases in law, philosophy, business, medicine, etc.

Mawson, Christopher Orlando. *Dictionary of Foreign Terms.* 2d ed. revised and updated by Charles Berlitz. New York: Thomas Y. Crowell Company, 1975. Explains words from more than fifty ancient and modern languages, from a wide variety of fields; the language of each word is identified.

Pei, Mario, and Ramondino, Salvatore. *Dictionary of Foreign Terms.* New York: Delacorte Press, 1974. Explains foreign terms and phrases that English-speaking people encounter in reading or listening; original language, pronunciation, and definition are given for each term; some usage labels are given.

Historical Development of Words

Craigie, William, and Hulbert, James R. (eds.). *A Dictionary of American English on Historical Principles.* 2d ed. Chicago: University of Chicago Press, 1938–1944. 4 vols. Indicates words which originated in America or which are in greater use here than elsewhere and words which are important in the history of America; follows the plan of *The Oxford English Dictionary.*

A Dictionary of Canadianisms on Historical Principles. Produced by the Lexicographical Centre for Canadian English, University of Victoria, British Columbia. Scarborough, Ont.: W. J. Gage, Ltd., 1967. Modeled after *The Oxford English Dictionary;* covers the period from the sixteenth century to the present; each entry is "substantiated" with dates and quotations from books, periodicals, and newspapers; includes regional, political, historical, and proper names; does not claim that all entries originated in Canada, but all are original or are closely related to Canada.

Mathews, Mitford N. (ed.). *A Dictionary of Americanisms on Historical Principles.* Chicago: University of Chicago Press, 1956. Includes words which have been added to the English language in the United States from colonial times to the present.

———. *Americanisms: A Dictionary of Selected Americanisms on Historical Principles.* Chicago: University of Chicago Press, 1966. An abridgment of *A Dictionary of Americanisms on Historical Principles;* gives approximately 1,000 entries.

Morris, William, and Morris, Mary (eds.). *Dictionary of Word and Phrase Origins.* New York: Harper & Row, Publishers, 1962, 1967, 1971. 3 vols. Explains a variety of additions to the English language from many sources.

————. *Morris Dictionary of Word and Phrase Origins.* Harper & Row, Publishers, Inc., 1977. To some extent an abridgment of the three-volume work by these authors; presents the history of several thousand words and phrases with illustrative examples; some etymologies are given; does not give pronunciation.

Murray, James Augustus Henry, and others (eds.). *The Oxford English Dictionary.* London: Oxford University Press, 1933. 12 vols. and supplement. Presents the historical development of each word which has entered the English language since 1150.

A Supplement to the Oxford English Dictionary. Edited by R. W. Burchfield. Oxford: Clarendon Press, 1972– . 4 vols. (In progress.) Vol. I: A–G, 1972; Vol. II: H–N, 1976. The four-volume *Supplement* will incorporate the material in the 1933 *Supplement* and will contain all words that came into common use in English during the publication of the *OED*, 1884–1928, and words which have come into use from 1928 to the present. It aims to record the vocabulary of the twentieth century, including literary, scientific, and technical terminology; legal and other professional terminology; and popular, colloquial, and modern slang expressions.

Pronunciation

Bender, James Frederick. *NBC Handbook of Pronunciation.* 3d ed. revised by Thomas Lee Crowell, Jr. New York: Thomas Y. Crowell Company, 1964. Aims to record the pronunciations used by "educated persons in the greater part of the United States" (Preface); pronunciation indicated by the International Phonetic Alphabet and by phonetic re-spelling.

Kenyon, John S., and Knott, Thomas A. (eds.). *A Pronouncing Dictionary of American English.* Springfield, Mass.: G. & C. Merriam Company, 1953. Gives pronunciation only, according to the alphabet of the International Phonetic Association; records standard speech.

Lass, Abraham Harold, and Lass, Betty. *Dictionary of Pronunciation.* New York: Quadrangle/The New York Times Book Company, 1976. Lists some 8,000 words which are pronunciation problems and gives the recommended pronunciations found in four standard desk dictionaries;

the number of dictionaries that recognize each acceptable pronunciation is indicated; includes words of foreign origin.

Slang, Dialect, Colloquialisms

Berrey, Lester V., and Van Den Bark, Melvin (eds.). *The American Thesaurus of Slang.* 2d ed. New York: Thomas Y. Crowell Company, 1953. A collection of colloquialisms, slang, and vulgarisms arranged according to the ideas which they express; has an alphabetical word index for ease of use.

Flexner, Stuart B. *I Hear America Talking: An Illustrated Treasury of American Words and Phrases.* New York: D. Van Nostrand Company, Inc., 1976. Discusses origins, meanings, uses, and other aspects of words and phrases that the author thinks reveal America's political and social history; words and phrases are grouped around historical periods, ethnic groups, and types of words.

Partridge, Eric. *A Dictionary of Slang and Unconventional English.* 7th ed. New York: The Macmillan Company, 1971. Covers colloquialisms, catchphrases, nicknames, vulgarisms, naturalized Americanisms.

Wentworth, Harold, and Flexner, Stuart B. (comps. and eds.). *Dictionary of American Slang.* 2d supplemented edition. New York: Thomas Y. Crowell Company, 1975. First published in 1960, and reprinted in 1967 with a forty-eight-page supplement; this edition retains all words in the two earlier editions and adds about 1,500 new slang words that have become current since 1967; gives brief definition of the term, and multiple meanings if appropriate; notes the group which uses the term; gives synonyms and antonyms.

Synonyms and Antonyms

Hayakawa, S. I. (comp.). *Funk & Wagnalls Modern Guide to Synonyms and Related Words.* New York: Funk & Wagnalls Company, 1968. In more than 1,000 essays or articles, discusses, defines, compares, and contrasts over 6,000 synonyms and related words in the context of the American 1960s; gives concise definitions and illustrative quotations.

Roget's International Thesaurus. 4th ed. Revised by Robert L. Chapman. New York: Thomas Y. Crowell Company, 1977. Lists about 250,000 words and phrases arranged in categories by their meanings; reflects modern vocabulary.

Webster's Collegiate Thesaurus. Springfield, Mass.: G. & C. Merriam Company, Publishers, 1976. Alphabetically arranged; has some 20,000 entries; each entry is defined briefly, with an illustrative phrase if needed; definition is followed by a group of exact synonyms, a group of related words, and a group of contrasted words and antonyms.

Webster's New Dictionary of Synonyms. Springfield, Mass.: G. & C. Merriam Company, 1973. "A dictionary of discriminated synonyms with analogous and contrasted words" (subtitle); has illustrative quotations from old and new authors.

Usage

Copperud, Roy H. *American Usage: the Consensus.* New York: Van Nostrand Reinhold Company, 1970. Compares seven current dictionaries of usage as well as the conventional dictionaries and presents a consensus on some of the common problems in usage; readers may decide for themselves from the statements given.

Follett, Wilson. *Modern American Usage: A Guide.* Edited and completed by Jacques Barzun in collaboration with Carlos Baker and others. New York: Hill & Wang, 1966. Arranged in dictionary format; explains words and phrases, giving recommended forms of usage; articles vary in length; treats matters of style.

Fowler, H. W. *A Dictionary of Modern English Usage.* 2d ed. revised by Ernest Gowers. Oxford: Clarendon Press, 1965. Gives definitions of terms, sometimes with disputed spellings and plurals; brief essays on use and misuse of words and expressions; reflects the author's personal opinions; many new articles; modernized and brought up to date in light of current usage; some terms dropped; new ones added.

Morris, William, and Morris, Mary. *Harper Dictionary of Contemporary Usage.* New York: Harper & Row, Publishers, Incorporated, 1975. Treats idioms, slang words, regionalisms, spelling, pronunciation; articles range in length from a few sentences to several pages; opinions of a panel of expert writers and speakers are cited on certain points; aims to direct attention to incorrect or awkward oral or written language, but does not prescribe usage.

Sykes, J. B. (ed.). *The Concise Oxford Dictionary of Current English.* Based on *The Oxford English Dictionary* and its *Supplements.* 6th ed. Oxford: Clarendon Press, 1976. First edition by H. W. Fowler and H. G. Fowler; includes words in current speech, scientific and technical terms, many colloquial and slang expressions; gives attention to North American usage; does not give dates of usage.

BIOGRAPHICAL DICTIONARIES[5]

Directory of American Scholars. 7th ed. Vol. III: *Foreign Languages, Linguistics, and Philology.* Edited by the Jaques Cattell Press. New

---

[5]See also Chapter 10, Biographical Dictionaries.

York: R. R. Bowker Company, 1978. Includes living persons in the field of language.

EXAMPLES OF PROFESSIONAL JOURNALS[6]

American Speech, A Quarterly of Linguistic Usage. New York: Columbia University Press, 1925– . (Quarterly.) Provides general and scholarly studies of English language in North America; covers dialect, current usage, structural linguistics, phonetics, dialects, geography, semantics, names, and vocabulary.

Modern Language Journal. Buffalo, N.Y.: S.U.N.Y. at Buffalo, 1916– . (Bimonthly, September–May.) Published by the National Federation of Modern Language Teachers Association; devoted to methods, pedagogical research, and topics of interest to all language teachers.

Modern Language Quarterly. Seattle: University of Washington, 1940– . (Quarterly.) Contains critical studies of literary works and forms in English, Romance, and Germanic languages; covers use of language and form in literary works; gives book reviews.

PMLA. New York: Modern Language Association of America, 1884– . (Six times a year.) The journal of MLA; presents scholarly and critical articles, professional news and notes, and bibliography.

Studies in Philology. Chapel Hill: University of North Carolina Press, 1906– . Reports research in the classical and modern languages and literatures.

[6]See also *Ulrich's International Periodicals Directory*, 17th ed., and *Magazines for Libraries*, 3d ed., edited by Bill Katz and Berry Richards.

CHAPTER TWENTY

SCIENCE
AND TECHNOLOGY

The word "science," deriving from a Latin word which means "to learn" or "to know," is in its broadest sense synonymous with learning and knowledge, and in general usage it means an organized body of knowledge. In a more restricted meaning, science is organized knowledge of natural phenomena and of the relations between them. Sciences are commonly classified as exact or descriptive. Exact sciences are those characterized by the possibility of exact measurement—for example, physics. Descriptive sciences are those which have developed a method of description or classification that permits precise reference to the subject matter—for example, zoology.

The 500 class of the Dewey Decimal System, class Q in the Library of Congress classification, is assigned to pure sciences and includes mathematics, astronomy and allied sciences, physics, chemistry and allied sciences, earth sciences, paleontology, anthropology and biological sciences, botanical sciences, and zoological sciences.

Technology—applied science—is concerned with the tools (machines, instruments) and the techniques (methods, ways) for carrying out the plans, designs, etc., created by science. It has been defined as "the totality of the means employed to provide objects necessary for human sustenance and comfort."[1]

---

[1] *Webster's Seventh New Collegiate Dictionary* (Springfield, Mass.: G. & C. Merriam Company, Publishers, 1967), p. 905.

Technology (applied science) is placed in the 600 class, which comprises the medical sciences, engineering and allied operations, agriculture and agricultural industries, domestic arts and sciences, business and related enterprises, chemical technology, manufactures, and buildings. The Library of Congress classification devotes parts of classes R, S, and T to these areas.

Books in science and technology become outdated more quickly than those in other subject fields, and the student who seeks material on a topic in any of these areas must consult periodicals, abstract journals,[2] and original sources—such as papers read at scientific meetings, reports, and patent applications—for the latest information. In addition to these sources, there are reference books designed to provide answers to the many questions which arise in this broad subject area. Among the most useful kinds of reference sources are bibliographies and guides, professional journals, abstract journals, indexes, handbooks, dictionaries and glossaries (both English and foreign-language), encyclopedias, yearbooks, directories, biographical dictionaries, and general histories.

The importance of frequently consulting the bibliographies in periodicals and abstract journals and the library card catalog in order to keep up with new materials in this rapidly changing field cannot be overemphasized.

USEFUL REFERENCE SOURCES IN SCIENCE AND TECHNOLOGY

BIBLIOGRAPHIES[3]

Dick, Elie M. *Current Information Sources in Mathematics: An Annotated Guide to Books and Periodicals, 1960–1972.* Littleton, Colo.: Libraries Unlimited, 1973. Lists the most important monographs published in English from 1960 to 1972.

Jenkins, Frances Briggs. *Science Reference Sources.* 5th ed. Cambridge, Mass.: The M.I.T. Press, 1969. A selected list of science reference sources by subject—mathematics, physics, chemistry, earth sciences, etc.—arranged by kind of reference source.

McGraw-Hill Basic Bibliography of Science and Technology. New York: McGraw-Hill Book Company, 1966. Lists English language titles on more than 7,000 subjects compiled and annotated by the editors of the *McGraw-Hill Encyclopedia of Science and Technology* under subject headings corresponding with encyclopedia articles; refers to readings beyond the encyclopedia articles; arranged by subject.

---

[2]An abstract journal lists and provides digests or summaries of periodical articles and other literature. Abstracts may be in the original language in which the article appeared, or they may be translated into English or another language.

[3]See also Chapter 13, Bibliographies.

Malinowsky, H. Robert, and others. *Science and Engineering Literature: A Guide to Reference Sources.* 2d ed. Littleton, Colo.: Libraries Unlimited, 1976. Describes the nature of the various fields of science and engineering; offers discussions of basic types of scientific literature; annotates a selective list of sources in these areas; includes guidance in literature searching.

New Technical Books. New York: New York Public Library, 1915– . (Monthly except August and September.) A selective list with descriptive annotations of current noteworthy titles in the pure and applied sciences and related fields; chiefly American publications.

Science Books: A Quarterly Review. Vol. I– . April, 1965– . Washington, D.C.: American Association for the Advancement of Science, 1965– . Provides informative descriptive annotations both positive and negative; indicates appropriate age levels for which each book is suitable; includes first two years of college; covers trade books, textbooks, and reference works.

Scientific and Technical Books and Serials in Print, 1977. 4th ed. New York: R. R. Bowker Company, 1977. (Annual.) Lists by author, title, and subject titles in print in all areas of the physical and biological sciences, engineering, and technology; the fourth edition lists some 17,000 periodicals.

Walford, A. J. (ed.). *Guide to Reference Materials.* Vol. I, *Science and Technology.* 3d ed. London: The Library Association, 1973. Aims to provide a signpost to reference books and bibliographies published mainly in recent years; international in scope but with emphasis on items published in Britain; for both general and specialized use.

Ward, Dedrick C., and Wheeler, Marjorie W. *Geologic Reference Sources.* Metuchen, N.J.: Scarecrow Press, Inc. 1972. "A subject and regional bibliography of publications and maps in the geological sciences" (subtitle); gives some annotations.

GUIDES
Bottle, R. T. (ed.). *The Use of Chemical Literature,* 2d ed. (Information Sources for Research and Development.) London: Butterworth & Company (Publishers), Ltd., 1969. Covers primary sources, abstracts, translations, dictionaries, monographs, tables, patent literature, and government publications; gives information about libraries and their use.

———. and Wyatt, H. V. (eds). *The Use of Biological Literature.* 2d ed. (Information Sources for Research and Development.) Hamden, Conn.: Archon Books, 1971. Includes primary sources, translations, patents, abstracts in general and by specific subjects such as botany, zoology, ecology, genetics; treats the use of libraries in research.

Dick, Elie M. *Current Information Sources in Mathematics: An Annotated Guide to Books and Periodicals; 1960–1972.* Littleton, Colo.: Libraries Unlimited, Inc., 1973. Lists and describes books published in English during the period indicated; arranged by subject with author and subject indexes; includes list of important mathematics periodicals.

Mellon, Melvin Guy. *Chemical Publications, Their Nature and Use.* 4th ed. New York: McGraw-Hill Book Company, 1965. Describes the principal sources for reference and research, including both primary and secondary sources; suggests library problems for practice in searching chemical literature.

Parke, Nathan Grier. *Guide to the Literature of Mathematics and Physics.* 2d revised ed. New York: Dover Publications, 1958. Includes works in related fields; emphasizes the usefulness of each kind of reference material; gives points on the use of the library and on finding material on a subject.

Smith, Roger C., and Reid, W. Malcolm. *Guide to the Literature of the Life Sciences.* 8th ed. Minneapolis: Burgess Publishing Company, 1972. Formerly *Guide to the Literature of the Zoological Sciences;* has been expanded to include botany; provides introductory essays on topics related to the life sciences; gives information on using the library; gives annotations.

INDEXES[4]

Applied Science and Technology Index. New York: The H. W. Wilson Company, 1958– . (Monthly except August.) One of two indexes which replaced *Industrial Arts Index;* indexes by subject periodicals in aeronautics, automation, physics, chemistry, engineering, industrial and mechanical arts, electricity and electronics, and related fields.

The Biological and Agricultural Index. New York: The H. W. Wilson Company, 1964– . (Monthly except August.) Formerly *The Agricultural Index;* is a subject index to eighty-eight periodicals in the field of agriculture, biology, and related areas; includes book reviews.

Engineering Index. 1906– . New York: Engineering Index, Inc., 1934– . (Monthly.) Continues the *Engineering Index* begun in 1884; international in scope; indexes literature in more than 1,500 professional and trade journals; includes publications of engineering societies, scientific and technical associations, and government agencies; papers of conferences and of selected books are covered; is available on magnetic tape.

General Science Index. New York: The H. W. Wilson Company, 1978– . (Monthly, except June and December; annual cumulation.) Indexes by

---

[4]See also Chapter 9, Indexes.

subject eighty-eight general science periodicals published in the English language covering pure and applied science; each issue contains an index to book reviews.

Index Medicus. Washington, D.C.: National Library of Medicine, 1960– . (Monthly.) Published in various forms and by various publishers since 1879. A comprehensive index to the world's medical literature; indexes completely or selectively 2,300 biomedical journals by subject and name; is cumulated annually into the *Cumulated Index Medicus;* journal articles are cited under the subject headings which represent the most important concepts discussed; all citations are stored in MEDLARS (Medical Literature Retrieval and Analysis System), the computer-based file of the National Library of Medicine, for future use in machine retrieval.

Technical Book Review Index, 1935– . Compiled and edited in the Technology Department, Carnegie Library of Pittsburgh. Pittsburgh: The JAAD Publishing Company, 1977– . (Monthly.) From 1935 through 1976, published by the Special Libraries Association. Indexes reviews of new technical, scientific, and medical books in all fields of science, life sciences, medicine, and technology; covers more than 3,000 reviews a year; gives complete citation for the reviews and brief quotations from the reviews.

DICTIONARIES—SCIENCE

Challinor, John. *A Dictionary of Geology.* 5th ed. New York: Oxford University Press, 1978. Aims to give a critical and historical review of the subject; defines some 1,500 terms, giving both meaning and usage; illustrative quotations showing usage are from geological literature.

Collocott, T. C. (ed.). *Dictionary of Science and Technology.* London: W. & R. Chambers, Ltd., 1971. Successor to *Chambers's Technical Dictionary;* records the basic language of communication of those engaged in scientific activity today.

The Condensed Chemical Dictionary. 9th ed. New York: Van Nostrand Reinhold Company, 1977. Covers up-to-date developments; describes trademarked products used in the chemical industries; defines chemical entities, phenomena, and terminology; gives technical descriptions of chemicals, raw materials, and processes; covers chemical and biological aspects of pollution and environmental control.

Grant, Julius (ed.). *Hackh's Chemical Dictionary (American and British Usage).* 4th ed. New York: McGraw-Hill Book Company, 1969. Contains the words generally used in chemistry and many of the terms used in related sciences; emphasizes the interrelationship of chemistry and related fields; offers more than 50,000 terms drawn from recent chemical literature.

Gray, H. J., and Isaacs, Alan (eds.). *A New Dictionary of Physics*. Rev. ed. London: Longmans, Green & Co., Ltd., 1975. Gives brief definitions of technical terms, biographical sketches of physicists, and data tables.

Gray, Peter. *The Dictionary of the Biological Sciences*. New York: Reinhold Publishing Corporation, 1967. Contains definitions or synonyms of nearly all taxa of ordinal rank and above and the great majority of families; definitions are in customary biological terms and, where possible, reference is made to the English or vernacular names of the plants or animals.

Hampel, Clifford A., and Gessner, G. Hawley. *Glossary of Chemical Terms*. New York: Van Nostrand Reinhold, 1976. Provides lengthy definitions of 2,000 terms that cover substances, processes, and phenomena.

James, Glenn, and James, Robert C. (eds.). *James & James Mathematics Dictionary*. 4th ed. New York, N.Y.: Van Nostrand Reinhold Company, 1976. Definitions range from terms in high school algebra and geometry to more advanced university topics in topology and analysis; designed for use by persons with some background in the field; includes brief biographical entries.

Lapedes, Daniel N. (ed.). *McGraw-Hill Dictionary of the Life Sciences*. New York: McGraw-Hill Book Company, 1976. Defines more than 20,000 terms in the biological sciences and related disciplines; includes many recent terms; is illustrated.

———. *McGraw-Hill Dictionary of Scientific and Technical Terms*. New York: McGraw-Hill Book Company, 1974. Provides almost 100,000 definitions, each definition identified with a field of science or technology; has many illustrations. 2d ed., 1978.

Leftwich, A. W. *A Dictionary of Zoology*. 3d ed. Princeton, N.J.: D. Van Nostrand Company, 1973. For students as well as naturalists; includes brief, concise definitions of the principal phyla and classes of animals as well as a large number of orders, suborders, and families.

Pennak, Robert William. *Collegiate Dictionary of Zoology*. New York: The Ronald Press Company, 1964. Gives brief, concise definitions of only the most common meanings; covers all areas of zoology; includes many biographical entries; aims to help students acquire a working vocabulary in zoology.

Stenesh, J. *Dictionary of Biochemistry*. Philadelphia: Interscience Publishers, a division of John Wiley & Sons, Inc., 1975. Has some 12,000 entries covering terms in biochemistry and related fields.

Thewlis, J. *Concise Dictionary of Physics and Related Sciences*. New York:

Pergamon Press, 1973. Emphasizes short definitions of terms from physics and related fields such as astronomy, astrophysics, meteorology, geophysics, physical chemistry, etc.; intended for college-level students, teachers, and educated nonspecialists.

———. *The Encyclopaedic Dictionary of Physics.* New York: Pergamon Press, 1961–1963. 9 vols. Supplements I and II, 1966, 1967. An international work; presents the whole of physics and its related subjects; brief to lengthy articles, each complete in itself; provides bibliographies for further study; Vol. 9 is a multilingual glossary; annual supplements.

Thomson, Sir Arthur L. (ed.). *A New Dictionary of Birds.* New York: McGraw-Hill Book Company, 1964. Worldwide in scope; designed for both British and North American readers; provides long articles as well as short articles which define terms; includes bibliography; intended for both the general reader and the ornithologist; many illustrations in color and black and white.

Usher, George. *A Dictionary of Botany.* Princeton, N.J.: D. Van Nostrand Company, 1966. Includes terminology in biochemistry, soil science, and statistics.

DICTIONARIES—TECHNOLOGY

Black's Medical Dictionary. 31st ed. Edited by William A. R. Thompson. New York: Barnes & Noble, Inc., 1977. The standard British dictionary; includes many new sections on drugs and new subjects in medicine.

Brussel, James A., and Cantzlaar, George. *The Layman's Dictionary of Psychiatry.* New York: Barnes & Noble, 1967. Defines the more frequently encountered terms.

De Vries, Louis. *French-English Science and Technology Dictionary.* 4th ed. Rev. and enl. by Stanley Hochman. New York: McGraw-Hill Book Company, 1978. Includes 4,500 terms; emphasizes new developments in electronics, automotive technology, astronautics.

———. and Devries, Herrmann (eds.). *German-English Technical and Engineering Dictionary.* 2d ed. revised and enlarged. New York: McGraw-Hill Book Company, 1966. For the engineer, research worker, translator, and student; offers over 225,000 terms; includes new words in the fields of nuclear physics, space flight, and plastics.

Dorland's Illustrated Medical Dictionary. 25th ed. Philadelphia: W. B. Saunders Company, 1978. Frequently revised, provides broad coverage of the field; gives pronunciation; claims that it is not just a record of usage, but maintains "certain standards of etymological propriety and selection" (Preface).

Graf, Rudolf F. *Modern Dictionary of Electronics*, 5th ed. New York: Howard W. Sams & Co., 1977. Includes new terms in special fields; has special pronunciation guide; includes most widely used symbols and abbreviations; features popular type of writing.

Hinsie, Leland E., and Campbell, Robert J. *Psychiatric Dictionary*. 4th ed. New York: Oxford University Press, 1970. Includes terminology from psychiatry and related sciences; gives pronunciation, illustrations, quotations, and some bibliography.

Jordain, Philip B. *Condensed Computer Encyclopedia*. New York: McGraw-Hill Book Company, 1969. Defines computer terms in the language of the nonspecialist except for complex entries; definitions include statement of concepts; divided into generic, specific, and specialized terms; includes bibliography.

Lingeman, Richard R. *Drugs from A to Z: A Dictionary*. 2d ed. New York: McGraw-Hill Book Company, 1974. Discusses drugs from a pharmacological and sociological point of view; gives definitions and some encyclopedic information on drugs and drug use; defines some current slang expressions.

Marks, Robert W. (ed.). *The New Dictionary & Handbook of Aerospace, with Special Sections on the Moon and Lunar Flights*. New York: Frederick A. Praeger, Publishers, 1969. Aims to introduce the general reader to the structural topography and vocabulary of aerospace science; defines terms; explains abbreviations; gives brief biographies of persons in the field; has a special section on Project Apollo and a lunar glossary.

Markus, John. *Electronics and Nucleonics Dictionary*. 4th ed. New York: McGraw-Hill Book Company, 1978. Provides easy-to-understand and up-to-date definitions for some 16,000 terms used in television, radio, engineering, nuclear science, etc.

Rogers, Harold A. (ed.). *Funk and Wagnalls Dictionary of Data Processing Terms*. New York: Funk & Wagnalls Company, 1970. Intended for the beginner; gives brief definitions of terms and concepts; covers equipment, software, programming, logic, Boolean algebra; includes some related fields.

Sarnoff, Paul (comp.). *The New York Times Encyclopedic Dictionary of the Environment*. New York: Quadrangle Books, 1971. Explains terminology and concepts of the environmentalist; gives illustrations; stresses social implications of environmental pollution.

Stedman's Medical Dictionary. 23rd ed. Baltimore: The Williams & Wilkins Company, 1976. "A vocabulary of medicine and its allied sciences with pronunciation and derivation" (subtitle); includes biographical sketches of persons important in the history of medicine.

ENCYCLOPEDIAS—SCIENCE AND TECHNOLOGY

Above and Beyond: the Encyclopedia of Aviation and Space Science. Chicago: New Horizons Publications, Inc., 1967–1969. 14 vols. Covers the full range of topics related to aviation and space from the earliest mythology into the predictable future; Aims to be the world's first complete encyclopedia of aviation and space; includes biographies.

Besançon, Robert M. (ed.). *The Encyclopedia of Physics.* 2d ed. New York: Van Nostrand Reinhold Company, 1974. Provides short introductory articles on physics, the history of physics, measurements, symbols, and terminology; general articles on the major areas of physics.

The Cambridge Encyclopaedia of Astronomy. By the Institute of Astronomy at the University of Cambridge. New York: Crown Publishing Company, 1977. Presents a broad survey of astronomy, past and present, with the latest astronomical findings; has a glossary.

Clark, George L. (ed.). *The Encyclopedia of Chemistry.* 2d ed. New York: Reinhold Publishing Corporation, 1966. Offers concise definitions, well-written essay-type articles, some photographs and diagrams; does not include biography.

Fairbridge, Rhodes W. *Encyclopedia of Atmospheric Sciences and Astrogeology* (Encyclopedia of Earth Sciences, vol. II). New York: Reinhold Book Corporation, 1967. Covers in original articles by world authorities meteorology, aeronomy, climatology, geophysics, and astrogeology; has many illustrations.

———. *The Encyclopedia of Geomorphology* (Encyclopedia of Earth Sciences, vol. III). New York: Reinhold Book Corporation, 1968. An encyclopedic treatment of the terminology, history, and principles of the science of geomorphology; gives bibliographical references.

———. *The Encyclopedia of Oceanography* (Encyclopedia of Earth Sciences, vol. I). New York: Reinhold Publishing Corporation, 1966. For all scientists, but provides general articles for the novice; has short, selective bibliographies and cross references to highly technical areas; includes diagrams and charts.

———. *The Encyclopedia of World Regional Geology.* Part I: *Western Hemisphere.* New York: John Wiley & Sons, Inc., 1975. Includes Antarctica and Australia; gives geologic and geomorphic data by continent, region, country, and island group; for persons with a background in the subject.

Gray, Peter (ed.). *The Encyclopedia of the Biological Sciences.* 2d ed. New York: Van Nostrand Reinhold Company, 1970. Aims to provide succinct and accurate information for biologists in those fields in which they are not experts; defines and explains subjects; has lengthy articles; gives biographical information on some individuals in the field.

Grzimek's Encyclopedia of Ecology. Edited by Bernhard Grzimek. New York: Van Nostrand Reinhold Company, 1977. Covers almost every concept pertinent to ecology, including pesticides, atomic energy, and oxygen distribution.

Hampel, Clifford, and Hawley, Gessner G. (eds.). *The Encyclopedia of Chemistry.* 3d ed. New York: Van Nostrand Reinhold Company, 1973. Offers concise definitions and well-written essay-type articles; has some biographical sketches; for students and nonscientists.

Hunter, David E., and Whitten, Phillip (eds.). *Encyclopedia of Anthropology.* New York: Harper & Row, Publishers, Incorporated, 1976. Covers concepts, theories, terminology, leading anthropologists; has bibliographies, maps, diagrams; is intended for beginners.

Hurlbut, C. S., Jr. (ed.). *The Planet We Live On: An Illustrated Encyclopedia of the Earth Sciences.* New York: Harry N. Abrams, Inc., 1976. Covers all aspects of the earth sciences—geology, meteorology, oceanography—as well as lunar science; has many drawings, photographs, and diagrams.

International Encyclopedia of Chemical Science. Princeton, N.J.: D. Van Nostrand Company, 1964. For chemists and nonchemists; gives definitions and emphasizes facts, principles, concepts, theoretical and descriptive topics; glossaries of terms in French, German, Russian, and Spanish into English.

Kingzett's Chemical Encyclopaedia. 9th ed. Princeton, N.J.: D. Van Nostrand Company, 1966. A digest of chemistry and its industrial applications; can be used by all "classes of the community" (Preface).

Lapedes, Daniel N. (ed.). *The Encyclopedia of Environmental Science.* New York: McGraw-Hill Book Company, 1974. Treats a broad range of topics that include ecology, conservation, oceanography, meteorology, and mining in relation to environmental problems; gives definitions, discussion, and bibliographies; written for the nonspecialist.

————. *McGraw-Hill Encyclopedia of Energy.* New York: McGraw-Hill Book Company, 1976. Presents various aspects of energy; includes articles on energy outlooks and alternatives such as coal mining and solar power; defines terms; has many illustrations, graphs, and charts.

Larousse Encyclopedia of the Animal World. Edited by A. R. Waterston. New York: Larousse and Company, Inc., 1975. Surveys the animal kingdom from protozoans to mammals; treats each order, class, or genus and gives typical species; has 1,000 photographs.

The McGraw-Hill Encyclopedia of Science and Technology. 4th ed. New York: McGraw-Hill Book Company, 1977. 15 vols. Presents factual, concise, basic data in all the physical sciences, earth sciences, life sciences, engineering; covers new developments in space travel, oceanography, geophysics, electronics, ecology, and many other areas; is kept up to date by *McGraw-Hill Yearbook of Science and Technology*; usefulness is further enhanced by the *McGraw-Hill Basic Bibliography of Science and Technology* (p. 196) and the *McGraw-Hill Modern Men of Science* (p. 208).

The McGraw-Hill Encyclopedia of Space. New York: McGraw-Hill Book Company, 1968. Covers all aspects of space science and exploration, space history, and technology; is written in nontechnical language.

Newman, James R. (ed.). *The Harper Encyclopedia of Science*. Rev. ed. New York: Harper & Row, Publishers, 1967. 4 vols. Intended for the nonspecialist and planned as a work of moderate length, covering almost every aspect of pure and applied science, including scientific thought, history, and achievement; provides long articles; includes biographical sketches of leading scientists; has many illustrations; gives a bibliography in the final volume.

Ralston, Anthony, and Meek, C. L. (eds.). *Encyclopedia of Computer Science*. New York: Petrocelli Books, Mason/Charter Publishers, Inc., 1976. Covers both theoretical and practical topics, including the science, technology, uses, history, and social setting of computers; has many illustrations; intended for nonspecialist.

Ridpath, Ian (ed.). *Illustrated Encyclopedia of Astronomy and Space*. New York: Thomas Y. Crowell Company, 1976. Has short articles on a wide range of topics; has tables, charts, photographs, and biographical sketches.

Satterthwaite, Gilbert E. (ed.). *Encyclopedia of Astronomy*. New York: St. Martin's Press, 1971. Covers a wide range of topics on all aspects of the subject; gives biographical notes on distinguished astronomers of the past; has photographs.

Todd, David Keith (ed.). *The Water Encyclopedia, A Compendium of Useful Information on Water Resources*. Port Washington, N.Y.: Water Information Center, 1970. Gives a variety of information on water resources from many sources; presents facts, statistics, information regarding climate, hydrology, surface and ground water, resources agencies, water use, water quantity, and pollution control; is presented in tabular form; the only text is explanatory notes and footnotes.

Van Nostrand's Scientific Encyclopedia. 5th ed. Edited by D. M. Considine. New York: Van Nostrand Reinhold Company, 1976. Covers all science and technology; provides clear definitions, well-written articles, many illustrations and diagrams; has more than 7,000 entries and some bibliographies.

Williams, Roger J., and Lansford, Edwin M., Jr. (eds). *The Encyclopedia of Biochemistry*. New York: Reinhold Publishing Corporation, 1967. Provides explanatory information and broad discussions for the biochemist, more technical and detailed information for the specialist; serves as an introduction to a much larger body of literature; bibliographies follow articles; brief biographical information on famous biochemists.

HANDBOOKS

Burington, Richard Stevens. *Handbook of Mathematical Tables and Formulas.* 5th ed. New York: McGraw-Hill Book Company, 1973. Provides quick reference source to mathematical information, including large collection of most frequently needed tables.

Condon, Edward Uhler, and Odishaw, Hugh. *Handbook of Physics.* New York: McGraw-Hill Book Company, 1968. Reviews and surveys the entire field of physics; chapters written by specialists.

Considine, Douglas M. (ed.). *Energy Technology Handbook.* New York: McGraw-Hill Book Company, 1977. Gives data in all areas of energy production where progress can be expected in the next few years; emphasizes scientific and engineering aspects; discusses projects from all over the world; has bibliographies.

Gray, Asa. *Gray's Manual of Botany.* 8th ed. New York: American Book Company, 1950. Identifies the flowering plants and ferns of the central and northeastern United States and nearby Canada. Centennial edition of a standard handbook.

Handbook of Chemistry and Physics. Cleveland, Ohio: Chemical Rubber Company, 1914– . (Annual.) A ready-reference book of chemical and physical data; contains tables, graphs, and property information.

Howard, Neale E. *The Telescope Handbook and Star Atlas.* Rev. 2d ed. New York: Thomas Y. Crowell Company, 1975. Describes celestial phenomena; gives photographs and diagrams of astronomical instruments; identifies and locates 239 stars; designed for amateur astronomers.

Korn, Granino A., and Korn, Theresa M. *Manual of Mathematics.* New York: McGraw-Hill Book Company, 1967. Introduces modern mathematical methods and presents in concise form comprehensive, connected outlines of basic mathematical subjects; permits rapid review of an entire mathematical subject.

Lange, Norbert Adolph. *Lange's Handbook of Chemistry.* Edited by John A. Dean. 11th ed. New York: McGraw-Hill Book Company, 1973. A compilation of facts, data, tabular material, and experimental findings, provides ready access to every aspect of chemistry; for students and professionals.

Perry, Robert H. (ed.). *Engineering Manual.* 3d ed. New York: McGraw-Hill Book Company, 1976. For students, engineers, and technical people in general; covers standard fields of engineering in individual chapters.

The Peterson Field Guide Series. Boston: Houghton Mifflin Company, 1934– . Under the editorship of Roger Tory Peterson; each title treats a specific subject, such as birds, shells, butterflies, mammals, rocks and minerals, animal tracks, ferns, trees and shrubs, reptiles and amphibians, wildflowers, stars and planets; usually regional in coverage; useful for identification purposes; illustrated.

"Putnam's Nature Field Books." New York: G. P. Putnam's Sons, 1928– This series includes separate volumes on specific scientific subjects. Titles include *Field Book of American Wild Flowers*, by F. S. Mathews; *Field Book of the Stars*, by W. T. Olcott; and *Field Book of Common Rocks and Minerals*, by F. B. Loomis.

Rickett, Harold William (ed.). *Wildflowers of the United States.* New York: McGraw-Hill Book Company, 1966–1973. 6 vols. in 14. Prepared in cooperation with the New York Botanical Gardens; provides full-color photographs of thousands of wildflowers, most of them shown in their natural habitats; gives both Latin and common names. Vol. I: *The Northeastern States* (2 vols.). Vol. II: *The Southeastern States* (2 vols.). Vol. III: *Texas* (2 vols.). Vol. IV: *The Southwestern States* (3 vols.). Vol. V: *The Northwestern States* (2 vols.). Vol. VI: *The Central Mountains and Plains* (3 vols.).

Sippl, Charles J. *Computer Dictionary and Handbook.* 2d rev. ed. Indianapolis: Howard W. Sams Company, 1972. Is designed to aid in identifying, classifying, and interpreting terms and concepts concerned with electronic data processing, information technology, computer science, and the many types of automation.

Walker, Ernest P., and others (eds.). *Mammals of the World.* 2d ed. Baltimore: The Johns Hopkins Press, 1968. 3 vols. Constitutes a basic source concerning all mammals; provides photographs of a representative of almost every genus. Vol. 3 is a bibliography.

YEARBOOKS[5]

McGraw-Hill Year Book of Science and Technology. New York: McGraw-Hill Book Company, 1961– . (Annual.) Planned as an annual supplement to the *McGraw-Hill Encyclopedia of Science and Technology;* summarizes the significant events and advances of the previous year in every area of science and technology and serves to keep the *Encyclopedia* up to date.

[5]Most of the societies in the subject fields issue a yearbook—e.g., *The Yearbook of Mathematics.* Some encyclopedias issue a science supplement—e.g. *Science Year,* issued to supplement *World Book Encyclopedia* (1965–) and *Encyclopedia Science Supplement,* issued by Grolier (1965–). Other yearbooks and annuals provide information on activities in the fields of science and technology during the preceding year. These titles are examples of yearbooks which treat many subdivisions of science and technology.

U.S. Department of Agriculture. *Yearbook of Agriculture.* Washington, D.C.: Government Printing Office, 1894– . Covers a specific subject in each issue, such as soil, water, food, trees.

U.S. Department of Interior, Bureau of Mines. *Minerals Yearbook.* Washington D.C.: Government Printing Office, 1933– . Reviews performance and developments in the nation's mineral industries; includes statistical summaries.

BIOGRAPHICAL DICTIONARIES[6]

American Men and Women of Science. 13th ed. Edited by Jaques Cattell Press. New York: R. R. Bowker Company, 1976. 7 vols. Gives biographical information on American and Canadian men and women now working and teaching in the physical, biological, and selected social sciences.

Asimov, Isaac. *Asimov's Biographical Encyclopedia of Science and Technology.* New rev. ed. Garden City, N.Y.: Doubleday & Company, 1972. Describes "the lives and achievements of 1,195 great scientists from ancient times to the present: chronologically arranged" (subtitle.)

Dictionary of Scientific Biography. Published under the auspices of the American Council of Learned Societies. New York: Charles Scribner's Sons, 1970–76. 14 vols., Vol. XV, *Supplement,* 1977; Vol. XVI, *Index,* 1978. Describes and evaluates the lives of more than 5,000 scientists from all regions and periods; does not include living persons; gives biographical information and information on the contributions of each person in relation to other scientists; each biography has a bibliography of works by and about the biographee; comparable in treatment to *Dictionary of American Biography* and *Dictionary of National Biography.*

McGraw-Hill Modern Men of Science. New York: McGraw-Hill Book Company, 1967. Supplements the *McGraw-Hill Encyclopedia of Science and Technology,* which does not contain biography; can also be used as biographical dictionary of twentieth-century scientists; gives essential biographical data and describes the most significant contributions.

EXAMPLES OF PROFESSIONAL JOURNALS IN SCIENCE AND TECHNOLOGY[7]

American Chemical Society Journal. Washington, D.C.: American Chemical Society, 1879– . (Semimonthly.) Reports significant research in all branches of chemistry; has a section on short preliminary studies of importance; gives book reviews.

[6]See also Chapter 10, Biographical Dictionaries.

[7]See also *Ulrich's International Periodicals Directory,* 17th ed., and *Magazines for Libraries,* 3rd ed., edited by Bill Katz and Berry Richards.

American Journal of Physics. New York: American Institute of Physics, 1933– . (Monthly.) Published by the American Association of Physics Teachers; represents the entire field; reports on new techniques and apparatus; includes some abstracts; gives book reviews.

American Journal of Public Health. Washington, D.C.: American Public Health Association, 1911– . (Monthly.) Covers all aspects of public health; written for the expert but has information of interest to nonexperts; discusses current issues in health; gives book reviews.

American Mathematical Monthly. Washington, D.C.: MathematicalAssociation of America, 1894– . (Ten times a year.) The official journal of the association; aimed at the college-level mathematics student; presents papers and notes, including reports of research; includes book reviews.

American Medical Association Journal. Chicago: American Medical Association, 1848– . (Weekly.) The official journal of the association; reviews current research; reports advances in the field of medical science; gives selected abstracts of world's medical literature; gives information on current topics of interest to the medical profession; includes news, views, and reviews of the profession.

Geological Society of America. *Bulletin.* Boulder, Colo.: Geological Society of America, 1888– . (Monthly.) The official publication of the society; is concerned with original research on any facet of geology, including geochemistry, geophysics, mineralogy, etc.; has long and short articles; is illustrated.

Journal of Geology. Chicago: University of Chicago Press, 1893– . (Bimonthly.) Concerned with original studies in all aspects of geology; some issues are devoted to a single subject; has book reviews; is international in scope.

Natural History. New York: American Museum of Natural History, 1900– . (Monthly, October–May; bimonthly, June–September.) Issued by the American Museum of Natural History; provides a popular approach to many topics of interest to nature lovers, including conservation, anthropology, geography, astronomy, etc.; authoritative articles are written in semipopular style; has many photographs.

Nature. London: Macmillan Journals, Ltd., 1869– . (Three weekly editions.) A British publication; represents all branches of science; gives essay and review articles by leading scientists and some studies on original research; provides both general and specialized treatment; includes book reviews.

Science. Washington, D.C.: American Association for the Advancement of Science, 1880– . (Weekly.) Discusses important issues related to developments in all the sciences; has short reports of original research; includes book reviews.

Scientific American. New York: Scientific American, 1845– . (Monthly.) Reports scientific and technical advances and theories; for both general readers and specialists; has many illustrated articles; gives book reviews.

Sky and Telescope. Cambridge, Mass.: Sky Publishing Corporation, 1941– . (Monthly.) For beginners in astronomy; features articles by experts; includes information on telescope accessions, observations, celestial calendars, etc.; has news notes.

ABSTRACT JOURNALS[8]

Biological Abstracts. Philadelphia: Biological Abstracts, 1926– . (Semimonthly.) Covers the world's biological research literature in agriculture, genetics, behavioral sciences, and other related fields, including periodical publications, books, government reports, and reports of conferences; is the major abstracting source for the biological sciences; entries are arranged under broad subject headings with many subdivisions.

Chemical Abstracts. Washington, D.C.: American Chemical Society, 1907– . (Weekly.) Provides abstracts from about 12,000 journals covering fifty languages, patents from twenty-five countries, and theses, books, conference proceedings, and government reports; makes available some 240,000 abstracts annually; is not confined to chemistry but covers all scientific and technical literature; reports new chemical information from patent literature; covers all scientific and technical papers; now on machine-readable tape.

Mathematical Reviews. Providence, R.I.: American Mathematical Society, 1940– . (Monthly.) Abstracts and reviews mathematical literature appearing in some 1,200 journals and books, conference proceedings, and translations grouped under general subject headings; is international in scope.

Pollution Abstracts. La Jolla, Calif.: Pollution Abstracts, 1970– . (Six times a year.) Divided into chapters by subject (such as air, fresh water, land, noise pollution) or by type of document cited (such as government documents, patents). Includes books, journals, papers, government reports.

Science Abstracts. London: Institution of Electrical Engineers 1898– . (Monthly.) Includes physics abstracts, electrical and electronics abstracts, and computer and control abstracts; covers journals, papers, books, conference proceedings; arranged by classified subject headings; available on magnetic tape for computer searches.

[8]This is just a sample; there are abstract journals in every major area of science and technology.

CHAPTER TWENTY-ONE
THE FINE ARTS

Art—the word is derived from the Latin *ars*—is any skill or aptitude which enables its possessor to perform in a superior manner. This meaning of the word covers (1) the fine arts, which express ideas, emotions, and experiences in beautiful or significant forms; (2) the useful arts, which are both utilitarian and artistic; (3) the decorative arts, which adorn rather than create; and (4) the recreational arts, which afford relaxation and amusement.

The fine arts, as a branch of knowledge, are those arts (skills or aptitudes) concerned with creating, producing, or expressing what is beautiful, imaginative, or appealing for its own sake, rather than for some utilitarian purpose. Traditionally, the fine arts include music, painting, sculpture, dance, drama, architecture, and poetry.

In the fine arts class of the Dewey Decimal System (700), all the above-named fine arts are included except poetry. Landscape and civic arts, drawing and decorative arts, prints and printmaking, photography, and recreation are also placed in the 700 class. In the Library of Congress classification, M is music and N is fine arts. Recreation is placed in the G class (GV).

Works of art—that is, paintings, sculpture, musical scores, dramatic productions, etc.—constitute the primary source materials in the fine arts subject field. There are, however, many reference books designed to aid the student in understanding and appreciating works of art; the artists who produced them; the technical terminology of the several areas; the historical backgrounds of schools, movements, and trends; and the actual techniques employed. Those reference aids include bibliographies, guides and catalogs, indexes to periodical literature and to paintings and illustrations, dictionaries and encyclopedias, biographical dictionaries, handbooks, histories, and professional journals.

USEFUL REFERENCE SOURCES IN THE FINE ARTS

PAINTING, SCULPTURE, ARCHITECTURE, DECORATIVE ARTS
Bibliographies, Guides, and Indexes[1]
The Art Index. New York: The H. W. Wilson Company, 1929– . (Quarterly.) Indexes selected art journals, museum publications, domestic art publications, and foreign journals by author and subject; includes both fine arts and applied arts.

Chamberlin, Mary. *Guide to Art Reference Books.* Chicago: American Library Association, 1959. Annotates and evaluates some 2,500 works on art in English and in other languages.

Clapp, Jane. *Sculpture Index.* Metuchen, N.J.: Scarecrow Press, Inc., 1970–1971. 2 vols. Indexes pictures of sculpture in some 950 art publications; traces sculpture from prehistoric times to the present; for each work, gives the present location of the sculpture, dimensions, materials of construction, and picture sources; Vol. I covers Europe and the contemporary Middle East; Vol. II covers the Americas, the Orient, Africa, the Pacific, and the Classical world.

Ehresmann, Donald L. *Applied and Decorative Arts: A Bibliographic Guide to Basic Reference Works, Histories, and Handbooks.* Littleton, Colo.: Libraries Unlimited, 1977. Includes both scholarly and popular works written in Western European languages from 1875–1975; is annotated; includes works on ceramics, toys, furniture, folk art, ornament.

———. *Fine Arts: A Bibliographic Guide to Basic Reference Works, Histories, and Handbooks.* Littleton, Colo.: Libraries Unlimited, 1975. Annotates a basic list of some 1,200 titles published since 1900, with emphasis on works published 1958–1973; covers Oriental as well as Western art; is arranged by geographical regions.

Ellis, Jessie Croft. *Index to Illustrations.* Boston: F. W. Faxon Company, 1967. Indexes paintings, people, places, symbols in books and in some periodicals; does not include nature illustrations.

Monro, Isabel S., and Monro, Kate M. *Index to Reproductions of American Paintings.* New York: The H. W. Wilson Company, 1948. Lists by name of artist, by title, and sometimes by subject the reproductions of

[1]See also Chapter 9, Indexes, and Chapter 13, Bibliographies.

American paintings in more than 800 books and exhibition catalogs. *First Supplement*, 1964.

———, and———. *Index to Reproductions of European Paintings*. New York: The H. W. Wilson Company, 1956. Lists by name of artist, title of painting, and often by subject European artists reproduced in more than 300 books.

Vance, Lucile E., and Tracey, Esther M. *Illustration Index*. New York: Scarecrow Press, Inc., 1966. Covers the period 1950 to June 1963; indexes illustrations in periodicals in many fields for many types of users; emphasizes costume. A companion volume, *Illustration Index*, 3d ed., by Roger C. Greer, covers the period July 1963 through December 1971.

Dictionaries and Encyclopedias

Adeline, Jules. *The Adeline Art Dictionary*. Translated from the French, with a supplement of new terms, by Hugo G. Beigel. New York: Frederick Ungar Publishing Company, 1966. A republication of the *Adeline Art Dictionary* with a supplement of new terms, gives brief, clear definitions and explanations; many illustrations; includes terms in architecture, heraldry, and archaeology.

Encyclopedia of World Art. New York: McGraw-Hill Book Company, Inc., 1959–1968. 15 vols. Includes biographies of artists; has monographic treatments of periods, movements, and areas of art; gives discussions of types, media, technology, concepts, and problems of art; provides bibliographies.

Fleming, John, and Honour, Hugh. *Dictionary of Decorative Arts*. New York: Harper & Row, Publishers, Incorporated, 1977. A guide to the decorative arts of the West from the Middle Ages to the present; emphasizes European and American art but gives attention to China, Japan, Turkey, and Persia; covers all forms of art; defines and explains stylistic and technical terms; has many illustrations.

The Focal Encyclopedia of Photography. Rev. ed. New York: McGraw-Hill Book Company, 1969. Covers new techniques, new subjects, new terminology; includes some statistical, historical, geographical, and biographical information; discusses the major developments in the field; provides practical information for both professional and amateur.

Harris, Cyril M. (ed.). *Dictionary of Architecture and Construction*. New York: McGraw-Hill Book Company, 1975. Provides clear definitions of current basic terminology in architecture and construction; has many illustrations.

———. *Historic Architecture Sourcebook*. New York: McGraw-Hill Book Company, 1977. Defines more than 5,000 terms in both Eastern and

Western architecture covering some 5,000 years; has many line drawings.

Huyghé, René (ed.). *Larousse Encyclopedia of Modern Art, from 1800 to the Present Day.* New York: Prometheus Press, 1965. One of a series, translated from the French *L'Art et L'Homme,* which includes *Larousse Encyclopedia of Prehistoric and Ancient Art* (1962), *Larousse Encyclopedia of Byzantine and Medieval Art* (1963), *Larousse Encyclopedia of Renaissance and Baroque Art* (1964). Each volume shows the art of the period in relation to philosophy, literature, science, and social and economic conditions; gives factual material on artists, schools, dates, and techniques.

McGraw-Hill Dictionary of Art. New York: McGraw-Hill Book Company, 1969, 5 vols. Gives worldwide coverage of concepts, styles, periods, movements, and works of art; includes biographies.

Mayer, Ralph (ed.). *A Dictionary of Art Terms and Techniques.* New York: Thomas Y. Crowell Company, 1969. Covers painting, drawing, sculpture, printmaking, ceramics, and some other related fields; gives definitions, history, description of periods, schools, etc.; represents all major art forms.

Murray, Peter, and Murray, Linda. *Dictionary of Art and Artists.* Rev. ed. New York: Penguin Books, Inc., 1972. Limited to the arts of painting, sculpture, drawing, and other graphic processes, chiefly in Western Europe; treats schools of art, artists, individual works of art, and art terms; includes biographical entries; gives at least one reproduction for each artist.

Myers, Bernard S. (ed.). *Encyclopedia of Painting.* 3d rev. ed. New York: Crown Publishers, 1970. Gives brief articles on more than 3,000 artists; identifies schools of painting; is arranged chronologically.

The Phaidon Dictionary of Twentieth Century Art. London and New York: Phaidon Press, Ltd., 1973. Gives brief biographies of artists of this century; treats concepts, movements, terms in modern art.

Praeger Encyclopedia of Art. New York: Praeger Publishers, Inc., 1971. 5 vols. Aims to provide a comprehensive and authoritative reference guide for students and general readers to the history of world art; includes biographies, chronological surveys, and articles on periods, styles, schools; gives articles on civilizations for which no artists' names are known.

Read, Herbert (ed.). *Encyclopedia of the Arts.* New York: Meredith Press, 1966. Discusses fine arts, applied arts, performing arts, literature, philosophy, history, works of art, movements and groups, techniques and materials; provides biographical information; intended for readers in the Western world, but includes artists in other parts of the world who have influenced Western art.

Savage, George. *Dictionary of Antiques*. New York: Praeger Publishers, Inc., 1970. Emphasizes style and fashion in art; has articles on almost every aspect of American and European decorative art; gives definitions for terms and explains techniques; provides biographical information on individual artisans; is designed to help readers recognize fakes in antiques; includes bibliographies.

Walker, John A. *Glossary of Art, Architecture and Design Since 1945*. London: Clive Bingley, 1977. Covers contemporary art terminology with emphasis on painting, sculpture, and architecture; groups and styles are discussed; international in scope but emphasizes Anglo-American terminology.

Handbooks

Hamilton, George Heard. *19th and 20th Century Art, Painting, Sculpture, Architecture*. New York: Harry N. Abrams, Inc., 1970. Provides authoritative articles by well-known art scholars with a list of books for each article; has many illustrations, including sixty-four color plates; reproductions of paintings and sculpture give medium and size.

Osborne, Harold (ed.). *The Oxford Companion to Art*. Oxford: Clarendon Press, 1970. "Nonspecialist introduction to the fine arts" (Preface); has only introductory articles; includes visual arts, but excludes arts of the theater and cinema; covers all parts of the world from earliest times to the present; includes brief historical articles; some bibliographies are given.

The Oxford Companion to the Decorative Arts. Oxford: Clarendon Press, 1975. Some 1,000 illustrated articles written by experts cover prehistoric crafts and technologies to modern times; includes some biographies; gives information on schools, styles, processes, and ornamentation; emphasis is on the Western world.

Biographical Dictionaries and Directories[2]

American Architects Directory. 3d ed. Sponsored by the American Institute of Architects. New York: R. R. Bowker Company, 1970. Gives information on architects in general practice or in specialized areas of architectural forms.

American Art Directory. Washington, D.C.: American Federation of Arts, 1898– . Published in New York by R. R. Bowker Company, 1952– .

[2]See also Chapter 10, Biographical Dictionaries

(Triennial.) Includes art associations and museums, periodicals, scholarships, art schools, and people and places in United States and Canadian art; has section devoted to major museums and art schools in foreign countries.

Cederholm, Theresa A. (comp. and ed.). *Afro-American Artists: A Bio-bibliographical Directory.* Boston: Boston Public Library, 1973. Provides biographical information on some 2,000 American artists; identifies media used, titles of works, locations of permanent collections.

Cummings, Paul. *A Dictionary of Contemporary American Artists.* 3d ed. New York: St. Martin's Press, 1977. Covers living and deceased artists who have been active in the United States during the past twenty-five years; gives personal data and bibliographical references for further study.

―――. *Fine Arts Market Place.* New York: R. R. Bowker Company, 1973– . (Biennial.) Gives information about art associations, exhibitions, organizations, suppliers, services, dealers, publishers, auction houses, photographers, and bookstores.

Richards, J. M. (ed.). *Who's Who in Architecture from 1400 to the Present.* New York: Holt, Rinehart and Winston, Inc., 1977. Covers the period from the early Renaissance to the present, emphasizing the West; other areas are included; both factual and critical articles are provided; has many illustrations.

Who's Who in American Art. Edited by the Jaques Cattell Press. New York: R. R. Bowker Company, 1937– . (Revised biennially.) Gives biographies of American and Canadian artists including professional painters, sculptors, illustrators, graphic artists, executives, collectors, patrons, scholars, and critics.

Examples of Professional Journals[3]

Art Bulletin. New York: College Art Association of America, 1913– . (Quarterly.) Contains articles for students of art history written by faculty members of the association and covering all facets and periods of fine arts.

Art in America. New York: Art in America Company, Inc., 1913– . (Bimonthly.) International in scope; emphasis is on contemporary art; includes some historical articles; covers painting, sculpture, architecture, design, and photography.

―――――――

[3]See also *Ulrich's International Periodicals Directory*, 17th ed., and *Magazines for Libraries*, 3d ed., edited by Bill Katz and Berry Richards.

MUSIC
Bibliographies, Guides, and Indexes[4]

Duckles, Vincent Harris (comp.). Music Reference and Research Materials: An Annotated Bibliography. 3d ed. New York: The Free Press of Glencoe, Inc., 1974. Points out and describes the resources of the field with emphasis on dictionaries, encyclopedias, histories, chronologies, bibliographies of music and music literature, guides to research methods in musicology, and catalogs of major music libraries and collections throughout the world; does not include biographical material.

Ewen, David (ed.). *American Popular Songs from the Revolutionary War to the Present.* New York: Random House, Inc., 1966. Includes songs originating in the theater and motion pictures, jazz, folk songs, American national ballads, patriotic songs, and some European song hits; gives factual information about the composers and about the performers who introduced them.

Horn, David (comp.). *The Literature of American Music in Books and Folk Music Collections: A Fully Annotated Bibliography.* Metuchen, N.J.: Scarecrow Press, Inc., 1977. Aims to include all English language material—scholarly, historical, or popular—and a sample of books in other languages.

Music Index: The Key to Current Music Periodical Literature. Detroit: Information Coordinators, Inc., 1949– . (Monthly; annual cumulations.) A subject and author guide to almost 200 periodicals treating various aspects of the music field; also includes selective indexing of nonmusical periodicals; book reviews are listed under that heading.

Shapiro, Nat (ed.). *Popular Music, An Annotated Index of American Popular Songs.* 5 vols. New York: Adrian Press, 1964–1969. Aims to provide selective annotated lists by decades of significant American popular songs, giving discussions of the decades in question and, for each song, information about the composer, lyricist, current publisher, recordings, film or stage show in which it was introduced, and performers associated with it. Covers the period 1920–1964.

Dictionaries

Ammer, Christine. *Harper's Dictionary of Music.* New York: Harper & Row, Publishers, Incorporated, 1972. Defines the most commonly used musical terms; gives material on music history and biographical material about composers; emphasizes popular music; includes information about musical forms and musical instruments.

[4]See also Chapter 9, Indexes, and Chapter 13, Bibliographies.

Apel, Willi (ed.). *Harvard Dictionary of Music.* 2d ed., revised and enlarged. Cambridge, Mass.: Belknap Press of Harvard University Press, 1969. Gives lengthy discussions of terms, music in different countries, trends, movements, forms; includes a discussion of music education in the United States; gives bibliographies and short musical illustrations; does not include biographies.

Everyman's Dictionary of Music. 5th revised and enlarged ed. compiled by Eric Blom, revised by Jack Westrup and others. New York: St. Martin's Press, 1972. Aims to provide "the maximum amount of information possible in a limited space" (Preface); includes living composers and composers not living, but does not include all composers; defines terms, identifies works, gives musical illustrations.

Fink, Robert, and Ricci, Robert. *The Language of Twentieth Century Music: A Dictionary of Terms.* New York: Schirmer Books, a Division of Macmillan, Inc., 1975. Defines basic terminology in current use by composers and performers in computer music, electronic music, jazz, film music, rock, etc.

Grove's Dictionary of Music and Musicians. 5th ed. Edited by Eric Blom. London: Macmillan & Co., Ltd., 1954. 9 vols. *Supplement,* 1961. Covers the whole field of music and musicians from earliest times; includes music history, theory, practice, terms, biographies, musical instruments. *The New Grove Dictionary of Music and Musicians,* in twenty volumes, edited by Stanley Sadie, is scheduled for publication in 1979 by Grove's Dictionaries of Music, Inc., Washington, D.C.

Picerno, Vincent J. *Dictionary of Musical Terms.* Brooklyn: Haskell House Publishers, Ltd., 1976. Gives simple definitions of contemporary musical terms in all languages; does not give biographical information; intended for college students taking undergraduate courses in music and for nonspecialists; gives pronunciation and brief definition of terms; has a selected annotated bibliography.

Rosenthal, Harold, and Warrack, John Hamilton. *Concise Oxford Dictionary of Opera.* New York: Oxford University Press, 1964. Includes plots, biographies, terms, characters, and first lines of the better-known arias.

Scholes, Percy A. (ed.). *The Concise Oxford Dictionary of Music.* 2d ed. edited by John Owen Ward. New York: Oxford University Press, 1964. For the ordinary listener; is illustrated; gives brief information on composers, musical compositions, performances, and terminology.

Vinton, John (ed.). *Dictionary of Contemporary Music.* New York: E. P. Dutton & Company, Inc., 1974. Covers stylistic and technical aspects of concert music in the Western tradition of the present day and of the last several decades; gives biographical information and list of works for some 1,000 composers who were living after 1930; provides survey articles on technical and special topics of current importance in music.

Encyclopedias

Ewen, David. *The New Encyclopedia of the Opera.* New York: Hill and Wang, Inc., 1971. Gives stories of the most significant operas in detail; others are given briefly; identifies characters of operas; gives passages from operas, history of opera, some biographies, and literary sources of operas.

Feather, Leonard G., and Gitler, Ira. *The Encyclopedia of Jazz in the Seventies.* New York: Horizon Press, 1977. Covers the period 1966–1976; examines all forms of jazz; includes biographical information and bibliography.

Kinkle, Roger D. *The Complete Encyclopedia of Popular Music and Jazz: 1900–1950.* New Rochelle, N.Y.: Arlington House Inc., 1974. 4 vols. Emphasizes performers who were established before 1950; covers Broadway and movie musicals, popular songs, popular and jazz recordings, and biographies of major figures; summarizes important events and dates during the period covered.

Logan, Nick, and Woffinden, Bob (comps.). *The Illustrated Encyclopedia of Rock.* New York: Crown Publishers, Inc., 1977. Gives information on groups associated with rock music from its beginning to 1976, biographies, career information, discographies.

Nite, Norm N. *Rock On: The Illustrated Encyclopedia of Rock 'n' Roll, the Solid Gold Years.* New York: Thomas Y. Crowell Company, 1974. Provides brief biographical and career information on major and minor recording artists who had a hit record in the 1950s and 1960s; includes country, western, and pop music.

Orrey, Leslie (ed.). *The Encyclopedia of Opera.* New York: Charles Scribner's Sons, 1976. Contains information on a limited number of operas and persons concerned with their production: composers, librettists, singers, conductors, designers; includes operatic characters and opera companies; includes terminology; has some entries for musical comedies and their composers; is illustrated.

Shestack, Melvin. *The Country Music Encyclopedia.* New York: Thomas Y. Crowell Company, 1974. Covers the stars of country music; gives biographical information and an assessment of each star's career; includes some coverage of groups and country music forms.

Stambler, Irwin (ed.). *Encyclopedia of Pop, Rock, and Soul.* New York: St. Martin's Press, 1974. Covers individual groups, terms, types of music, and events; gives biographical information on persons and some critical evaluations; includes year-by-year listings of Gold Record Awards from 1965 to 1973.

————. *Encyclopedia of Popular Music and Rock.* Rev. ed. New York: St. Martin's Press, 1973. Presents popular music from 1925, the people responsible for it, and its effects on modern life; gives definitions, biographical information, and synopses of musicals; lists award winners.

————, and Landon, Grelun. *Encyclopedia of Folk, Country and Western Music.* New York: St. Martin's Press, 1969. Emphasizes biographical information on current and past performers; defines terms; describes instruments; gives some historical background; includes items of general interest in this field.

Thompson, Oscar (ed.). *The International Cyclopedia of Music and Musicians.* 10th ed. Edited by Bruce Bohle. New York: Dodd, Mead & Company, 1975. Provides definitions, bibliography, biography, synopses of opera plots, pronunciation of names; has short articles, lengthy discussions; international in scope, but has strong emphasis on American music and the American scene.

Westrup, J. A., and Harrison, F. L. *The New College Encyclopedia of Music.* Rev. ed. by Conrad Wilson. New York: W. W. Norton & Company, Inc., 1976. Includes musical works, American popular music, jazz, early music, and musicals; aims to reflect current tastes and attitudes in the 1970s and 1980s.

Handbooks

Ewen, David. *All the Years of American Popular Music.* Englewood Cliffs, N.J.: Prentice-Hall, Inc., 1977. Attempts to cover every style and field of popular music from colonial days to rock musicals; includes brief biographies of composers, lyricists, and librettists.

Fuld, James J. *The Book of World-famous Music—Classical, Popular and Folk.* Revised and enlarged ed. New York: Crown Publishers, Inc., 1971. Gives information about many hundreds of the best-known musical compositions from twenty-five countries; includes music and words of songs, date of first appearance, and brief biographical information for composer, librettist, and lyricist; traces each melody to its original printed source; gives first line of music and words of each work in original key.

Haggin, B. H. (ed.). *The New Listener's Companion and Record Guide.* New York: Horizon Press, 1977. New, up-to-date edition; gives critical evaluation, meaning of music, music producers, forms, analyses of works.

Jacobs, Arthur, and Sadie, Stanley. *Great Operas in Synopsis.* New York: Thomas Y. Crowell Company, 1966. Covers sixty-one of the recognized classics of opera by thirty-two composers from the seventeenth to the early twentieth century and mentions many others; includes a general introduction, synopsis, and musical commentary.

Kobbé, Gustav. *The New Kobbé's Complete Opera Book.* Edited and revised by the Earl of Harewood. New York: G. P. Putnam's Sons, 1976. Traces the development of opera; gives stories of more than 300 operas; gives brief notes on composers; includes older and modern works; is arranged chronologically by century and subdivided by the native country of the composer; includes musical examples.

Marcuse, Sibyl. *A Survey of Musical Instruments.* New York: Harper & Row, Publishers, Incorporated, 1975. Offers historical and technical information on the musical instruments of the world, tracing the development of individual instruments from their origin to the present; quotations from scholarly works and bibliographical references are given.

Sandberg, Larry, and Weissmann, Dick. *The Folk Music Sourcebook.* New York: Alfred A. Knopf, Inc., 1976. Lists and analyzes significant folk and folk-based music and performers; gives wide coverage, including the blues, North American Indian music, Chicano music; has lists of songbooks, instructional books, records, musical instruments, films, periodicals, videotapes, and music festivals.

Scholes, Percy A. (ed.). *The Oxford Companion to Music.* 10th ed. revised and reset. Edited by John Owen Ward. New York: Oxford University Press, 1970. Designed for a wide range of readers, offers definitions of terms, surveys of history of music, plots of operas; discussions of musical instruments; biographical information; covers forms of music.

Slonimsky, Nicolas. *Music since 1900.* 4th ed. New York: Charles Scribner's Sons, 1971. Presents chronologically the occurrences of musical importance in Europe and North America from January 1, 1900, through July 20, 1969; includes information on composers and their works and other items of musical interest; covers electronic music and instruments; includes a glossary.

Biographical Dictionaries[5]

Anderson, E. Ruth (comp.). *Contemporary American Composers: A Biographical Dictionary.* New York: G. K. Hall & Co., 1976. Gives brief biographical information for some 4,000 composers born in 1870 or later

[5]See also Chapter 10, Biographical Dictionaries.

who did the major part of their work in the United States; includes information about career, compositions, etc.

Baker's Biographical Dictionary of Musicians. 6th ed. Revised by Nicolas Slonimsky. New York: Schirmer Books, 1978. Gives up-to-date information on performers, composers, critics, librettists, publishers, instrument makers, scholars, and patrons of music; includes musicians of all countries and periods; gives list of works and selective bibliographies; indicates pronunciation.

Ewen, David (comp. and ed.). *Great Composers, A Biographical and Critical Guide: 1300–1900.* New York: The H. W. Wilson Company, 1966. Supplies detailed biographical, historical, and analytical information on 198 composers of the past whose works are significant in the development of music; includes lesser masters and composers. *Composers since 1900* (1969), companion volume to *Great Composers*, contains biographical sketches of 220 principal composers of the twentieth century.

————. *Great Men of American Popular Song.* Englewood Cliffs, N.J.: Prentice-Hall, Inc., 1970. Tells the "history of American popular song through the lives, careers, achievements, and personalities of its foremost composers and lyricists from William Billings of the Revolutionary War to Bob Dylan" (subtitle).

————. *Popular Composers from Revolutionary Times to the Present: A Biographical Guide, First Supplement.* New York: The H. W. Wilson Company, 1972. First edition was published in 1962; covers composers in rock, country, and western music, except folk; gives biographies, bibliographies; includes only the best-known names.

Examples of Professional Journals[6]

High Fidelity. New York: Billboard Publishing Company, 1951– . (Monthly.) Covers current music performances, music, performing artists; has articles about music and musicians; gives critical reviews of recordings of all kinds of music—classical, folk, jazz, and pop.

Music Journal: Educational Music Magazine. New York: Music Journal, Inc., 1943– . (Monthly, September-June.) Presents current thinking on a wide variety of musical topics; gives critical reviews of books, records, and music.

The Musical Quarterly. New York: G. Schirmer, Inc., 1915– . (Quarterly.) Aims to present the best musical thought throughout the world; publishes research in the field of serious music; gives reviews of recordings and musical examples.

[6]See also *Ulrich's International Periodicals Directory*, 17th ed., and *Magazines for Libraries*, 3d ed., edited by Bill Katz and Berry Richards.

PERFORMING ARTS
Indexes[7]

The Art Index. (See p. 212)

Humanities Index. (See p. 232.)

Dictionaries and Encyclopedias

Brown, Les. *The New York Times Encyclopedia of Television.* New York: Quadrangle/The New York Times Book Company, Inc., 1977. Covers the history of television, personalities, technology, regulations, networks, cable TV, pay TV, public television, legal cases; gives evaluative comments.

Chujoy, Anatole, and Manchester, P. W. *The Dance Encyclopedia.* Revised ed. New York: Simon and Schuster, 1967. Covers history, dances, dancers.

Clarke, Mary, and Vaughan, David (eds.). *The Encyclopedia of Dance and Ballet.* New York: G. P. Putnam's Sons, 1977. Discusses ballet and contemporary dance, especially of the twentieth century; traces the development of the major ballet companies; describes more than 300 ballets and modern dance works; gives biographical information on the choreographers, composers, designers, and dancers who created them; has numerous photographs and a glossary of terms.

Dictionary of Modern Ballet. New York: Tudor Publishing Company, 1959. Presents a complete record of modern dance from Diaghilev and Isadora Duncan to the late 1950s.

Esslin, Martin (ed.). *The Encyclopedia of World Theater.* New York: Charles Scribner's Sons, 1977. Based on the German *Friedrichs Theaterlexikon* (1969); covers all facets of the theater; many strictly German-oriented articles have been removed and more English and American articles added; gives biographies and definitions of literary characters; is illustrated.

Green, Stanley. *Encyclopedia of the Musical Theatre.* New York: Dodd, Mead & Company, 1976. Gives brief information on plots, costs, and background of about 200 musicals; has short biographies of composers, lyricists, librettists, performers, directors, choreographers, and producers; gives a list of awards through 1975.

Koegler, Horst. *The Concise Oxford Dictionary of Ballet.* New York: Oxford University Press, 1977. Covers all aspects of ballet for the past four centuries: ballets and their sources, dancers, choreographers, schools, theaters, companies, cities important to ballet; defines terms; includes information on ethnic, ballroom, and modern dancing.

[7]See also Chapter 9, Indexes.

McGraw-Hill Encyclopedia of World Drama. New York: McGraw-Hill Book Company, 1972. 4 vols. International in scope; gives articles on 910 dramatists and important movements and schools in world drama; has biographical articles; includes critique of the work of all dramatists listed and synopses of their most important plays.

Raffé, W. G., and Purdon, M. E. (eds.). *Dictionary of the Dance.* New York: A. S. Barnes and Co., Inc., 1965. Concentrates on the art of dance (not on dancers and dancing); deals with the meanings and aims of dance; represents more than 100 countries from ancient Assyria to the present day.

Terry, Walter. *Ballet Guide.* New York: Dodd, Mead & Company, 1976. Gives background, listings, credits, and description of more than 500 of the world's major ballets.

Wilson, G. B. L. *A Dictionary of Ballet.* 3d ed. New York: Theatre Arts Books, 1974. Emphasizes dance in English-speaking countries, with special emphasis on classical ballet; covers individual ballets, dancers, steps, technical terms.

Handbooks

Anderson, Michael, and others (eds.). *Crowell's Handbook of Contemporary Drama.* New York: Thomas Y. Crowell Company, 1971. A guide to developments in the drama in Europe and the Americas since World War II, and in Spain since the Civil War; emphasizes drama rather than theater; gives surveys of national drama by country; defines terms; identifies styles; gives information about selected playwrights and plays.

Bawden, Liz Anne. *The Oxford Companion to Film.* New York: Oxford University Press, 1977. A guide to feature films; gives information about the art of films; has biographies of actors, actresses, directors, and producers; provides histories of major film companies and discussions of movements and genres; includes some critics; gives history of films in each country.

Ewen, David. *New Complete Book of the American Musical Theater.* New York: Holt, Rinehart and Winston, Inc., 1970. Gives information about the cast, date, producer, composer, story, production, songs, etc., of some 500 musicals.

Hartnoll, Phyllis (ed.). *The Oxford Companion to the Theatre.* 3d ed. New York: Oxford University Press, 1967. Provides information on every aspect of the theater; deals with the theater in all ages and in all countries; includes new playwrights and players.

McDonagh, Don. *The Complete Guide to Modern Dance.* New York: Doubleday & Company, Inc., 1976. Traces modern dance from the last decade of the nineteenth century to the present; gives biographies of individual artists and describes their more outstanding performances and the works they created; describes dancers in terms of their worth and variety of approaches; gives stories of modern dances; lists the choreography of each artist.

Biographical Dictionaries[8]

Notable Names in the American Theatre. Clifton, N.J.: James T. White & Company, 1976. A new and revised edition of *The Biographical Encyclopedia & Who's Who of the American Theatre;* gives biographical sketches of those important in the American theater as performers, writers, directors, producers, etc.; includes awards, premieres, information about theater groups, and theater buildings.

Directory of American Scholars. 7th ed., Vol. II: *English, Speech, and Drama.* Edited by the Jaques Cattell Press. New York: R. R. Bowker Company, 1978.

Who's Who in the Theatre: A Biographical Record of the Contemporary Stage. 16th ed. Detroit: Gale Research Company, 1976. Gives biographical sketches of actors, actresses, producers, directors, playwrights, designers; includes a list of notable productions, principal theaters, and long runs of the Broadway, off-Broadway, and London stage from 1870; contains playbills.

Examples of Professional Journals[9]

Dance Magazine. New York: Dance Magazine, Inc., 1926– . (Monthly.) Devoted to theory and practice of dance; gives reviews of performances, photographs of dancers, international information about activities of dance companies and dancing schools; covers ballet and modern, variety, and ethnic dancing; includes biographies.

Drama and Theatre, 1961–62– . Fredonia, N.Y.: State University of New York, 1962– . (Quarterly.) Offers 365 short plays a year, usually one-act; has articles on contemporary theater around the world; gives interviews with theatrical personalities.

SPORTS AND RECREATION
Encyclopedias, Dictionaries, and Handbooks

Arlott, John (ed.). *The Oxford Companion to World Sports and Games.* New York: Oxford University Press, 1975. Traces the development of specific sports; introduces the sports that are played in national or international competition; explains the way a sport is played; gives a digest of

---

[8]See also Chapter 10, Biographical Dictionaries.

[9]See also *Ulrich's International Periodicals Directory.* 17th ed., and *Magazines for Libraries,* 3d ed., edited by Bill Katz and Berry Richards.

the rules of each game, line drawings and diagrams, and action photographs; provides information on prominent players, teams, and stadiums; traces the historical development of each sport; intended to help the reader understand a sport when watching it for the first time.

The Baseball Encyclopedia: The Complete and Official Record of Major League Baseball. Bicentennial ed. (3d ed.). New York: Macmillan Publishing Co., Inc., 1976. Provides statistical information on all aspects of professional baseball: special achievements, awards and records, teams and players, all-star games, World Series, etc.

Hickok, Ralph. *New Encyclopedia of Sports.* New York: McGraw-Hill Book Company, 1977. Gives full information on more than 100 sports; includes related topics; has many illustrations.

Hollander, Zander (ed.). *The Modern Encyclopedia of Basketball.* New York: Four Winds Press, 1969. A comprehensive record of basketball with emphasis on the period since 1930; includes history, all forms of the game, and records of professional players.

Menke, Frank G. *The Encyclopedia of Sports.* 5th rev. ed. Revisions by Suzanne Treat. New York: A. S. Barnes and Co., Inc., 1975. Gives information about the background of sports, rules, records, players, and awards; covers nearly eighty sports.

Pratt, John Lowell, and Benagh, Jim. *The Official Encyclopedia of Sports.* New York: Franklin Watts, Inc., 1965. Covers thirty-three sports: their history, stars, coaches, rules, equipment, playing fields, associations, outstanding teams, and official records; includes a history of the Olympic Games.

Treat, Roger. *The Encyclopedia of Football.* 14th rev. ed. Edited by Pete Palmer. New York: A. S. Barnes and Co., Inc., 1976. Gives comprehensive coverage of football, with complete AFL, NFL, and AAFC records; has Hall of Fame information; includes the 1975–1976 season.

Webster's Sports Dictionary. Springfield, Mass.: G. & C. Merriam Company, 1976. Defines briefly and concisely terms used in the principal sports of the English-speaking countries; gives common sports abbreviations, specifications for playing fields, and discussions of sports equipment, officials' signals, and scoring; has many drawings.

Examples of Professional Journals[10]

Sports Illustrated. Chicago: Time, Inc., 1954– . (Weekly.) Covers all the usual spectator sports; includes information about sports personalities, sports records, news of interest; has many illustrations.

---

[10]See also *Ulrich's International Periodicals Directory,* 17th ed., and *Magazines for Libraries,* 3d ed., edited by Bill Katz and Berry Richards.

Journal of Health, Physical Education, Recreation. Washington, D.C.: American Association for Health, Physical Education, and Recreation, 1930– . (Monthly, September–June.) Since 1975, the title is *Journal of Physical Education and Recreation.* Covers physical education and related areas, such as dance, intramural sports, athletics; gives some history.

CHAPTER TWENTY-TWO
LITERATURE

Any discussion of reference sources in the field of literature must be prefaced by a definition and a delimiting of the term "literature."

In its broadest sense, "literature" includes all preserved writings. In a more limited but still general denotation, it is the total written works of a people, such as the literature of America or the literature of England. It is also the name given to all writings upon a particular subject, such as the literature of geography, the literature of education, or the literature of history.

Specifically and as a subject area, literature is that class of writing which is notable for imaginative and artistic qualities, form, or expression. The forms of literature are poetry, drama, prose fiction, and essay. The Dewey Decimal class assigned to literature is 800. In the Library of Congress classification literature and language share class P.

Reference sources in the field of literature are more numerous than in any other subject field. There are reference materials which cover all forms of literature, and there are reference materials in each of the literary genres, such as poetry, drama, and fiction.

Since each reference source is designed to serve a particular purpose, the representative titles listed below are grouped according to the purposes they serve and the kinds of questions they answer. Distinguishing features are noted with the bibliographical entry.

BIBLIOGRAPHIES[1] AND GUIDES

Bibliographies and guides in literature, as in other areas of knowledge, are designed to locate and evaluate the literature of a field. They may group works according to form, such as poetry, drama, fiction, essay; they may be complete and include all works; or they may be selective, listing only a part of the literature. Not all bibliographies and guides do all these things.

Altick, Richard Daniel, and Wright, Andrew. *Selective Bibliography for the Study of English and American Literature.* 5th ed. New York: The Macmillan Company, 1974. Provides a guide to a highly selective group of materials for research; about 590 items are included.

Bateson, Frederick Wilse, and others (eds.). *A Guide to English and American Literature.* 3d ed. New York: Gordian Press, Inc., 1976. Formerly *A Guide to English Literature;* now includes American literature and American authors; is arranged chronologically according to periods; is intended for the serious student of English literature.

Blanck, Jacob (comp.). *Bibliography of American Literature.* New Haven: Yale University Press, 1955–1973. Vols. 1–6. (In progress.) A selective bibliography limited to the past 150 years of American literature; describes but does not evaluate.

Dyson, A. E. (ed.). *The English Novel: Select Bibliographical Guides.* London: Oxford University Press, 1974. A group of bibliographical essays on selected English novelists; includes information about recommended editions, critics, biographies.

Fiction Catalog. 9th ed. New York: The H. W. Wilson Company, 1975. (Four annual supplements.) A guide to works of adult fiction found most useful in representative libraries in the United States and Canada; lists works of fiction by author, title, and subject, with full bibliographical information and annotations; indicates books suitable for young people; intended as a companion to the *Public Library Catalog.*

Gohdes, Clarence. *Bibliographical Guide to the Study of the Literature of the U.S.A.* 4th ed. Durham, N.C.: Duke University Press, 1976. Lists types and sources of bibliography, biography, and other materials on forms and periods of the literature of the United States; includes allied fields such as folklore, theater, history, and literature on or by racial and other minorities, and materials on methods of research.

Handbook of Latin American Studies. (Annual.) A guide to books published in the Latin American countries, excluding science and technology, with critical notes.

Jones, Howard Mumford, and Ludwig, Richard M. *Guide to American Literature and Its Backgrounds since 1890.* 3d ed. revised and en-

[1]See also Chapter 13, Bibliographies.

larged. Cambridge, Mass.: Harvard University Press, 1964. A selective bibliography and outline of American literature since 1890; presents works reflecting the intellectual, sociological, and political backgrounds of American literary history; includes reading lists on various aspects and schools in American literature since 1890; covers developments in science, social history, and popular amusement.

Leary, Lewis Gaston. *Articles on American Literature 1950–1967.* Compiled with the assistance of Carolyn Bartholet and Catharine Roth. Durham, N.C.: Duke University Press, 1970. Based on the quarterly checklists of articles appearing in *American Literature;* supplements author's volume which covered articles from the first half of the century (1900–1950), published in 1954.

————, and Auchard, John (eds.). *American Literature: A Study and Research Guide.* New York: St. Martin's Press, 1976. For beginning college students; presents essential works of the past 40 years; treats the study and teaching of the subject and the schools of criticism; gives criticism of selected major authors; includes information on writing a research paper.

The Literary History of the United States. Edited by Robert E. Spiller and others. *Bibliography Supplement II.* Edited by Richard M. Ludwig. New York: The Macmillan Company, 1972. Covers period 1958–1970.

The Literary History of the United States Bibliography. Edited by Robert E. Spiller and others. New York: The Macmillan Company, 1963. This is vol. 2 of *Literary History of the United States.* Edited by Robert E. Spiller and others. 3d ed. revised. New York: The Macmillan Company, 1963. 2 vols. Classifies literature by author, period, and literary type; describes and evaluates. A 4th edition revised was published in 2 vols. in 1974.

Modern Humanities Research Association. *Annual Bibliography of English Language and Literature.* Cambridge: Cambridge University Press, 1920– . (Annual.) Lists books, pamphlets, and periodical articles in English and American literature with references to reviews of works; arranged chronologically.

Rubin, Louis D., Jr. (ed.). *A Bibliographical Guide to the Study of Southern Literature* (Southern Literary Studies). Baton Rouge: Louisiana State University Press, 1969. Aims to be "a compilation of some of the most useful materials available for the student who would begin work in the field of Southern literary study" (Preface); gives discussions of general topics and historical periods and 100 selected writers; covers folklore, drama, popular literature, local color; gives checklist of aids to the study of each area.

Watson, George (ed.). *The Concise Cambridge Bibliography of English Literature, 600–1950.* 2d ed. Cambridge: Cambridge University Press,

1965. Lists books (and a few articles) about some 400 English writers; includes significant works by and about each writer; provides a concise statement of the bibliography of all periods of English literature through the early twentieth century; includes only writers who are native to or mainly resident in the British Isles.

————. *The New Cambridge Bibliography of English Literature*. Cambridge: Cambridge University Press, 1969–1977. 5 vols. Covers works by and about authors in both primary and secondary sources; covers belles lettres, philosophy, book publication, religion, history, travel, education, sports, newspapers, and magazines; the location of manuscripts and papers of some authors is given; Vol. V, *Index*, compiled by J. D. Pickles, 1977. Supersedes *The Cambridge Bibliography of English Literature*, edited by F. W. Bateson, (1941, 4 vols.), and *Supplement*, A.D. *600–1900*, ed. by George Watson (1957).

INDEXES[2]

An index in the field of literature locates an article in a periodical or locates a poem, quotation, fairy story, play, essay, or other work in an anthology. Since the person seeking information does not always know the title and the author of a poem, play, or essay, a means of locating these items by subject is also necessary. It may be necessary to locate quotations by means of key words. The following indexes provide some or all of these kinds of listings; they are representative of the indexes available.

British Humanities Index. London: The Library Association, 1962– . Succeeds the *Subject Index to Periodicals*, which had been published until 1962, and incorporates the *British Technology Index;* indexes material relating to the arts and politics in periodicals and in society proceedings.

Essay and General Literature Index. New York: The H. W. Wilson Company, 1934– . (Semiannual.) Indexes by author and subject collections of essays and other collected works; covers all areas of the humanities, but emphasizes literary criticism; indexes only twentieth-century publications, but includes authors of all ages and nationalities; first volume covered the period 1900–1933.

Granger's Index to Poetry. 6th ed. Edited by William J. Smith. New York: Columbia University Press, 1973. Indexes by title, first line, subject, and author (when known) poems appearing in 514 anthologies published through 1970. *Granger's Index to Poetry, 1970–1977*. Edited by William J. Smith. New York: Columbia University Press, 1978. Provides first-

[2]See also Chapter 9, Indexes.

line, title, author, and subject indexes to poems in 119 major anthologies published between 1970 and 1977.

Humanities Index. New York: The H. W. Wilson Company, 1974– . (Quarterly.) Indexes by author and subject 260 periodicals in the humanities; has an index to book reviews. (See also *Social Sciences and Humanities Index*, p. 174.)

Ottemiller's Index to Plays in Collections. 6th ed., revised and enlarged. Edited by John M. Connor and Billie M. Connor. Metuchen, N.J.: Scarecrow Press, Inc., 1976. Indexes by author and title plays which appear in collections published from 1900 through early 1975.

Play Index. New York: The H. W. Wilson Company, 1953–1978. 5 vols. Published 1949–1977; includes plays in collections, single plays, radio, television, and Broadway plays, and plays for children and young adults; gives plot, cast, set, and other information; plays are listed under author, title, and subject.

Short Story Index. New York: The H. W. Wilson Company, 1953– . (Annual since 1974; five-year cumulations.) Indexes by author, title, and subject short stories in more than 8,000 collections published from 1900 to 1978 and in about 45 periodicals indexed in *Readers' Guide to Periodical Literature* and *Humanities Index.*

Sutton, Roberta B. *Speech Index*, 4th ed. revised and enlarged. New York: Scarecrow Press, 1966. Indexes world-famous orations and speeches for various occasions found in more than 250 collected works; covers works published through 1965; two *Supplements* cover period 1966–1975.

BOOK REVIEWS[3]

A book review is a notice, usually in a periodical publication, of a current book or play. Its purpose is to tell enough about the work under consideration to enable the reader to decide whether or not to read it. Therefore, it describes the subject matter, discusses the method and technical qualities, and may examine its value or usefulness when it is compared with similar works. A book review may be only descriptive; it may also be critical and evaluative. Among the sources of book reviews are the book review sections of newspapers, notably *The New York Times Book Review;* professional and scholarly journals which review materials in specific subject fields, for example, *The American Historical Review;* trade publications, which announce and sometimes promote newly published books (see Chapter 13, Bibliographies); and bibliographies in the subject fields. The sources below

[3]See also Chapter 9, Indexes.

cover book reviews in several fields and in several kinds of publications.

Book Review Digest. New York: The H. W. Wilson Company, 1905– . (Monthly except February and July.) Indexes reviews of current books which appear in more than seventy periodicals and journals; each book reviewed is entered by author, with a descriptive note, citations to all reviews (which appear in the journals indexed), and excerpts from selected reviews; has a title and subject index in each issue; gives length of review. A cumulated subject and title index every five years, covering the preceding five-year period, are aids in using this reference source. *Book Review Digest: Author/Title Index* 1905–1974. 4 vols. 1976.

Book Review Index. Detroit: Gale Research Company, 1965– . (Bimonthly; annual cumulations.) An index to reviews appearing in more than 300 periodicals (both magazines and newspapers) including the major adult and children's book reviewing media and many special-interest magazines; gives book title, name, date, and pages of the publication in which the review is located; does not give excerpts from the reviews. Since 1976, has a title index.

Current Book Review Citations. New York: The H. W. Wilson Company, 1976. (Monthly, except August.) Gives citations to book reviews from more than 1,200 book reviewing periodicals and subject periodicals; fiction and nonfiction, juvenile literature, foreign language books, and new editions are included; books reviewed are listed under author and title; gives names of publications in which the book was reviewed, volume, pages, date, and name of reviewer, if known.

An Index to Book Reviews in the Humanities. Vol. 1, No. 1, March, 1960– . Detroit: Philip Thomson, 1960– . (Quarterly; annual cumulation. Since 1963, annual.) Indexes reviews appearing in English in some 700 periodicals, American and foreign; does not include theology and archaeology; does not give excerpts from reviews.

Nineteenth Century Readers' Guide to Periodical Literature. Includes an index to book reviews which appeared in the periodicals indexed.

DICTIONARIES AND ENCYCLOPEDIAS

Dictionaries and encyclopedias of literature define words and phrases; identify references to fictional, mythical, and legendary places, characters, and events; explain the historical, geographical, social, economic, and cultural backgrounds of literature; provide biographical and critical information about authors and their works; and in some cases give pronunciation, summaries of plots, and bibliographical references. Some useful dictionaries and encyclopedias of literature follow.

DICTIONARIES

Beckson, Karl, and Ganz, Arthur (eds.). *Literary Terms: A Dictionary*. New York: Farrar, Straus, and Giroux, Inc., 1975. Defines and illustrates terms from poetry, drama, criticism, fiction, and rhetoric; identifies literary movements.

Cuddon, J. A. (ed.). *A Dictionary of Literary Terms*. Garden City, N. Y.: Doubleday & Company, Inc., 1977. Covers technical terms, forms of literature, movements, well-known phrases, styles, and themes; has illustrative examples; gives sources for further reading; includes some foreign terms.

Eagle, Dorothy (ed.). *Concise Dictionary of English Literature*. New York: Oxford University Press, 1970. Covers authors, literary terms, characters, works, recently established authors; notes scholarly developments and research since the 1939 edition.

Fuchs, J. W. *Classics Illustrated Dictionary*. New York: Oxford University Press, 1974. Covers briefly a wide range of information about Greco-Roman civilization, including literature, mythology, history, grammar, geography, clothing and other objects, philosophy, the arts, education, costume, the early Christians, etc.

Hammond, N. G. L., and Scullard, H. H. (comps.). *The Oxford Classical Dictionary*. 2d ed. Oxford: Clarendon Press, 1970. Revised in light of new discoveries and recent scholarship; covers ancient Greek and Roman periods; includes archaeology, geography, history, literature, mythology, philosophy, religion, science; arranged alphabetically by topic; includes bibliographies.

Lazarus, Arnold, and others. *Modern English: A Glossary of Literature and Language*. New York: Grosset & Dunlap, Inc., 1971. Provides a summary of concepts that writers, critics, and scholars have used to discuss and to describe the language and its literature; includes terminology of literature, rhetoric, and linguistics.

Reed, Joyce M. H. (ed.). *The Concise Dictionary of French Literature*. New York: Oxford University Press, 1976. An abridgment and updated version of the *Oxford Companion to French Literature* (1959); reflects developments since 1959; gives essential facts on writers, works, forms, genres, and trends that have influenced French literature.

Scott, Arthur F. *Current Literary Terms: A Concise Dictionary of Their Origin and Use*. New York: St. Martin's Press, 1965. Gives the etymology and a concise definition of the principal terms used in all branches of literature; quotations are used to illustrate many definitions; includes schools and movements; describes literary forms and techniques.

Shaw, Harry (ed.). *Dictionary of Literary Terms*. New York: McGraw-Hill Book Company, 1972. Defines, explains, and illustrates more than

2,000 literary terms, references, and allusions likely to be encountered by the general reader in any kind of literature, including magazines, newspapers, plays, and television programs.

ENCYCLOPEDIAS

Cassell's Encyclopedia of World Literature. Rev. and enl. ed. Edited by J. Buchanan-Brown. New York: William Morrow & Company, Inc., 1973. 3 vols. Provides general articles on literary genres, movements, terms; brief histories of national literature, biographical articles; aims to cover all periods and peoples.

Fleischmann, W. B. (ed.). *Encyclopedia of World Literature in the 20th Century.* New York: Frederick Ungar Publishing Co., 1967–1971. 3 vols. Designed mainly for English-speaking readers; covers twentieth-century literature, movements, authors; gives surveys of national literature. Vol. IV, *Supplement and Index,* 1975.

Gassner, John, and Quinn, Edward (eds.). *The Reader's Encyclopedia of World Drama.* New York: Thomas Y. Crowell Company, 1969. Emphasizes drama as literature, not as theater; does not include entries on actors or theatrical troupes; includes all countries; gives biographies and criticism of playwrights, plots of plays, articles on genres, and historical surveys of national drama.

Herzberg, Max J., and others (eds.). *Reader's Encyclopedia of American Literature.* New York: Thomas Y. Crowell Company, 1962. Gives essential information on writers writing in America; touches on almost every subject which is related to the literature of the United States and Canada from colonial times to the present, including authors, works, characters, historical settings and personages, editors, periodicals, and literary trends; provides biographical, bibliographical, and critical information and a glossary of literary terms.

McGraw-Hill Encyclopedia of World Drama. New York: McGraw-Hill Book Company, 1972. 4 vols. Includes articles on theatrical subjects and terms, movements, and styles; for 300 selected major dramatists, gives critique, synopsis of most important plays, and biography; a synopsis is given for each play of such master dramatists as Sophocles, Shakespeare, Racine, Molière, Ibsen; lists all the plays of the world's major dramatists with date of writing, first performance, and first publication of each play; includes bibliographies, illustrations, photographs.

Matlaw, Myron (ed.). *Modern World Drama: An Encyclopedia.* New York: E. P. Dutton & Company, Inc., 1972. Attempts to cover the work of all major nineteenth-century playwrights who lived in that century as well as those of notable twentieth-century playwrights up to the present time; includes brief biographies of playwrights, synopses of plots of plays, surveys of national literature; has illustrations.

Preminger, Alex, and others (eds.). *Princeton Encyclopedia of Poetry and Poetics*. Enl. ed. Princeton, N.J.: Princeton University Press, 1974. Covers the full range of poetry from oral tradition to the latest trends: history, theory, technique, and criticism; international in scope; provides entries on the history of each major body of world poetry.

HANDBOOKS

Handbooks provide short, concise answers to questions about literary authors, terminology, works, and trends; movements affecting literature; and events, places, and characters referred to in literature. The Oxford Companion Series, which is listed below, provides this kind of information, although each volume in the series may vary in points of emphasis. The other handbooks listed provide some or all of the types of information mentioned above.

Benét, William Rose. *The Reader's Encyclopedia*. 2d ed. New York: Thomas Y. Crowell Company, 1965. Covers all nations and all peoples; explains literary expressions and terms; identifies literary schools and movements, plots, and characters; gives information on musical compositions, works of art, writers, philosophers, scientists; pays special attention to the Orient, the Soviet Union, Latin America, and the Near East and to literary developments since 1948 (date of first ed.).

Brewer's Dictionary of Phrase and Fable. Centenary ed. Revised by Ivor H. Evans. London: Cassell & Company, Ltd., 1972. Emphasizes the unusual; includes words which are not in the traditional dictionary; defines, identifies, and explains words, phrases, and allusions in nonfiction, folklore, and legend; gives pronunciation for some words; is universal in scope.

Burke. W. J., and Howe, Will D. (eds.). *American Authors and Books*. 3d rev. ed. Revised by Irving Weiss and Anne Weiss. New York: Crown Publishers, 1972. Has articles on authors, books, periodicals, newspapers, publishing firms, literary societies, regions, and locations in the United States; primarily about authors and their works; secondarily about aspects of American literature; covers all types of writing, including western and detective stories; limited to the United States; covers the period 1640–1970.

Campbell, Oscar James, and Quinn, Edward G. (eds.). *The Reader's Encyclopedia of Shakespeare*. New York: Thomas Y. Crowell Company, 1966. A comprehensive view of Shakespearean criticism from Shakespeare's time to the present; provides convenient reference to persons, places, literary works, and other subjects relevant to Shakespeare.

Deutsch, Babette. *Poetry Handbook: A Dictionary of Terms.* 4th ed. New York: Funk & Wagnalls Company, 1974. Defines and explains literary terms; arranged alphabetically.

Feder, Lillian (ed.). *Crowell's Handbook of Classical Literature.* New York: Thomas Y. Crowell Company, 1964. Aims to help people interested in Greek and Roman civilization understand and enjoy classical literature; provides summaries, definitions, and factual material on authors, myths, and places; gives critical commentaries.

Hart, James David. *The Oxford Companion to American Literature.* 4th ed. New York: Oxford University Press, 1965. Treats writers and their works and the major nonliterary aspects of the American mind and the American scene as they are reflected and influenced by American literature; new edition adds more than 200 authors and sixty-two summaries of literature; in appendix, lists literary and social history side by side in chronological order.

Harvey, Paul (ed.). *The Oxford Companion to English Literature.* 4th ed. Revised by Dorothy Eagle. Oxford: Clarendon Press, 1967. Broad in scope; provides information about classical allusions found in literature; gives biographical and background material; identifies characters; gives synopses of literary works; brings entries for twentieth century up to date; has useful appendices, including information regarding censorship, English copyright law, and the calendar.

———, and Heseltine, Janet E. (eds.). *The Oxford Companion to French Literature.* New York: Oxford University Press, 1959. Surveys French literary life from the emergence of the vernacular to 1939.

Hathorn, Richmond Y. (ed.). *Crowell's Handbook of Classical Drama.* New York: Thomas Y. Crowell Company, 1967. Gives synopses of plays, biographical information on dramatists, short articles on dramatic forms, criticisms, mythology, and other topics; includes lost and fragmentary works.

Holman, C. Hugh. *A Handbook to Literature.* Based on the original by William Flint Thrall and Addison Hibbard. 3d ed. New York: The Odyssey Press, 1972. Explains words, phrases, movements peculiar to English and American literature; emphasizes terminology related to literary study; includes an outline of the literary history of England and America; gives winners of major literary awards.

Malkoff, Karl (ed.). *Crowell's Handbook of Contemporary American Poetry.* New York: Thomas Y. Crowell Company, 1974. Aims to be a guide to the actual reading of contemporary American poetry; gives some poetry explication; includes only poets who have published since 1940; traces development of major movements and identifies poets associated with each movement; gives brief biographical information on each poet.

The Penguin Companion to World Literature. New York: McGraw-Hill Book
Company, 1971. 4 vols. The four volumes cover English literature,
European literature, American literature, and classical, Oriental, and
African literature; includes biography and critical evaluation of work,
plots, and bibliography for each entry.

Story, Norah. *The Oxford Companion to Canadian History and Literature.*
New York: Oxford University Press, 1967. Provides both literary and
historical entries. *Supplement,* 1973.

LITERATURE IN COLLECTIONS (ANTHOLOGIES)

BOOK DIGESTS

Magill, Frank N. (ed.). *Masterpieces of World Literature in Digest Form.*
4th series. New York: Harper & Brothers, 1968. First series,
1952. Second series, 1956. Third series, 1960. Emphasizes poetry and
philosophical works; has some essay-type reviews; is universal in
scope.

Magill, Frank N. (ed.). *Masterplots.* Story editor, Dayton Koehler. Rev. ed.
Englewood Cliffs, N.J.: Salem Press, 1976. 12 vols. "2,010 plot stories
and essay reviews from the world's fine literature" (subtitle); begun in
1949; now covers more than 1,000 authors; arranged alphabetically by
title, gives plot summaries and essay-reviews of each; identifies form,
author, period, type of plot, locale, date of first publication, principal
characters, and themes; gives an evaluation of the work; poems, philosophy, and speeches have essay-reviews only.

Sprinchorn, Evert (ed.). *20th Century Plays in Synopsis.* New York: Thomas
Y. Crowell Company, 1965. Summarizes act by act more than 130
representative dramas by more than sixty modern playwrights; gives
brief biographical notes on playwrights.

BOOKS OF QUOTATIONS

Books of quotations provide (1) quotations on a subject for speeches or
papers and (2) the correct wording and source of a given quotation. There
are many collections of quotations; each one includes some quotations
omitted in others, and thus they supplement each other. The usefulness of a
book of quotations depends on (1) the kind of quotations included, (2) the
kind of reference provided (name of author, work from which the quotation
is taken, collection in which it can be located, with page, stanza, or line), and
(3) the ways each quotation is indexed (author, title, subject, first line, key
word). Some useful collections of quotations follow.

Bartlett, John (ed.). *Familiar Quotations*. 14th ed.; revised and enlarged by E. M. Beck. Boston: Little, Brown & Company, 1968. Presents familiar quotations arranged chronologically, beginning with ancient Egypt; has key word index.

Bohle, Bruce. *The Home Book of American Quotations*. New York: Dodd, Mead & Company, 1967. Companion volume to Stevenson's *Home Book of Quotations;* emphasizes distinctly American subjects and American writers and speakers who have commented on them; quotations are exclusively American and chiefly contemporary; sources are American or deal specifically with America.

Evans, Bergen (ed.). *Dictionary of Quotations*. New York: Delacorte Press, 1968. Presents the familiar and unfamiliar with historical and explanatory notes; arranged by subject and chronologically under subject.

Magill, Frank Northen. *Magill's Quotations in Context*. New York: Harper & Row, Publishers, 1966. 2 vols. Offers quotations of prose, poetry, and proverbs from all periods of Western literature in context with emphasis on English and American writers; arranged alphabetically with historical background information. Second Series. 1969.

The Oxford Dictionary of English Proverbs. 3d ed. revised by F. P. Wilson. Oxford: Clarendon Press, 1970. Arranged alphabetically; gives dated uses in chronological order.

Stevenson, Burton Egbert (ed.). *The Home Book of Quotations, Classical and Modern*. 10th ed. New York: Dodd, Mead & Company, 1967. Includes classical and modern selections; provides quotations from important contemporary figures; arranged alphabetically by subject.

Tripp, Rhoda T. (ed.). *International Thesaurus of Quotations*. New York: Thomas Y. Crowell Company, 1970. Arranges 16,000 brief quotations under subject; about one-third of the quotations are from the twentieth century; original sources are given when known.

BIOGRAPHICAL DICTIONARIES[4]

General encyclopedias, biographical dictionaries, handbooks, and histories of literature provide much information on the lives and works of authors. In addition to these sources, there are biographical dictionaries which are devoted exclusively to authors.

Contemporary Authors. Detroit: Gale Research Company, 1962– . (Four-volume cumulations.) Vols. 1 to 76 in print 1978; aims to be an up-to-date source of bio-bibliographical information on authors in many fields and of many nationalities; includes little-known authors.

[4]See also Chapter 10, Biographical Dictionaries.

Kunitz, Stanley J. (ed.). *Twentieth Century Authors.* New York: The H. W. Wilson Company, 1942. For each author, gives a lengthy biography, list of principal works, list of works about the author, and a portrait of the author. *Twentieth Century Authors: First Supplement* was published in 1955.

————, and Colby, Vineta (eds.). *European Authors: 1000–1900: A Biographical Dictionary of European Literature.* New York: The H. W. Wilson Company, 1967. Contains 967 biographies of European authors representing thirty-one different literatures; gives both biographical and critical information on each author; includes some portraits; lists principal works translated into English.

————, and Haycraft, Howard (eds.). *American Authors: 1600–1900.* New York: The H. W. Wilson Company, 1938. Presents some 1,300 biographies of American authors, including politicians, religious leaders, educators, and professional persons, with lists of principal works, biographical and critical sources, and 400 portraits.

————, and ————. *British Authors before 1800.* New York: The H. W. Wilson Company, 1952. Gives biographies of authors from the beginning of English literature to Cowper and Burns with lists of principal works by and about each author; includes 220 portraits.

————, and————. *British Authors of the Nineteenth Century.* New York: The H. W. Wilson Company, 1936. Contains more than 1,000 biographies of British authors from William Blake to Aubrey Beardsley with lists of principal works, biographical and critical sources, and some portraits of authors.

————, and————. *The Junior Book of Authors.* 2d ed. rev. New York: The H. W. Wilson Company, 1951. Covers the lives of writers and illustrators of books for young readers from Lewis Carroll and Louisa M. Alcott to the present time. Companion volumes are *More Junior Authors* (1963), *Third Book of Junior Authors* (1972), *Fourth Book of Junior Authors and Illustrators* (1978).

Murphy, Rosalie (ed.). *Contemporary Poets of the English Language.* Chicago: St. James Press, 1970. Provides biographical and bibliographical information about poets now writing in the English language in all parts of the world; covers 1,100 poets; gives brief biographical information, list of publications, and something about each poet's particular interest or some comment by each poet.

Rush, Theressa Gunnels, and others. *Black American Writers Past and Present: A Biographical and Bibliographical Dictionary.* Metuchen, N.J.: Scarecrow Press, Inc., 1975. 2 vols. Covers the period from the early eighteenth century to the present; gives brief biographical information, list of works, some quotations from the author, and references to critical materials on the author; includes more than 2,000 authors; writers from Africa and the West Indies who live in or publish in the United States are included.

Wakeman, John, and Kunitz, Stanley J. (eds.). *World Authors, 1950–1970.* New York: The H. W. Wilson Company, 1975. A companion volume to *Twentieth Century Authors.* Includes more than 900 authors (living and not living), most of whom became prominent between 1950 and 1970; gives biographical material, a survey of critical opinions on the writings, and a bibliography of works by and about each author.

REFERENCE HISTORIES[5] AND CRITICISM

Literary criticism is concerned with the description, analysis, comparison, and evaluation of works of literature. There are a number of sources of critical articles: indexes to periodical literature (under the heading "literary criticism"); indexes to newspapers; indexes to collected works; general bibliographies (under literary criticism); bibliographies in the field of literature; biographical works which provide critical commentary or list sources of critical works, bibliographies which treat literary criticism exclusively, and histories of literature.

REFERENCE HISTORIES

The Cambridge History of English Literature. London: Cambridge University Press, 1907–1927. 15 vols. Emphasizes movements in English literature, influence of foreign literature on the literature of England, and bibliographies.

The Cambridge History of American Literature. New York: G. P. Putnam's Sons, 1917–1921. 4 vols. Gives trends, evaluation, and extensive bibliographies.

The Oxford History of English Literature. New York: Oxford University Press, 1947–1978– . 12 vols. (In progress.). Each volume or half volume is an independent book; the twelve volumes provide a continuous and comprehensive history of English literature; includes bibliographies. Each volume includes a bibliography and chronological tables.

Sampson, George. *The Concise Cambridge History of English Literature.* 3d ed. Revised by R. C. Churchill. Cambridge: Cambridge University Press, 1970. Has sections on Indian, Canadian, Australian, and South African literature; has a new chapter on the United States from the colonial period to Henry James, giving attention to the relations be-

[5]See p. 154.

tween American and British literature and the ways each has influenced the other.

CRITICISM

Coleman, Arthur, and Tyler, Gary R. *Drama Criticism.* Denver: Alan Swallow, 1966, 1971. 2 vols. A checklist of interpretation of English and American plays in a variety of journals published since 1940.

Combs, Richard E. *Authors: Critical and Biographical References.* Metuchen, N.J.: Scarecrow Press, Inc., 1971. "A guide to 4,700 critical and biographical passages in books" (subtitle); includes a large number of books published in the past twenty-five years.

Contemporary Literary Criticism. Detroit: Gale Research Company, 1973– . "Excerpts from criticism of the works of today's novelists, poets, playwrights, and other creative writers" (subtitle); covers authors living or deceased since 1960; gives excerpts from criticism of each author; each volume covers some 200 well-established and minor authors. Vols. 1 to 9 in print 1978.

Curley, Dorothy Nyren, and others. *Modern American Literature (A Library of Literary Criticism).* 4th enlarged ed. New York: Frederick Ungar Publishing Company, 1969. 3 vols. An index to hundreds of critical books, essays, articles, and reviews dealing with works of some 300 important twentieth-century American poets, novelists, dramatists, essayists; includes excerpts from the criticism. Vol. IV: *Supplement* to the 4th ed., 1976.

Eichelberger, Clayton L. (comp.). *A Guide to Critical Reviews of United States Fiction 1870–1910.* Metuchen, N.J.: Scarecrow Press, Inc., 1971. Lists reviews from thirty American and English periodicals, including some regional sources, of the period covered. Vol. II, 1974.

Gerstenberger, Donna (comp.). *The American Novel: A Checklist of Twentieth Century Criticism on Novels Written since 1789.* Chicago: The Swallow Press, 1970. 2 vols. Vol. I: *The American Novel 1789–1959;* Vol. II: *Criticism Written 1960–1968.* Does not include reviews; is a listing by novelist of critical writings on particular works.

Kearney, Elizabeth, and Fitzgerald, Louise S. (comps.). *The Continental Novel: A Checklist of Criticism in English, 1900–1966.* Metuchen, N.J.: Scarecrow Press, Inc., 1968. Lists criticism from books and periodicals of the period covered.

Moulton, Charles Wells (ed.). *The Library of Literary Criticism of English and American Authors.* Buffalo: Moulton Publishing Company, 1901– 1905. 8 vols. (Reprinted in 1934 by Peter Smith, New York.) Chronologically arranged by authors; includes both obscure and prominent writers; is a compilation of materials by numerous authors; gives biographical information on authors and excerpts from criticisms.

Palmer, Helen H. *European Drama Criticism 1900–1975.* Hamden, Conn.: The Shoe String Press, Inc., 1977. A checklist of criticism in books and periodicals in English and foreign languages; extends coverage through 1975.

——, and Dyson, Anne Jane (comps.). *American Drama Criticism.* Hamden, Conn.: The Shoe String Press, Inc., 1967. *Supplement I* (1970), *Supplement II* (1976), compiled by Floyd E. Eddleman. A checklist of critical articles arranged alphabetically by author; covers the period 1890–1975.

—— and ——. *English Novel Explication: Criticisms to 1972.* Hamden, Conn.: Shoe String Press, Inc., 1972. A checklist of critical articles arranged alphabetically by author and then by novel; lists criticism from 1957 to 1972 which is found in books and journals. *Supplement I* to 1975, edited by Peter Abernethy and others.

Salem, James M. (comp.). *A Guide to Critical Reviews.* New York: Scarecrow Press, Inc., 1966, 1967, 1971. 5 vols. Part I: *American Drama from 1909 to 1969,* 2d ed., 1973; Part 2: *The Musical from Rodgers and Hart to Lerner and Loewe;* Part 3: *British and Continental Drama from Ibsen to Pinter;* Part 4 (in 2 volumes): *The Screen Play from The Jazz Singer to Dr. Strangelove.* Gives a checklist of reviews from American and Canadian periodicals but does not include critical articles from scholarly journals.

Temple, Ruth Z., and Tucker, Martin (eds.). *Modern British Literature (A Library of Literary Criticism).* New York: F. Ungar Publishing Co., 1966. 3 vols. Presents over 400 twentieth-century British and Commonwealth authors, giving excerpts from criticism of their works found in British and American sources; includes bibliography of author's works. Vol. IV, 1975.

——, and —— (comps.). *Twentieth Century British Literature, A Reference Guide and Bibliography.* New York: F. Ungar Publishing Co., 1968. Lists works about criticism, poetry, drama, and fiction; has some annotations.

Tucker, Martin (ed.). *The Critical Temper: A Survey of Modern Criticism on English and American Literature from the Beginnings to the Twentieth Century.* New York: Frederick Ungar Publishing Co., 1969. 3 vols. Gives a view of the best twentieth-century criticism; shows wide range of thought within the criticism; gives excerpts from criticism and bibliographical references.

Walcutt, Charles C., and Whitesell, J. Edwin. *The Explicator Cyclopedia.*

Chicago: Quandrangle Books, 1966. 3 vols. Covers modern poetry (Vol. 1), traditional poetry, medieval to late Victorian (Vol. 2), and prose (Vol. 3); is a compilation of essays which explicate notable British and American poems.

Walker, Warren S. *Twentieth Century Short Story Explication.* 3d ed. Hamden, Conn.: The Shoe String Press, Inc., 1977. Arranged alphabetically by name of short story author under each title; explications are listed alphabetically by critic's name; coverage is through 1975.

YEARBOOKS

American Literary Scholarship. 1963– . Durham, N.C.: Duke University Press, 1963– . (Annual.) Reviews the year's work in American literature.

Year's Work in English Studies. London: English Association, 1921– . (Annual.) Surveys studies of English literature appearing in books and periodicals published in Britain, Europe, and America; includes material on the English language and on American literature.

EXAMPLES OF PROFESSIONAL AND LITERARY JOURNALS[6]

American Literature: A Journal of Literary History, Criticism and Bibliography. Durham, N.C.: Duke University Press, 1929– . (Quarterly.) Published with the cooperation of the American Literature Section of the Modern Language Association, gives research articles on history, criticism, and bibliography of American literature; includes critical book reviews; reports dissertations completed or under way and research in progress.

Criticism: A Quarterly for Literature and the Arts. Detroit: Wayne State University Press, 1959– . (Quarterly.) Designed to advance the study of literature and the fields of fine arts and music and to be a medium for scholarly explication and evaluation of artists and their works; examines the arts and literatures of all nations and periods; gives book reviews.

Poetry. Chicago: Poetry Magazine, 1912– . (Monthly.) Publishes work of poets from the least-known to the best-established; offers essays on poetry and critical reviews of books about poetry.

Sewanee Review. Sewanee, Tenn.: University of the South, 1892– . (Quarterly.) The oldest literary magazine in the United States; contains

---

[6]See also *Ulrich's International Periodicals Directory*, 17th ed., and *Magazines for Libraries*, 3d ed., edited by Bill Katz and Berry Richards.

original fiction, poetry, book reviews, essays, and recent criticism on literary figures.

ABSTRACT JOURNAL

Abstracts of English Studies. Boulder, Colo.: National Council of Teachers of English, 1958– . (Ten times a year, September–June.) Contains abstract articles on English and American literature from both American and foreign journals; each issue has a subject index.

CHAPTER TWENTY-THREE
HISTORY
AND GEOGRAPHY

The discovery of writing and the beginnings of the measurement of time made possible the preservation of temple records which form the first historical annals.[1]

History is that area of study which is concerned with the recording of past events and with the interpretations of the relationships and significance of these events. It is divided into ancient, medieval, and modern, and each of these divisions may be subdivided geographically, as the history of medieval Europe or the history of modern England. History can be subdivided further into its economic, cultural, social, political, military, and literary aspects. The history class of the Dewey Decimal System, 900, includes geography. G is assigned to geography in the Library of Congress classification; C, D, E, and F are the classes assigned to history and its subdivisions.

Many of the general reference sources—encyclopedias, dictionaries, handbooks, atlases, gazetteers, indexes, and bibliographies—provide material in the field of history. There are, however, specialized reference materials that have been prepared for the primary purpose of aiding

[1]T. R. Glover, "Historiography: Antiquity," *Encyclopaedia of the Social Sciences*, VII (1932), p. 368.

students of history. They include bibliographies, guides, indexes, encyclopedias, chronologies, handbooks, dictionaries, historical atlases, general
histories, and professional journals.

REPRESENTATIVE REFERENCE SOURCES IN HISTORY

HISTORY
Bibliographies, Guides, and Indexes[2]

America: History and Life: A Guide to Periodical Literature. Santa Barbara,
Calif.: American Bibliographical Center, Clio Press, 1964– . (Quarterly.) Gives abstracts of articles from some 650 American and Canadian
periodicals which cover all aspects of the nation's history from earliest
times to current events; arranged by subject. (*See Historical Abstracts.*)

American Historical Association. *Guide to Historical Literature.* George
Frederick Howe, Chairman, Board of Editors, New York: The Macmillan Company, 1961. Aims to list the more satisfactory sources for
historical study.

Freidel, Frank (ed.). *Harvard Guide to American History.* Rev. ed. Cambridge: Belknap Press of Harvard University, 1974. 2 vols. A selection
of the more important works; covers research methods and materials,
biographies, general histories, and histories of special subjects; includes political science, constitutional, and economic history; intended
for the intelligent general reader, student, and scholar.

*Historical Abstracts: Bibliography of the World's Periodical Literature,
1775– .* Santa Barbara, Calif.: American Bibliographical Center, Clio
Press, 1955– . (Quarterly.) Arranged by country; covers all aspects of
history; includes related subjects; before 1964 covered United States
and Canada. (See *America: History and Life.*)

Library of Congress, Reference Division. *A Guide to the Study of the United
States of America.* Washington, D.C.: Government Printing Office,
1960. "[Introduces] representative books reflecting the development of
American life and thought" (subtitle). *Supplement 1956–1965.* 1976.
Most of these titles are annotated.

Paetow, Louis John. *A Guide to the Study of Medieval History.* Revised ed.
prepared under the auspices of the Medieval Academy of America. New
York: Kraus Reprint Corporation, 1959. Lists general books useful in
the study of medieval history; provides readings to accompany the study
of major areas of medieval history; gives some critical notes.

Social Sciences Index. (See p. 174.)

---

[2]See also Chapter 9, Indexes, and Chapter 13, Bibliographies.

Dictionaries and Encyclopedias

Boatner, Mark Mayo. *Encyclopedia of the American Revolution.* New York: David McKay Company, 1966. Similar in style to Boatner, *Civil War Dictionary* (McKay, 1959); covers American history of the period 1763–1783, including British, French, and German participation; gives biographical material; emphasizes military aspects.

Bray, Warwick, and Trump, David. *The American Guide to Archaeology.* New York: The American Heritage Press, 1971. Designed to aid nonspecialists and students; is worldwide in coverage; emphasizes the prehistoric; entries are brief; provides illustrations including photography; has maps and graphs; is available also as *Penguin Dictionary of Archaeology* (1970).

Carruth, Gorton, and Associates (eds.). *The Encyclopedia of American Facts and Dates.* 6th ed. New York: Thomas Y. Crowell Company, 1972. Presents in one volume a vast number of interesting events from the earliest times in America to the present; includes events in four fields of interest—politics and government, literature and art, sciences, and sports—arranged in parallel columns in chronological order.

Daniel, Glyn (ed.). *The Illustrated Encyclopedia of Archaeology.* New York: Thomas Y. Crowell Company, 1977. Treats the ancient cultures of the Middle East, the Far East, Africa, Australia, and the Americas from the Stone Age to the beginnings of modern times; includes information on major sites, key processes, pioneer archaeologists, technical terms, and allied sciences.

Dictionary of American History. Rev. ed. New York: Charles Scribner's Sons, 1976. 8 vols. Revised and brought up to date, this edition provides coverage of almost all aspects of American history; does not include biographical entries. Vol. 8 is the index.

Dupuy, R. Ernest, and Dupuy, Trevor N. *The Encyclopedia of Military History from 3500 B.C. to the Present.* Rev. ed. New York: Harper & Row, Publishers, 1977. A survey of the history of wars and military affairs, it offers a series of narratives on these topics; organized chronologically by period; each period is prefaced by an essay on military trends and followed by a chronological arrangement of events and battles; gives a list of nations that have achieved independence since World War II.

Eggenberger, David. *A Dictionary of Battles.* New York: Thomas Y. Crowell Company, 1967. Seeks to provide "essential details of all the major battles in recorded history" (Preface); covers more than 1,500 battles from 1479 B.C. to the fighting in Vietnam in the 1960s; gives brief treatments; provides some maps and additional readings.

Everyman's Dictionary of Dates. 6th ed. Revised by Audrey Butler. (Everyman's Reference Library.) New York: E. P. Dutton & Company, Inc.,

1971. Proposes to make useful dates easily accessible; arranged alphabetically by subject—ancient, medieval, and modern—and chronologically within the subject; some subjects have discussions; is designed for the general reader.

Langer, William Leonard (ed.). *An Encyclopedia of World History, Ancient, Medieval, and Modern Chronologically Arranged.* 5th ed. revised and enlarged. Boston: Houghton Mifflin Company, 1972. Covers all aspects of world history through 1970, including political, social, educational, and cultural events; gives attention to space, scientific, and technological advances; has maps and genealogical tables.

Morris, Richard B., and Irwin, Graham W. (eds.). *Harper Encyclopedia of the Modern World: A Concise Reference History from 1760 to the Present.* New York: Harper & Row, Publishers, 1970. Arranged in two parts: a basic chronology of political, military, and diplomatic history divided by geographical area, and a topical section which covers education, government, society, literature, the arts, and science, with subdivisions of each topic.

Morris, Richard B., and Morris, Jeffrey B. (eds.). *Encyclopedia of American History.* Bicentennial Edition. New York: Harper & Row, Publishers, Incorporated, 1976. Gives essential historical facts about American life and institutions in both chronological and topical arrangements from the period of discovery through 1973; attention is given to recent developments in science and technology, to minorities and ethnic groups, and to film, dance, and popular music; gives biographical information for notable Americans.

The Praeger Encyclopedia of Ancient Greek Civilization. New York: Frederick A. Praeger, 1967. Originally published in French as *Dictionnaire de la Civilisation Greque* (Paris, 1966); is the combined effort of an archaeologist, a literary historian, a philosopher, and a professor of Greek; covers cities, legendary heroes, writers, statesmen, gods, goddesses, etc., and focuses on the "civilization that took shape in Greece during the second millennium B.C., spread throughout the civilized world, and remained a living force well into the Christian era" (Preface).

Stillwell, Richard (ed.). *The Princeton Encyclopedia of Classical Sites.* Princeton, N.J.: Princeton University Press, 1976. Presents more than 2,200 articles on the archaeology of Greek and Roman civilization covering the period 750 B.C. to A.D. 565; gives sources for further reading.

Handbooks

Avery, Catherine B. *The New Century Italian Renaissance Encyclopedia.* New York: Appleton-Century-Crofts, Educational Division, Meredith

Corporation, 1972. Is broad in scope; covers many minor Renaissance figures as well as the major ones; has articles on art and music; provides many illustrations; does not include bibliography.

Breach, R. W. (ed.). *Documents and Descriptions: the World since 1914.* Oxford: Oxford University Press, 1966. Presents main events since 1914; arranged geographically by country; includes international organizations.

Clements, John (comp.). *Chronology of the United States.* New York: McGraw-Hill Book Company, 1972. Gives a year-by-year guide to the history of the United States, covering important people and events from 1789 to 1970; includes information on growth, important happenings, territorial expansion and development, population, business, and economic development.

Collison, Robert (comp.). *Newnes Dictionary of Dates.* 2d revised ed. London: Newnes, 1966. Emphasizes scientific and technological achievements and cultural and sociological leaders; divided into two parts: a dictionary of dates and anniversaries, and people and events.

Dupuy, Trevor Nevitt, and Blanchard, Wendell (eds.). *The Almanac of World Military Power.* 3d ed. New York: T. N. Dupuy Associates in association with R. R. Bowker Company, 1975. Arranged by geographical area; gives information about the military and defense structure of every nation and summaries of factors that affect its military potential; includes maps and a glossary of military terms.

Freeman-Grenville, G. S. P. *Chronology of World History: A Calendar of Principal Events from 3,000 B.C to A.D. 1976.* Totowa, N.J.: Rowman and Littlefield, Publishers, 1978. Outlines year by year the principal dates and events of the period covered; ancient history and regions beyond Europe and the Americas are covered.

Grun, Bernard. *The Timetables of History: A Horizontal Linkage of People and Events.* New York: Simon and Schuster, 1975. Presents a columnar listing of major events in seven areas for each year from about 5000 B.C. through A.D. 1974; history, literature, theater, religion, philosophy, science and technology, music and visual arts are represented; emphasis is on the Western world.

Johnson, Thomas H., in consultation with Harvey Wish. *The Oxford Companion to American History.* New York: Oxford University Press, 1966. A sister volume to *The Oxford Companion to American Literature;* summarizes lives, events, and places of significance in the founding of the nation; gives attention to social, political, and labor movements; includes the fields of art, science, commerce, education, law, sports and entertainment; provides some bibliographies.

Steinberg, Sigfrid H., and others (eds.). *Steinberg's Dictionary of British*

History. London: Edward Arnold Publishers, Ltd., 1970. Covers countries that are or were part of the British Empire; gives political, constitutional, economic, legal, and administrative events; does not include literature and art.

Story, Norah (ed.). *The Oxford Companion to Canadian History and Literature.* New York: Oxford University Press, 1967. Designed as an aid in understanding any Canadian book in English or in French; includes biographies of numerous historical and literary figures; 450 literary entries; 1,500 historical entries; bibliographic essays; brief articles and long discussions; also treats places, periodicals, societies. *Supplement.* 1973.

U.S. Bureau of the Census. *Historical Statistics of the United States: Colonial Times to 1970.* Washington, D.C.: Government Printing Office, 1975. 2 vols. Includes and brings up to date the material in *Historical Statistics of the United States, Colonial Times to 1957* (1960) and its *Supplement* (1965) and adds new material; has tables, statistics, descriptive text, annotations, and sources for further reading.

Historical Atlases

Atlas of American History. Rev. ed. Kenneth T. Jackson, Editor in Chief. New York: Charles Scribner's Sons, 1978. Portrays in maps all facets of American history from the earliest settlement to 1976, including all twentieth-century wars, shifts in population, and recent changes in the political, social, and economic characteristics of the country.

Cappon, Lester J., and others (eds.). *Atlas of Early American History: The Revolutionary Era, 1760–1790.* Published for the Newberry Library and Institute of Early American History and Culture. Princeton, N.J.: Princeton University Press, 1976. Covers in maps all aspects of life in the period of the Revolution: political, economic, religious, cultural, demographic, and military.

Finley, M. I. (ed.). *Atlas of Classical Archaeology.* New York: McGraw-Hill Book Company, 1977. An introduction to classical sites, covers the Greco-Roman world of 1000 B.C. through A.D. 500; describes archaeological sites; has diagrams, maps, and photographs.

Hawkes, Jacquetta (ed.). *Atlas of Ancient Archaeology.* New York: McGraw-Hill Book Company, 1974. Traces the development of various civilizations throughout history; describes major sites; does not include classical Greece and Rome.

Heyden, A. A. M. Van Der, and Scullard, H. H. (eds.). *Atlas of the Classical World.* New York: Thomas Nelson & Sons, 1959. Includes maps, illustrations, and text relating to the religious, economic, military, literary, artistic, and political history of Greece and Rome.

Lord, Clifford L., and Lord, Elizabeth H. (eds.) *Historical Atlas of the United States.* Revised ed., New York: Henry Holt and Company, Inc., 1953. Provides maps of the political and economic history, population, and natural resources of the United States to 1950.

Sellman, R. R. *An Outline Atlas of World History.* New York: St. Martin's Press, 1970. Provides broad coverage of world history from ancient times to the middle 1960s; includes thematic maps.

Schwartzberg, Joseph E. (ed.). *A Historical Atlas of South Asia.* Chicago: The University of Chicago Press, 1978. Seeks to provide a comprehensive record in maps of the history of South Asia from the Old Stone Age to 1975; includes text, maps, bibliography, and charts; text is keyed to maps.

Shepherd, William R. (ed.). *Historical Atlas.* 9th revised ed. New York: Barnes & Noble, 1964. Provides maps of world history from 1450 B.C. to the 1960s; new maps since 1929.

The Times Atlas of World History. Maplewood, N.J.: Hammond, Inc. and The London Times, 1978. For the general reader and the student; covers world history from the earliest times through 1976; includes text, maps, glossary, indexes.

Documents

Boorstin, Daniel J. (ed.). *An American Primer.* Chicago: The University of Chicago Press, 1966. 2 vols. A selection of reprints of documents from 1620 to 1965 which are significant in American history.

Brownlee, Ian (ed.). *Basic Documents on Human Rights.* Oxford: Clarendon Press, 1971. Includes documents from 1688 to 1967.

Commager, Henry Steele (ed.). *Documents of American History.* 9th ed. New York: Appleton-Century-Crofts, 1973. Contains reprints of selected original documents designed to illustrate the course of American history from the age of discovery to the present time; arranged chronologically.

Biographical Dictionaries[3]

Directory of American Scholars. 7th ed. Vol. I, *History.* Edited by the Jaques Cattell Press. New York: R. R. Bowker Company, 1978.

Who Was Who in America, Historical Volume, 1607–1896. Chicago: Marquis—Who's Who, Inc., 1967. Provides biographical material on more than 13,000 persons from 1607 to 1896; historical and statistical

---

[3]See also Chapter 10, Biographical Dictionaries.

data on federal government, states, major cities; major American events.

Reference Histories

Cambridge Ancient History. New York: Cambridge University Press, 1929–1939. 12 vols. 5 vols. of plates.

Cambridge Mediaeval History. New York: Cambridge University Press, 1911–1936. 8 vols.

Cambridge Modern History. New York: Cambridge University Press, 1902–1922. 13 vols. and atlas.

The New Cambridge Modern History. New York: Cambridge University Press, 1957–1975. 13 vols. and atlas volume.

Examples of Professional Journals[4]

American Heritage: The Magazine of History. New York: American Heritage Publishing Company, 1954– . (Bimonthly.) Covers all aspects of American history, major and minor; social, educational, cultural trends; many illustrations in color.

American Historical Review. Washington, D. C.: American Historical Association, 1895– . (Quarterly.) The official journal of the American Historical Association; has scholarly articles based on original research; gives book reviews.

English Historical Review. London: Longmans Green & Company, Limited, 1886– . (Quarterly.) Covers history of all periods with some emphasis on Great Britain and the British Empire; offers scholarly articles, lengthy and critical book reviews.

Journal of American History. Bloomington, Ind.: Organization of American Historians, 1914– . (Quarterly.) Formerly *Mississippi Valley Historical Review;* the scope is almost entirely American; articles include biographical sketches as well as historical theory.

Journal of Modern History. Chicago: University of Chicago Press, 1929– . (Quarterly.) Published in cooperation with the Modern European History Section of the American Historical Association; articles cover European history from the Renaissance to the present; important documents are often published; has book reviews.

The Journal of Negro History. Washington, D.C.: The Association for the Study of Negro Life and History, Inc., 1916– . (Quarterly.) Aims to

[4]See also *Ulrich's International Periodicals Directory,* 17th ed., and *Magazines for Libraries,* 3d ed., edited by Bill Katz and Berry Richards.

promote historical research and writing; articles are concerned with Negro life and history; has book reviews.

GEOGRAPHY

Geography—the term is derived from *geo*, the Greek combining form for "earth," plus *graphia*, "writing"—is the science concerned with the description of the earth's surface, its form and physical features, its natural and political subdivisions, and its climate, products, and population. Geography is frequently divided into mathematical, physical, and political geography.

In addition to atlases and gazetteers, which are recognized as being essential aids in the study of geography, there are bibliographies of, and indexes to, the literature of geography, dictionaries of place names and terminology, and guidebooks which provide descriptive material and maps not usually found in gazetteers and atlases.

REPRESENTATIVE REFERENCE SOURCES IN GEOGRAPHY[5]
Bibliographies, Guides, and Indexes[6]

Brewer, J. Gordon. *The Literature of Geography: A Guide to Its Organization and Use.* Hamden, Conn.: Linnet Books. The Shoe String Press, Inc., 1973. Discusses geographical literature and describes and evaluates individual reference and research materials in the various categories: bibliographies, handbooks, histories, periodicals, government publications, etc.

Lock, Clara B. M. *Geography and Cartography: A Reference Handbook.* Hamden, Conn.: Linnet Books, The Shoe String Press, Inc., 1976. A revision of two earlier works; gives short articles on geographers (not living), societies, organizations, schools of geography, and journals, atlases, and other geographical sources.

Social Sciences Index. (See p. 174.)

Wright, John K., and Platt, Elizabeth (eds.). *Aids to Geographical Research.* 2d ed. completely revised. New York: Columbia University Press for the American Geographical Society, 1947. Lists and describes the literature of the field.

Atlases[7]

The Bartholomew/Scribner Atlas of Europe: A Profile of Western Europe. New York: Charles Scribner's Sons, 1974. Uses text, diagrams, maps,

---

[5]See also Chapter 11, Atlases and Gazetteers.
[6]See also Chapter 9, Indexes, and Chapter 13, Bibliographies.
[7]See also pp. 114–115.

and graphs to present a comprehensive picture of the eighteen countries of Western Europe; gives statistical information on business and industry, economic conditions, transportation, trade, and other topics in addition to the physical-political maps.

Fitzgerald, Ken (comp.). *The Space-Age Photographic Atlas: A Photographic Atlas of the Earth*. New York: Crown Publishers, 1970. Shows aerial photographs, supplied by government agencies in the United States and other countries, of the continents, the planet earth, and many landmarks; each photograph is accompanied by a map.

Moore, Patrick. *The Atlas of the Universe*. Chicago: Rand McNally & Company, 1970. Gives basic information on the origin of the earth, moon, solar system, and stars in short essays; offers views of the earth as seen from the Apollo flights; gives maps, charts, and diagrams.

Rand McNally Commercial Atlas and Marketing Guide. Chicago: Rand McNally & Company, 1876– . (Annual.) Gives general information about each state in the United States and the territories and possessions regarding agriculture, communications, manufacturing, population, business centers, transportation, distance; covers the United States, Canada, and the world; has maps, tables, etc.

Gazetteers
For a discussion of gazetteers and examples, see pp. 113, 115.

Dictionaries, Encyclopedias, and Handbooks
British Association for the Advancement of Science. Research Committee. *A Glossary of Geographical Terms*. 2d ed. Edited by L. Dudley Stamp. New York: John Wiley & Sons, 1966. Limited to terms used in current geographical literature written in English; gives agreed-upon definitions and source of definitions; includes reference to origin and to current use and misuse; uses quotations from original and standard sources to clarify several meanings of a term.

Harder, Kelsie B. (ed.). *Illustrated Dictionary of Place Names, United States and Canada* (Hudson Group Book). New York: Van Nostrand Reinhold Company, 1976. Has more than 15,000 place names, including towns, villages, cities, counties, states, provinces, parks, and historic sites.

Monkhouse, F. J. (ed.). *A Dictionary of Geography*. 2d ed. London: Edward Arnold, 1970. Covers terms relating to landforms, oceanography, climate, soil, vegetation, archaeology, and cartography.

Rand McNally and Company. *The Earth and Man*. Chicago: Rand McNally & Company, 1976. Describes the planet earth; discusses the preservation of the environment; uses colored illustrations to show the history of the earth and its present condition; includes diagrams, text, and maps.

Schmieder, Allen A., and others. *A Dictionary of Basic Geography.* Boston: Allyn and Bacon, Inc., 1970. Covers basic geographic terminology needed for an understanding of general geography; includes a brief, basic annotated bibliography.

Stamp, Sir Laurence Dudley. *Dictionary of Geography.* New York: John Wiley & Sons, 1966. Serves as a companion to the textbooks of students; gives concise definitions of terms based on explanations of terms in *A Glossary of Geographical Terms;* has some gazetteer entries; includes biographical information on many geographers; has a selected bibliography of geography books.

Stewart, George R. *American Place Names: A Concise and Selective Dictionary for the Continental United States of America.* London: Oxford University Press,1970. Has 12,000 American place names; gives derivation, state, historical, geographical, or other interpretation of the name; includes unusual names.

Guidebooks

Other sources of geographical information are guidebooks. Produced by local or state chambers of commerce, state development commissions, local historical societies, travel bureaus, airlines, railroads, hotels, commercial publishers, and other sources, they are designed for the tourist and traveler, to attract trade and industry, or for purposes of historical record or local interest. They include certain types of information not found in gazetteers or atlases, such as maps of small towns and areas, places of strictly local or historical interest, information about schools, churches, hotel accommodations, communications, transportation, natural resources, etc. If they are produced locally, they reflect the local interpretation of the social, economic, cultural, industrial, and other advantages of a given area.

Guidebooks are available from the local, state, or national agencies which are responsible for industrial development and tourism, from historical societies, tourist bureaus, and bookstores, and from other sources which produce them. They are usually paperbacks. Examples of the kinds of guidebooks available and of sources of guidebooks are:

Baedeker Handbook for Travellers. Various publishers. 1828– . Published in English, French, and German editions, these handbooks cover Europe, North and South America, Egypt, and the Near East, giving information useful to the sightseeing traveler.

Fodor's Modern Guides. Edited by Eugene Fodor. New York: David McKay Company, Inc., 1953– . Cover Europe, Asia, South America, Japan and other countries, giving information useful to the sightseeing traveler.

Neal, J. A. (ed.). *Reference Guide for Travellers.* New York: R. R. Bowker Company, 1969. Arranged geographically; lists and annotates more than 1,200 English-language travel books covering some seventy countries and all the United States.

Examples of Professional Journals[8]

Association of American Geographers. *Annals.* Washington, D.C.: Association of American Geographers, 1911– . (Quarterly.) Provides a scholarly approach to any geographical subject—human, historical, economic, cultural—in articles by professional geographers; illustrated with maps, photographs, tables, charts; includes abstracts of papers given at professional meetings.

Economic Geography. Worcester, Mass.: Clark University, 1925– . (Quarterly.) For geographers, economists, generalists in education and the professions; covers economic and urban geography; gives maps, tables, black-and-white illustrations, book reviews.

Geographical Review. New York: American Geographical Society, 1913– . (Quarterly.) Offers scholarly articles on all aspects of geography, historical and current; includes illustrations, maps, charts; gives book reviews.

[8]See also *Ulrich's International Periodicals Directory*, 17th ed., and *Magazines for Libraries*, 3d ed., edited by Bill Katz and Berry Richards.

PART FIVE
USING THE LIBRARY
FOR A RESEARCH PAPER

CHAPTER TWENTY-FOUR
THE UNDERGRADUATE RESEARCH PAPER

The word "research" means "search, inquiry, pursuit" and comes from the French *rechercher*, "to seek again."

The true research paper involves not only studious inquiry into a subject but also critical and exhaustive investigation of that subject for the purpose of revising accepted conclusions concerning it in the light of facts uncovered by the investigation.

It may be said that elementary research begins when the first encyclopedia the student consults fails to provide the information which is needed to answer a question or to carry out an assignment, and it becomes necessary to consult several sources.

In general, the college research paper on the undergraduate level is an exposition designed to present, not evaluate, the results of the student's inquiry into, or investigation of, a chosen subject.

The undergraduate-level research paper—sometimes called a "term paper"—may be one of several kinds.

1 It may be a report which relates facts for the purpose of informing the reader or of showing progress over a period of time.
2 It may be a report, based on the student's investigations, which analyzes an event, a situation, or a period.

3 It may be a thesis,[1] that is, a paper which states and maintains by argument a position or a proposition.

4 It may be a thesis taking the form of presentation and evaluation of facts for the purpose of persuading or recommending.

The successful completion of any research paper depends upon the careful investigation of a subject; the ability to choose and evaluate materials and to take clear, well-documented notes; an understanding of the purpose and forms of footnotes and bibliography; and clear, logical, and orderly development and presentation of facts in keeping with the purpose of the paper.

PROCEDURE

Some of the basic steps in writing a research paper are listed below.

1 Select a subject. In making the choice of a topic, consider the following factors:

    a Is this a subject of sufficient interest to you that you can make it interesting to your readers?

    b Can you study it seriously in the length of time allotted for writing the paper?

    c Can you cover it adequately in the number of words prescribed by your instructor?

    d Is it likely that you will find sufficient material on it to write a paper, or is it too new, too highly specialized, or too limited in appeal to have received coverage in books, newspapers, or magazines?

2 Restrict your subject if the topic you have chosen is too broad or too general for the assigned paper.

    a Look in the card catalog under your subject and read the subject headings immediately following to see how that subject is subdivided. Notice the subject headings listed at the bottom of each card to find further subdivisions and related headings. For example, if your general topic is "books," you may find in the card catalog:

Books	Books—Miniature editions
Books—Best sellers	Books on microfilm
Books—Dedications	*See* Microphotography
Books—Facsimiles	Books—Pirated editions
Books—First editions	*See* Copyright—Unauthorized
Books for the blind	editions

[1]"Thesis" is also the name given to a dissertation presented by a candidate for an academic degree, usually the M.A. or M.S. degree.

    b Find the subject in a periodical index; notice subdivisions; e.g.:[2]

Literature	Literature—Themes
See also Authorship	*See also* Religion in literature
Censorship	Social problems in
Style, Literary	literature
Literature—Competitions	Literature and art
	Literature and science

    c See how a general encyclopedia and the index subdivide your subject.

    d You may restrict your topic according to period of time or geographical location or according to historical, social, cultural, or political significance; for example:

The Medieval Scriptorium
The Cultural Significance of the Invention of Printing
The Political Influence of the Printer in Colonial America
The Book in the 1970s
Paperback Books
Mystery Stories

In the following list of subjects, notice the progression from general to specific:

Medieval Civilization
Feudalism
Knighthood
Knightly Sports
Tournaments
Jousting

3 Choose the phase of your subject that you wish to investigate.

4 Decide upon the purpose of your paper.

    a Is it to inform?

    b Is it to show progress?

    c Is it to analyze an event, a situation, or a period?

    d Is it to persuade and recommend?

5 Make a tentative statement of your thesis—that is, the proposition you will attempt to defend, clarify, or develop. For example, "The institution of monasticism was of major importance in the preservation and development of literature during the Middle Ages," or "The printing press hastened the era of discovery and exploration."

    a Analyze your thesis as to the subject areas it includes or touches: geography, sociology, economics, history, literature, politics.

[2]From *Readers' Guide to Periodical Literature* (New York: The H. W. Wilson Company, March, 1966–February, 1967), pp. 682–683.

b Decide what kinds of sources will provide the information you will need to write your paper.
   (1) Primary sources[3]—interviews, questionnaires, letters, diaries, manuscripts, memoirs
   (2) Secondary sources—books, journals, encyclopedias, other reference books, and nonbook materials.
c Determine the chronological period in which your subject falls.

6 Begin your preliminary search for material. In the preceding chapters, reference sources have been discussed, with emphasis upon their usefulness in providing material on a subject. Since subject headings are the key to the card catalog, the indexes, and most reference books, it is necessary, before using any of these sources, to determine the headings under which your subject may be listed.[4]

a Consult the card catalog to find the books in your library in which your subject, or any relevant phase of it, is discussed. Read the entire card carefully to see what the book covers, the amount and kind of illustrative material it includes, the bibliographical references provided, the number of topics treated, and the topic which is given the greatest emphasis. (The first subject heading listed is the subject which is given the widest coverage.) Study the subject headings as an indication of other subjects which will lead to material on your subject. For example, if your subject is "The Book in the 1960s," some of the headings under which you will find material are:

Books	Libraries—History
Books—Format	Microfilm books
Books—History—Twentieth century	Microcards
Books—Statistics	Paperback books
Books, Talking	Printing—History

b Take the class number or numbers, and browse in these sections of the stacks, looking at the tables of contents and the indexes of books which may be helpful.
c Consult a printed bibliography or guide to find material on your subject which may not be listed in the card catalog, such as parts of books, pamphlets, and reports.
d Use a general dictionary for general definitions; use a subject dictionary for specialized definitions and terminology.

[3]Primary sources are those materials which have not been interpreted by another person. Secondary sources are materials which have been reported, analyzed, or interpreted by other persons.

[4]See pp. 56–59.

e Find an overview of your topic in a general encyclopedia, and then consult a subject encyclopedia for technical and specialized information. Consult the bibliography at the end of the article for additional readings and the index volume for other headings under which to look; remember that an encyclopedia is *only* the starting point.

f Use general and subject indexes to find recent material in periodicals and to find selections in collected works.

g Consult a handbook for statistical information or for identification of allusions to persons, events, dates, and legendary or mythological figures.

h Look up important persons connected with your subject in a biographical dictionary.

i Establish geographical locations and facts with the aid of an atlas or a gazetteer.

j Use primary sources whenever possible.

It is essential that you use a variety of sources in order to obtain a broad view of your subject; to see it in its various phases; to discover the factors which influenced or contributed to it; to know the individuals, groups, or organizations associated with it; to become acquainted with current thinking as well as with past opinion regarding it; and to have some understanding of the terminology of the field in question.

7 Begin preliminary reading

a Read a background or overview article in a textbook or in a history of the subject.

b Examine a general article in an encyclopedia.

c Read a popular article in a periodical.

d Skim through the material at first.

e Make brief notes of references for later serious reading, giving adequate information for finding these references easily.

8 As you examine material, make a tentative bibliography of the materials which you think you will use. (See Figure 19.)

a Make the bibliography on cards.

    (1) Use cards of uniform size.

    (2) Use a separate card for each bibliographical reference.

b Give basic information for each reference.

    (1) Author

    (2) Title

    (3) Facts of publication

    (4) Page or pages on which the information can be found

c Include a brief descriptive statement of each work, indicating the content and its usefulness for your subject.

9 Make a tentative outline of the major divisions of your paper. An outline

```
Ref
ML    New Oxford History of Music.  Vol. X:
160       The Modern Age 1890-1960.  London:
N4        Oxford University Press, 1974.

      The background of music in the United
States during the period 1918-1960 is
discussed on pp. 569-574.
```

```
Vinton, John.  "Change of Mind."
   Music Review, XXXV (November, 1974),
   301-318.


   Discusses changes in music in the
19th and 20th centuries.
```

```
Ref
ML    Fuld, James J.  The Book of World-
113       Famous Music —Classical, Popular
F8        and Folk.  Revised and enlarged edition.
          New York: Crown Publishers, 1971.


      Gives information about many hundreds of
the best known musical compositions.
```

Figure 19 Sample bibliography cards.

of the major divisions of Chapter 1, A Brief History of Books and Libraries, is as follows:

   I. Introduction

  II. Thesis: The story of books and libraries from earliest times to the present is closely interwoven with the story of writing and other methods of preserving and transmitting information and knowledge, with the materials and physical forms which have been used for these purposes, and with the methods of preserving them and of making them accessible for use.

 III. Writing, books, and libraries

      A. Antiquity

          1. The Sumerians, Babylonians, and Assyrians

          2. The Egyptians

          3. Other Semitic peoples

          4. The Chinese

          5. The Greeks

          6. The Romans

      B. The Middle Ages

          1. The monasteries

          2. The universities

          3. The Renaissance

          4. Printing with movable types

      C. 1500–1900

          1. Europe

          2. America

      D. The Modern Era: the Twentieth Century

10 Begin serious reading.

11 Take notes. (See Figure 20.)

    a The kinds of notes you may take include:

      (1) A restatement, in your own words, of the thought or thoughts of an author. It is important that in your paraphrase you do not lose the meaning of the original statement when you take it out of context.

      (2) A direct quotation, copied exactly, including punctuation. Any omission must be indicated by an ellipsis (. . .); any interpolation must be indicated by brackets ([ ]).

      (3) A critical or evaluative comment about a book or a person.

    b Use cards for your notes.

      (1) Use cards of uniform size throughout.

      (2) Give complete bibliographical information on the first card for each reference:

Ref
ML   Thompson, Oscar (ed.). <u>The International</u>
100   <u>Cyclopaedia of Music and Musicians</u>.
T47   10th ed. Edited by Bruce Bohle. New
             York: Dodd, Mead & Company, 1975.

          Before primitive man could speak
       intelligibly, he expressed feelings of
       joy, grief, and fear in bodily movements
       accompanied by rhythmic noises. (p. 990)

Ref
N   <u>Encyclopedia of World Art</u>. New York:
31   McGraw-Hill Book Company, 1959-
E533   1968. 15 vols.

          "Among the most important factors
       that influence the evolution of musical
       instruments are . . . the prevailing
       style of a period and . . . the status
       of technology." (Vol. X, p. 431)

Ref
ML   Fink, Robert, and Ricci, Robert. <u>The</u>
100   <u>Language of Twentieth Century Music:</u>
F55   <u>A Dictionary of Terms</u>. New York:
             Schirmer Books, A Division of Macmillan,
             1975.

          Useful for brief definitions of terms
       used in contemporary music.

Figure 20 Sample note cards: *(top)* restatement or paraphrase, *(center)* quotation, *(bottom)* evaluative comment.

      (a) Author's full name
      (b) Complete title
      (c) Imprint: place of publication, publisher, date
      (d) Pages and volume
      (e) Month, day, year, volume, and pages of periodical articles
      (f) Month, day, year, and pages of newspaper articles

  c Use one card for each reference. If more than one card is required to complete a note, number all cards and put the author's last name on all cards after the first.

  d Leave space at the top of the card for the subject headings, which will be the subdivisions of your outline.

12 Formulate your thesis.

  a State it simply, expressing the basic idea which you will develop.

  b Restrict it to one approach to the subject.

  c Avoid using ambiguous words or phrases.

13 Study your notes in order to restrict your subject further.

14 Make a preliminary detailed outline, either topical or in sentence form. Whatever form you choose, use it throughout your outline.

  a Make sure that your outline is organized in a logical manner, that each division and subdivision receives proper emphasis, and that each part of the outline is in the appropriate relationship to other parts of the outline.[5]

  b Fill in the gaps in your outline by additional reading and note taking.

  c Discard irrelevant material.

15 Remake your outline.

16 Write the first draft of your paper.

17 Use footnotes when necessary.

  a Give the source of a direct quotation.

  b Acknowledge the source of an opinion or a discussion which you have paraphrased or of any specific material which cannot be considered common knowledge.

  c Give credit for statistical information, graphs, and charts you have used.

  d Suggest additional reading on a particular point.

  e Add an explanation to clarify or expand a statement in the text of your paper.

  f Make cross references to other parts of your paper.

18 Make a bibliography.

---

[5] Show the relationship of subdivisions in an outline (or of items in an enumeration) by indentation and the use of letters and numerals in the following order: I, A, B, 1, a, b, (1), (a), (b), (i).

   a Give the sources of the materials which you have used in writing the paper.

   b Suggest additional reading materials.

   c Include an entry for each work mentioned in a footnote.

19 Revise your paper.

20 Evaluate the entire paper, as to clarity of purpose, proper emphasis of important ideas and divisions, elimination of gaps and irrelevant material, accuracy in presenting or in interpreting facts, appropriateness of the choice of words, correctness of grammatical structure and form, unity and coherence in writing, adequacy of documentation, and consistency of bibliographical and footnote form.

21 Write the final draft of your paper.

FOOTNOTES AND BIBLIOGRAPHY

Footnotes give the exact location of the sources of certain kinds of information used in the text of the research paper; bibliography describes, as a whole, the work or works from which the citations are taken. The forms for footnotes and bibliography—that is, the order of listing the items and the punctuation, capitalization, and underlining of words in the title—vary according to the manual of style[6] which is followed by a college or by a department within a college. Each department may adopt a different form. In general, the variations are not in the items included but in the style in which they are presented. Footnote and bibliographical forms are not the same, and entries for books, periodical and newspaper articles, encyclopedia articles, and for special materials differ from each other.

Before writing a research paper, students must understand the forms which they are required to use in making footnotes and bibliography, and they must follow those prescribed forms consistently.

FOOTNOTES

In general, footnotes are numbered consecutively and are placed at the bottom of the page, in numerical order, separated from the text by a solid line across the page. However, all footnotes may be placed at the end of the paper in a section for notes.

Arabic numerals are often used as footnote reference indexes, but

[6]Two manuals of style are Kate L. Turabian, *A Manual for Writers of Term Papers, Theses, and Dissertations*, 4th ed. rev. (Chicago: University of Chicago Press, 1973), and William Giles Campbell and Steven V. Baler, *Form and Style: Theses, Reports, Term Papers*, 4th ed. (Boston: Houghton Mifflin Company, 1974).

asterisks and other symbols may be used also. Whatever reference symbol is employed, it must follow the passage to which it refers and must be placed after it (following the punctuation mark if there is one), just above the line.

The first citation of a footnote reference must give complete information in logical order.

1 Author's name (usually not inverted)
2 Title of publication
3 Facts of publication: place, publisher, and date
4 Volume and page numbers
5 Date of periodicals

Listed below are examples of one form which may be used in making footnotes.

¹Ludwig Bieler, *Ireland, Harbinger of the Middle Ages* (New York: Oxford University Press, 1963), p. 24.

²Mabel M. Smythe (ed.), *Black American Reference Book* (Englewood Cliffs, N.J.: Prentice-Hall, Inc., 1976), p. 40.

³Edwin R. A. Seligman, "What Are the Social Sciences?" *Encyclopaedia of the Social Sciences*, I, 3–7.

⁴"Phoenicia," *The Encyclopedia Americana*, XXI (1958), 786–788.

Usually the complete form of a reference is not repeated after it is first given; a shortened form is used, as follows:

1 When references to the same work follow each other without any other reference in between, use the abbreviation *ibid.*, from the Latin *ibidem*, meaning "in the same place."

¹Louis B. Wright, *The Cultural Life of the American Colonies, 1607–1763* (New York: Harper & Brothers, 1957), p. 70.

²*Ibid.* (*Ibid.* is used in place of full reference and indicates that the source is exactly the same.)

³*Ibid.*, p. 87. (In this case, *ibid.* replaces everything except the page number.)

2 An abbreviation may be used in place of the title after a reference has been cited fully, unless there has been more than one reference by the same author. The shortened form would include the author's last name and the abbreviation *op. cit.*, which comes from *opere citato*, meaning in the work cited.

¹Charles H. Haskins, *The Rise of Universities* (Ithaca, N.Y.: Great Seal Books, 1957), p. 10.

[2]James W. Thompson, *The Medieval Library* (New York: Hafner Publishing Company, 1957), p. 49.
[3]Haskins, *op. cit.*, p. 40.

BIBLIOGRAPHY

There is no single correct form for making a bibliography, but there are several principles which must be adhered to in any form which is followed:

1 All bibliographical entries must be in accord with the purpose of the research paper.
2 All items must be presented accurately, clearly, and logically.
3 The bibliographical form which is prescribed for a given paper must be followed consistently in every entry.

The following items are included in a bibliographical entry:

1 Name of the author
2 Title of the book as it appears on the title page
3 Edition, if it is other than the first
4 Number of volumes in the set, if the entire set is used
5 Place of publication, name of publisher, and date of publication
6 Number of pages in the book and price, if these items are required by the instructor.

Bibliographical entries may be grouped according to kind—books, newspapers, periodicals—or according to the main divisions in the research paper. They are arranged alphabetically within the groups.

Some examples of one form for making a bibliography are given below.

BOOKS
One Author
Bieler, Ludwig. *Ireland, Harbinger of the Middle Ages.* New York: Oxford University Press, 1963.

Two Authors
Brown, James W., and Norberg, Kenneth D. *Administering Educational Media.* New York: McGraw-Hill Book Company, 1965.

Several Authors
Davis, Cullom, and others. *Oral History: From Tape to Type.* Chicago: American Library Association, 1977.

Organization or Institution as Author

American Institute of History and Art. *Hudson Valley Painting, 1700–1750.*
Albany, N.Y.: Albany Institute of History and Art, 1959.

Edition of an Author's Work

Deutsch, Babette. *Poetry Handbook: A Dictionary of Terms.* 4th ed. New
York: Funk & Wagnalls Company, 1974.

Author's Work Edited by Another Person

Cary, Joyce. *Selected Essays.* Edited by A. G. Bishop. New York: St.
Martin's Press, 1976.

Translation

Chastel, André. *The Age of Humanism:Europe, 1480–1530.* Translated by
Katherine M. Delavenay and E. M. Gwyer. New York: McGraw-Hill
Book Company, 1963.

Edited Work

Smythe, Mabel M. (ed.). *The Black American Reference Book.* Englewood
Cliffs, N.J.: Prentice-Hall, Inc., 1976.

Volume in a Series

Lunt, William Edward. *History of England.* 4th ed. (Harper's Historical
Series). New York: Harper & Brothers, 1957.

ARTICLES

Encyclopedia—Signed and Unsigned

Seligman, Edwin R. A. "What Are the Social Sciences?" *Encyclopaedia of
the Social Sciences,* I, 3–7.

"Phoenicia." *The Encyclopedia Americana* XXI (1958), 786–788.

Periodical Article

Trippett, Frank. "The Weather: Everyone's Favorite Topic." *Time,* CXI
(February 6, 1978), 76–77.

Essay, Article, or Chapter in a Collected Work

Morgan, E. "Women and the Future." In *Images of the Future: The
Twenty-first Century and Beyond,* pp. 143–151. Edited by R. F. Bundy.
Buffalo, N.Y.: Prometheus Books, 1976.

Newspaper

Jonas, Jack. "A Visit to a Land of Many Facets," *The Sunday Star* (Washington, D.C.), March 5, 1961, sec. F, p. 1.

Nonbook Materials

American Men in Space, The Story of Project Mercury (Phonodisc). Narration by John H. Powers and Fred Hanney. CMS Records, CMS 71000, 1964. 2 s, 12 in., 33⅓ rpm., microgroove, stereophonic.

The Book Takes Form (Motion Picture). Department of Cinema. University of Southern California, Los Angeles. Released by NET Film Service, 1956. 29 min., sd., b&w, 16mm. (The Written Word Series.)

Duché, Jacob. *Observations on a Variety of Subjects, Literary, Moral and Religious.* . . . Philadelphia: Printed by John Dunlap. 1764. (Microfilm.)

Hutchins, Robert Maynard. *A Vision of Athens* (Phonotape). Santa Barbara, Calif.: Center for the Study of Democratic Institutions, 1971. 1 reel, 5 in., 3 ¾ ips., 42 min., 15 sec.

An Inquiry Into the Future of Mankind: Designing Tomorrow Today (Slide set). Center for Humanities, 1974. 160 slides, color, 2×2 in., and 2 phonodiscs (2 s each), 12 in., 33 ⅓ rpm. 29 min.

Using Library Resources for a Research Paper (Filmstrip). McGraw-Hill Book Company, New York, 1966, 39 fr., col., 35mm. (The College Library Series.)

INDEX

Abbreviations Dictionary, 189
Above and Beyond: the Encyclopedia
    of Aviation and Space Science, 203
Abridged Readers' Guide to Periodical
    Literature, 96
ABS Guide to Recent Publications in
    the Social and Behavioral
    Sciences, The, 171–172
Abstract journal, 154, 196n.
    (See also specific subject fields)
Abstracts of English Studies, 245
Acronyms, Initialisms, and
    Abbreviations Dictionary, 189
Added entries, 59
Adeline Art Dictionary, The, 213
Africa Contemporary Record, 176
Afro-American Artists: A
    Bio-Bibliographical Directory, 216
Aids to Geographical Research, 254
Alcuin, 11
Alexandrian Library, 8–9
All the Years of American Popular
    Music, 220
Almanac, definition, 67, 116
Almanac of American Politics 1978,
    The, 176
Almanac of World Military Power, The,
    250
Alphabet, 6, 7
Alphabetical arrangement, card
    catalog, 60
America: History and Life, 247

American Academy of Political
    Science. Annals, 179-180
American Architects Directory, 215
American Art Directory, 215-216
American Authors: 1600–1900, 240
American Authors and Books, 236
American Behavioral Scientist, 180
American Book Publishing Record,
    127
American Chemical Society Journal,
    208
American Drama Criticism, 243
American Economic Review, 180
American Guide to Archaeology, The,
    248
American Heritage, 253
American Heritage Dictionary of the
    English Language, The, 76, 78
American Historical Review, 253
American Journal of Economics and
    Sociology, 180
American Journal of Physics, 209
American Journal of Psychology, 162
American Journal of Public Health,
    209
American Junior Colleges, 183
American Library Association, 17
American Literary Scholarship, 244
American Literature, 244
American Literature: A Study and
    Research Guide, 230
American Mathematical Monthly, 209

American Medical Association Journal,
209
American Men and Women of Science,
161, 179, 208
American Novel, The, 242
American Place Names, 256
American Political Dictionary, The,
175
American Political Science Review,
180
American Popular Songs from the
Revolutionary War to the Present,
217
American Primer, An, 252
American Psychological Association,
Biographical Directory, 161-162
American Record Guide, 140
American Reference Books Annual,
127
American Speech, 194
American Statistics Index, 147
American Thesaurus of Slang, The,
192
American Universities and Colleges,
183
American Usage: the Consensus, 193
Americana Annual, 118
Americanisms, 190-191
Anniversaries and Holidays, 120
Annual Bibliography of English
Language and Literature, 188, 230
Annual Register of World Events, The,
177
Annual Review of Psychology, 162
Anthologies, 153
Appendix, part of book, 24
Appleton's Cyclopaedia of American
Biography, 107
Appleton's New Cuyás
English–Spanish and
Spanish-English Dictionary, 78
Applied and Decorative Arts: A
Bibliographic Guide to Basic
Reference Works, Histories, and
Handbooks, 212
Applied Science and Technology
Index, 198
Art Bulletin, 216
Art in America, 216
Art Index, The, 170, 212, 223
Articles on American Literature
1950–1967, 230
Asheim, Lester, 163n.
Asia: A Handbook, 177

Asimov's Biographical Encyclopedia of
Science and Technology, 208
Association of American Geographers,
Annals, 257
Assurbanipal, 4, 5
Assyria, books and libraries, 5
Atlas of American History, 251
Atlas of Ancient Archaeology, 251
Atlas of Classical Archaeology, 251
Atlas of Early American History, 251
Atlas of the Classical World, 251
Atlas of the Universe, The, 255
Atlases, 111–115, 153
definition, 67, 112
examples, 114-115
selection and use, 112-113
Audio-Visual Equipment Directory,
138
Audiovisual Instruction, 140
Audiovisual Market Place: A
Multimedia Guide, 137
Audiovisual materials, 29, 131-132
kinds of, 131
organization and arrangement of, 132
sources of reviews, 140
Author card, 54–56
Authors: Critical and Biographical
References, 242
Automated information sources,
135-136
Automated reference service, 28, 135
Automation, 18, 19
AV Communication Review, 140
Ayer Directory of Publications, 125

Babylonia, books and libraries, 4-5
Baedeker Handbook for Travellers,
256
Baker's Biographical Dictionary of
Musicians, 222
Ballet Guide, 224
Bartholomew/Scribner Atlas of
Europe, 254-255
Baseball Encyclopedia, The, 226
Basic Documents on Human Rights,
252
Bay Psalm Book, The, 16
Behistun Inscription, 5
Bibliographic Index, The, 124
Bibliographic instruction, 27
Bibliographical Guide to the Study of
the Literature of the U.S.A., 229

*Bibliographical Guide to the Study of
Southern Literature, A,* 230
Bibliographies, printed, 122-128
examples of, 124-128
general, 124
of periodical publications, 125-126
selective and evaluative, 126-127
trade, 127-128
union catalogs, 124
usefulness of, 25, 123-124
(See also specific subject fields)
Bibliography:
definition, 24, 68, 122-123, 229
sample cards, 266
sample form, 272-274
for term paper, 265, 269, 272-274
Bibliography of American Literature,
229
Bibliothèque Nationale, La, 15
Binding, part of book, 22, 24
Biographical dictionaries, 101-110,
153
definition, 67, 102
examples of, 106-110
kinds of, 103
selection and use of, 103-105
(See also specific subject fields)
*Biographical Dictionaries Master
Index,* 110
Biography:
definition, 101
indexes to, 110
Biography Index, 94, 100, 104, 110
Biological Abstracts, 210
Biological and Agricultural Index, 198
Black American Reference Book, The,
177
*Black American Writers Past and
Present,* 240
Black's Law Dictionary, 174
Black's Medical Dictionary, 201
Bol'shaia Sovetskaia Entsiklopediia, 85
Book, parts of, 22-24
Book bindings, 115
Book catalogs, 52
Book forms, 4, 5, 7-9, 14-15, 19-20
Book of Kells, 11
Book of the States, The, 177
*Book of World-Famous
Music—Classical, Popular and
Folk, The,* 220
Book Review Digest, 95, 233
Book Review Index, 95, 233
Book reviews, 232-233

Booklist, The, 126
Books in Print, 127
Borsippa, 4
Boswell, James, 102
*Brewer's Dictionary of Phrase and
Fable,* 236
Britain: An Official Handbook, 177-178
Britannica Book of the Year, 118
British Authors before 1800, 240
*British Authors of the Nineteenth
Century,* 240
British Humanities Index, 231
British Museum, 15
*Brockhaus Enzyklopädie in Zwanzig
Bänden,* 85
*Brockhaus' Konversations-Lexikon.
Der Grosse Brockhaus,* 86
Bunge, Charles A., x
Business Information Sources, 172
Business Periodicals Index, 173

Caesar, Julius, 10
Call number, 27, 41, 45
Cambridge Ancient History, 253
*Cambridge Encyclopaedia of
Astronomy, The,* 203
*Cambridge History of American
Literature, The,* 241
*Cambridge History of English
Literature, The,* 241
Cambridge Mediaeval History, 253
Cambridge Modern History, 253
Canadian Almanac and Directory, 119
Card catalog, 37, 51-62, 87, 103
Carnegie, Andrew, 17
Carolingian Renaissance, 11
*Cassell's Encyclopedia of World
Literature,* 235
Cassell's German Dictionary, 77
*Cassell's Italian-English,
English-Italian Dictionary,* 77
Cassell's New Latin Dictionary, 77
Cassiodorus, 10
Catalog cards, 54-60
arrangement in catalog, 60-62
examples of, 55-57, 59, 60
kinds of, 54-60
Cathode-ray tube, 135
*Catholic Periodical and Literature
Index,* 95-96
Caxton, William, 14
*Celebrations: the Complete Book of
American Holidays,* 120

Chambers's Biographical Dictionary, 106

Chambers's Encyclopaedia, 84

Champollion, Jean Francois, 6

Charlemagne, 11

Chemical Abstracts, 135, 210

Chemical Publications, Their Nature and Use, 198

Chicago Tribune, The, 97

Children's Catalog, 126

Chinese books and libraries, 7

Chronological History of the Negro in America, The, 176

Chronology of the United States, 250

Chronology of World History, 250

Church History, 169

CIS/Annual, 147

Classics Illustrated Dictionary, 234

Classification, 35-50

Classification systems, purposes and characteristics, 36-37

Classified List of Periodicals for the College Library, 125

Clippings, 131

Codex, 8-10

College Blue Book, The, 183

Collegiate Dictionary of Zoology, 200

Collier's Encyclopedia, 84

Collier's Year Book, 118

Collison, Robert Lewis, 71, 78

Colombo's Canadian References, 176

Columbia-Lippincott Gazetteer of the World, 115

Commonwealth Universities Yearbook, 183

Community and Junior College Journal, 185

Compact Edition of the Dictionary of National Biography, The, 108

Companion, definition, 67, 117

Comparative Guide to American Colleges, 182

Comparative Guide to Two-Year Colleges and Career Programs, 182-183

Complete Concordance to the Bible (Douay Version), 165

Complete Concordance to the Holy Scriptures of the Old and New Testaments, A, 164

Complete Encyclopedia of Popular Music and Jazz: 1900-1950, The, 219

Complete Guide to Modern Dance, The, 224-225

Comprehensive Dictionary of Psychological and Psychoanalytical Terms, A, 161

Comprehensive Etymological Dictionary of the English Language, A, 189

Computer Dictionary and Handbook, 207

Computer searches, 135-136

Computers, 18, 19, 28

Concise Cambridge Bibliography of English Literature, 600-1950, The, 230-231

Concise Cambridge History of English Literature, The, 241-242

Concise Cambridge Italian Dictionary, The, 77

Concise Dictionary of American Biography, 108

Concise Dictionary of English Literature, 234

Concise Dictionary of French Literature, The, 234

Concise Dictionary of National Biography, 108

Concise Dictionary of Physics and Related Sciences, 200-201

Concise Encyclopedia of Western Philosophy and Philosophers, The, 158

Concise Oxford Dictionary of Ballet, The, 223

Concise Oxford Dictionary of Current English, The, 193

Concise Oxford Dictionary of Music, The, 218

Concise Oxford Dictionary of Opera, 218

Concordance, definition, 164n.

Condensed Chemical Dictionary, The, 199

Condensed Computer Encyclopedia, 202

Conspectus of American Biography, The, 107

Contemporary American Composers, 221-222

Contemporary Authors, 239

Contemporary Literary Criticism, 242

Contemporary Poets of the English Language, 240

Continental Novel, The, 242

Copyright, 23, 128

Country Music Encyclopedia, The, 219

Critical Temper, The, 243

Criticism, 244
Crowell's Handbook of Classical
    Drama, 237
Crowell's Handbook of Classical
    Literature, 237
Crowell's Handbook of Classical
    Mythology, 170
Crowell's Handbook of Contemporary
    American Poetry, 237
Crowell's Handbook of Contemporary
    Drama, 224
Cumulative Book Index, 104, 127
Current Biography, 106
Current Book Review Citations, 233
Current Career and Occupational
    Literature: 1973–1977, 172
Current Index to Journals in
    Education, 185
Current Information Sources in
    Mathematics, 196, 198
Current Literary Terms, 234
Cutter, C. A., 41

Dance Encyclopedia, The, 223
Dance Magazine, 225
Demographic Yearbook, 178
Depository libraries, 142n.
Descriptors, 59
Dewey, Melvil, 17, 36
Dewey Decimal Classification and
    Relative Index, 38
Dewey Decimal Classification System,
    38-42, 132n.
    excerpts from, 38–41
DIALOG, 136
Dictionaries, 71-79
    definition of, 66-67, 72, 152-153, 233
    determining usefulness of, 73
    examples of, 74-78
    excerpts from, 78-79
    kinds of, 74
    (See also specific subject fields)
Dictionaries of Foreign Languages,
    188
Dictionary of American Biography,
    102, 107-108
Dictionary of American English on
    Historical Principles, A, 74, 190
Dictionary of American History, 248
Dictionary of American Politics, 175
Dictionary of American Religious
    Biography, 169
Dictionary of American Slang, 192

Dictionary of Americanisms on
    Historical Principles, A, 190
Dictionary of Antiques, 215
Dictionary of Architecture and
    Construction, 213
Dictionary of Art and Artists, 214
Dictionary of Art Terms and
    Techniques, A, 214
Dictionary of Ballet, A, 224
Dictionary of Basic Geography, A,
    256
Dictionary of Battles, A, 248
Dictionary of Biochemistry, 200
Dictionary of Botany, A, 201
Dictionary of Canadian
    Biography/Dictionnaire
    Biographique du Canada, 108
Dictionary of Canadianisms on
    Historical Principles, A, 190
Dictionary of Christian Ethics, 166
Dictionary of Comparative Religion, A,
    165
Dictionary of Contemporary Artists, A,
    216
Dictionary of Contemporary Music,
    218-219
Dictionary of Decorative Arts, 213
Dictionary of Economics, 175
Dictionary of Education, 182
Dictionary of Foreign Phrases and
    Abbreviations, 190
Dictionary of Foreign Terms, 190
Dictionary of Foreign Words and
    Phrases in Current English, A,
    189-190
Dictionary of Geography, A, 255, 256
Dictionary of Geology, A, 199
Dictionary of Hymnology, A, 166
Dictionary of International Biography,
    106-107
Dictionary of Literary Terms, 234-235
Dictionary of Modern Ballet, 223
Dictionary of Modern English Usage,
    A, 193
Dictionary of Musical Terms, 218
Dictionary of National Biography, 102,
    108
Dictionary of Non-Christian Religions,
    A, 166
Dictionary of Philosophy, A, 158
Dictionary of Philosophy and
    Psychology, 157
Dictionary of Politics, A, 175
Dictionary of Pronunciation, 191-192
Dictionary of Psychology, 161

Dictionary of Quotations, 239
Dictionary of Religion and Ethics, A, 166
Dictionary of Religious Terms, The, 166
Dictionary of Science and Technology, 199
Dictionary of Scientific Biography, 208
Dictionary of Slang and Unconventional English, A, 192
Dictionary of the Bible, 165
Dictionary of the Biological Sciences, The, 200
Dictionary of the Dance, 224
Dictionary of the History of Ideas: Studies of Selected Pivotal Ideas, 158
Dictionary of the Social Sciences, A, 174
Dictionary of Universal Biography of All Ages and All Peoples, A, 110
Dictionary of Word and Phrase Origins, 191
Dictionary of Zoology, A, 200
Digest of Educational Statistics, 184
Digests, 117
Directories:
  definition, 67, 116
  examples of, 119–120
Directory of American Philosophers, 158–159
Directory of American Scholars, 159, 169, 193–194, 225, 252
Directory of Special Libraries and Information Centers, 120
Documentation in Education, 181
Documents and Descriptions: the World since 1914, 250
Documents of American History, 252
Dorland's Illustrated Medical Dictionary, 201
Drama and Theatre, 225
Drama Criticism, 242
Drugs from A to Z: A Dictionary, 202

Earth and Man, The, 255–256
Ebony Handbook, The, 176
Economic Almanac, 178
Economic Geography, 257
Edition, definition, 23
Education, 180–186
  definition, 181
  reference sources, 181–186

Education:
  reference sources:
    abstract journals, 185–186
    bibliographies, 181–182
    biographical dictionaries, 184
    dictionaries, 182
    directories, 182–183
    encyclopedias, 182
    guides, 181
    handbooks, 183–184
    indexes, 181
    professional journals, 184–185
    yearbooks, 183–184
Education Directory, 184
Education Index, 92, 181
Educational Leadership, 184
Educational Media Year Book 1978, 137
Educational Screen and Audio-Visual Guide, 141
Educators Guide to Free Films, 138
Educators Guide to Free Filmstrips, 139
Educators Guide to Free Tapes, Scripts, and Transcriptions, 140
Egyptians, books and libraries, 5–6
8mm Film Directory, 138
Eighth Mental Measurements Yearbook, The, 162
Electronics and Nucleonics Dictionary, 202
Enciclopedia Italiana di Scienze, Lettere ed Arti, 86
Enciclopedia Universal Ilustrada Europeo-Americana, 86
Encyclopaedia Britannica, 81, 84–85
Encyclopaedia Judaica, 166
Encyclopaedia of Religion and Ethics, 167
Encyclopaedia Universalis, 86
Encyclopaedic Dictionary of Physics, The, 201
Encyclopedia Americana, 81, 84
Encyclopedia annuals, 81, 116, 118
Encyclopedia of American Biography, 107
Encyclopedia of American Facts and Dates, The, 248
Encyclopedia of American History, 249
Encyclopedia of Anthropology, 204
Encyclopedia of Associations, 119
Encyclopedia of Astronomy, 205

Encyclopedia of Atmospheric Sciences and Astrogeology, 203
Encyclopedia of Biochemistry, The, 205–206
Encyclopedia of Careers and Vocational Guidance, The, 182
Encyclopedia of Chemistry, The, 203, 204
Encyclopedia of Computer Science, 205
Encyclopedia of Dance and Ballet, The, 223
Encyclopedia of Education, The, 182
Encyclopedia of Educational Research, 182
Encyclopedia of Environmental Science, The, 204
Encyclopedia of Folk, Country, and Western Music, 220
Encyclopedia of Football, The, 226
Encyclopedia of Geomorphology, The, 203
Encyclopedia of Human Behavior, The, 161
Encyclopedia of Jazz in the Seventies, The, 219
Encyclopedia of Mental Health, The, 161
Encyclopedia of Military History from 3500 B.C. to the Present, The, 248
Encyclopedia of Oceanography, The, 203
Encyclopedia of Opera, The, 219
Encyclopedia of Painting, 214
Encyclopedia of Philosophy, The, 158
Encyclopedia of Physics, The, 203
Encyclopedia of Pop, Rock, and Soul, 219–220
Encyclopedia of Popular Music and Rock, 220
Encyclopedia of Psychology, 161
Encyclopedia of Religious Quotations, The, 167
Encyclopedia of Sports, The, 226
Encyclopedia of the American Revolution, 248
Encyclopedia of the Arts, 214–215
Encyclopedia of the Biological Sciences, The, 203
Encyclopedia of the Lutheran Church, The, 166
Encyclopedia of the Musical Theatre, 223

Encyclopedia of the Social Sciences, 175–176
Encyclopedia of World Art, 213
Encyclopedia of World History, An, 249
Encyclopedia of World Literature in the 20th Century, 235
Encyclopedia of World Regional Geology, The, 203
Encyclopedia of World Theater, The, 223
Encyclopedias, 80–86
  continuous revision, 81
  definition, 67, 81, 153, 233
  examples of, 84–86
  judging usefulness of, 82–83
  (See also specific subject fields)
Encyclopedic Dictionary of Judaica, 166
Endpapers, part of book, 22
Energy Technology Handbook, 206
Engineering Index, 198
Engineering Manual, 206
English Historical Review, 253
English Novel Explication: Criticisms to 1972, 243
English Novel: Select Bibliographical Guides, The, 229
English-Russian Dictionary, 77
ERIC, 49, 136, 185n.
Essay and General Literature Index, 99, 100, 231
Etymology, definition, 187
Europa Year Book, 118
European Authors: 1000–1900, 240
European Drama Criticism 1900–1975, 243
Everyman's Dictionary of Dates, 248–249
Everyman's Dictionary of Music, 218
Everyman's Dictionary of Non-Classical Mythology, 170
Explicator Cyclopedia, The, 243–244

Facts on File, 178
Familiar Quotations, 238–239
Famous First Facts, 120
Far East and Australasia, The, 178
Fertile Crescent, 6
Fiction Catalog, 126, 229
Film Evaluation Guide, 138
Film Journal, The, 141

Fine arts, 211–227
  definition, 211
  music, reference sources, 217–222
    bibliographies, 217
    biographical dictionaries,
      221–222
    dictionaries, 217–219
    encyclopedias, 219–220
    guides, 217
    handbooks, 220–221
    indexes, 217
    professional journals, 222
  painting, sculpture, architecture,
    decorative arts, reference
    sources, 212–216
    bibliographies, 212
    biographical dictionaries,
      215–216
    dictionaries, 213–215
    directories, 215–216
    encyclopedias, 213–215
    guides, 212
    handbooks, 215–216
    indexes, 212
    professional journals, 216
  performing arts, reference sources,
    223–225
    biographical dictionaries, 225
    dictionaries, 223–224
    encyclopedias, 223–224
    handbooks, 224–225
    indexes, 223
    professional journals, 225
  primary source materials, 211
  reference sources, examples,
    212–227
*Fine Arts: A Bibliographic Guide to
  Basic Reference Works, Histories,
  and Handbooks*, 212
Fine Arts Market Place, 216
*Flags through the Ages and across the
  World*, 121
Fly-leaves, part of book, 23
*Focal Encyclopedia of Photography,
  The*, 213
Fodor's Modern Guides, 256
Folk Music Sourcebook, The, 221
Footnotes, 24
Forthcoming Books, 127
Foundation Directory, The, 119
Franklin, Benjamin, 16, 88
*French-English Science and
  Technology Dictionary*, 201

Frontispiece, part of book, 23
*Funk & Wagnalls Dictionary of Data
  Processing Terms*, 202
*Funk & Wagnalls Modern Guide to
  Synonyms and Related Words*, 192
*Funk & Wagnalls New Standard
  Dictionary of the English
  Language*, 74
*Funk & Wagnalls Standard College
  Dictionary*, 75–76
*Funk & Wagnalls Standard Desk
  Dictionary*, 76

Gazetteers, 67, 113, 115, 153, 255
General Science Index, 198–199
Geographia, The, 111
Geographical Review, 257
Geography, 254–257
  definition, 254
  reference sources, 254–257
    atlases, 254–255
    bibliographies, 254
    dictionaries, 255–256
    encyclopedias, 255–256
    gazetteers, 255
    guidebooks, 256
    guides, 254
    handbooks, 255
    indexes, 254
    professional journals, 257
*Geography and Cartography: A
  Reference Handbook*, 254
Geologic Reference Sources, 197
Geological Society of America.
  Bulletin, 209
*German-English Technical and
  Engineering Dictionary*, 201
Glossary, definition, 24, 72
*Glossary of Art, Architecture, and
  Design Since 1945*, 215
Glossary of Chemical Terms, 200
Glossary of Geographical Terms, A,
  255
Glossary of Linguistic Terminology,
  189
Glover, T. R., 246
Golden Bough, The, 170
Government documents, 51
Government publications, 141–148
  kinds of, 142
  organization and arrangement in
    libraries, 143–146

Government publications:
purpose of, 142
reference sources on, 146–148
usefulness of, 143
*Government Publications, A Guide to
Bibliographic Tools*, 148
*Government Publications and Their
Use*, 148
*Government Reference Books: A
Biennial Guide to U.S.
Government Publications*, 147
Grand Larousse Encyclopédique,
86
Grande Encyclopédie, La, 86
Granger's Index to Poetry, 231–232
Gray's Manual of Botany, 206
Great Composers, 222
Great EB, The, 81n.
Great Men of American Popular Song,
222
Great Operas in Synopsis, 221
*Great Soviet Encyclopedia: A
Translation of the Third Edition*,
86
Greek-English Lexicon, 77
Greeks, books and libraries, 7–9
*Grove's Dictionary of Music and
Musicians*, 218
Grzimek's Encyclopedia of Ecology,
204
*Guide to American Literature and Its
Backgrounds since 1890*, 229–
230
Guide to Art Reference Books, 212
Guide to Critical Reviews, A, 243
*Guide to Critical Reviews of United
States Fiction 1870–1910*, 242
*Guide to English and American
Literature, A*, 229
*Guide to Graduate Study: Programs
Leading to the Ph.D. Degree, A*,
183
Guide to Historical Literature, 247
Guide to Microforms in Print, 139
Guide to Reference Books, 126
Guide to Reference Material, 126–127,
157, 164, 173, 197
*Guide to the Literature of Mathematics
and Physics*, 198
*Guide to the Literature of the Life
Sciences*, 198
*Guide to the Study of Medieval
History, A*, 247

*Guide to the Study of the United
States of America, A*, 247
*Guide to U.S. Government
Publications*, 147
Guides, definition, 152, 229
Guides to Educational Media, 137–138
Gutenberg, Johann, 14
Gutenberg Bible, 14

Hackh's Chemical Dictionary, 199–200
Half-title page, part of book, 23
Hammond Medallion World Atlas, 114
Hammurabi, Code of, 4, 5
Handbook of Chemistry and Physics,
206
*Handbook of Denominations in the
United States*, 168
Handbook of Latin American Studies,
172, 229
*Handbook of Mathematical Tables and
Formulas*, 206
Handbook of Modern Accounting, 176
Handbook of Physics, 206
Handbook to Literature, A, 237
Handbooks, 117, 118, 120–121
definition, 67, 117, 153, 236
examples of, 120–121
selection and use of, 117–118
types of, 117
*Harper Dictionary of Contemporary
Usage*, 193
*Harper Dictionary of Modern Thought,
The*, 158
Harper Encyclopedia of Science, The,
205
*Harper Encyclopedia of the Modern
World*, 249
Harper's Bible Dictionary, 166
Harper's Dictionary of Music, 217
*Harrap's New Standard French and
English Dictionary*, 76–77
Harvard, John, 16
Harvard Dictionary of Music, 218
Harvard Guide to American History,
247
*Harvard List of Books in Psychology,
The*, 160
Harvard Theological Review, 169
High Fidelity, 222
Historia Naturalis, 80
Historic Architecture Sourcebook,
213–214

Historical Abstracts, 247
Historical Atlas of South Asia, A, 252
Historical Atlas of the Religions of the World, 168
Historical Atlas of the United States, 252
Historical Statistics of the United States: Colonial Times to 1970, 251
History, 246–257
  definition, 246
  reference sources, 247–254
    atlases, 251–252
    bibliographies, 247
    biographical dictionaries, 252–253
    dictionaries, 248–249
    documents, 252
    encyclopedias, 248–249
    guides, 247
    handbooks, 249–251
    indexes, 247
    professional journals, 253
    reference histories, 253–254
History of Religions, 169
Home Book of American Quotations, The, 239
Home Book of Bible Quotations, The, 167
Home Book of Quotations, Classical and Modern, The, 239
Humanities Index, 93, 223, 232

I Hear America Talking, 192
Illumination, 11, 15
Illustrated Dictionary of Place Names, 255
Illustrated Encyclopedia of Archaeology, The, 248
Illustrated Encyclopedia of Astronomy and Space, 205
Illustrated Encyclopedia of Rock, The, 219
Illustrated Encyclopedia of Rock 'n Roll, the Solid Gold Years, The, 219
Illustration Index, 213
Imprint, definition, 23
Incunabula, 14
Index, part of book, 24, 87
Index Medicus, 135, 161, 199
Index to Book Reviews in the Humanities, An, 233

Index to Educational Audio Tapes, 140
Index to Educational Overhead Transparencies, 140
Index to Educational Video Tapes, 140
Index to 8mm Cartridges, 138
Index to Illustrations, 212
Index to Legal Periodicals, 173
Index to Publications of the United States Congress, 147
Index to Religious Periodical Literature, 164
Index to Reproductions of American Paintings, 212–213
Index to Reproductions of European Paintings, 213
Index to 16mm Educational Films, 138
Index to the Times, 98
Index to 35mm Educational Filmstrips, 139
Index to Women, 110
Indexes, 87–100, 152
  definition, 67, 87
  examples of, 95–98, 100
  excerpts from, 91–93, 95, 99
  kinds of, 87
  to literature in collections, 98–100
  to newspapers, 96–98
  to periodicals, 89–96
  selecting and using, 91, 94
  (See also specific subject fields)
Industrial Arts Index, 173
Information Centers, 19
Information Please Almanac, Atlas, and Yearbook, 119
Information sources, general, 65–70
  (See also Reference books)
Instruction in use of library, 27
Interlibrary loan, 27, 123, 136
International Atlas, The, 114
International Cyclopedia of Music and Musicians, 220
International Directory of Philosophy and Philosophers, 159
International Encyclopedia of Chemical Science, 204
International Encyclopedia of the Social Sciences, 175
International Handbook of Universities and Other Institutions of Higher Education, 183
International Index, 173
International Relations Dictionary, The, 175

International Thesaurus of Quotations, 239
International Who's Who, 107
International Yearbook of Education, 183
Interpreter's Dictionary of the Bible, The, 165
Introduction, part of book, 24, 25
Introduction to United States Public Documents, 147
Irish, books and libraries, 11

James & James Mathematics Dictionary, 200
Jefferson, Thomas, 36
Johnson, Samuel, 72
Journal of American History, 253
Journal of Economic History, 180
Journal of General Psychology, 162
Journal of Geology, 209
Journal of Health, Physical Education, Recreation, 227
Journal of Higher Education, 185
Journal of Human Relations, 180
Journal of Modern History, 253
Journal of Negro History, The, 253–254
Journal of Philosophy, The, 159
Journal of the History of Ideas, 159
Journal of the History of Philosophy, 159
Junior Book of Authors, The, 240
Junior High School Library Catalog, The, 126

Katz, William A., 135*n*.
Keesing's Contemporary Archives, 178
Kingzett's Chemical Encyclopaedia, 204

Lange's Handbook of Chemistry, 206
Language, 187–194
  definition, 187
  reference sources, 188–194
    bibliographies, 188
    biographical dictionaries, 193–194
    dictionaries: kinds of, 188
      of special aspects of, 189–193
    indexes, 188
    professional journals, 194

Language of Cities: A Glossary of Terms, The, 174
Language of Twentieth Century Music: A Dictionary of Terms, The, 218
Larousse Encyclopedia of Modern Art from 1800 to the Present Day, 214
Larousse Encyclopedia of Mythology, 170
Larousse Encyclopedia of the Animal World, 204
Larousse World Mythology, 170
Layman's Dictionary of Psychiatry, The, 201
LC Classification Outline, 46
Leaders in Education, 184
Learning Directory, 137
Legislation, federal, 18–19
Libraries:
  academic, 18–19, 26–32
    college, 16, 31
    community college, 30–31
    university, 15–16, 31
  private, 6, 8, 10, 16
  public, 10, 17, 18
  research, 19
  school, 18
  special, 19
  state, 18
  subscription, 16
Library catalogs, 5, 12, 17, 52–54
Library of Congress, 17, 36, 42
Library of Congress Catalog. Books: Subjects, 125
Library of Congress Catalog: Motion Pictures and Filmstrips, 138–139
Library of Congress Catalog: Music and Phonorecords, 139
Library of Congress Catalogs: Subject Catalog, 1950– ., 124–125
Library of Congress Classification System, 42–49, 132*n*.
  excerpts from, 43, 44, 46–49
Library of Congress Subject Headings, 58
Library cooperation, 18, 27
Library of Literary Criticism of English and American Authors, The, 242–243
Library networks, 18
Library positions, 20
Library staff, 30
Library systems, 18
Linguistics, definition, 187

Literary criticism, definition, 241
Literary History of the United States,
  Bibliography, The, 230
Literary Terms: A Dictionary, 234
Literature, 228–245
  in collections, 98–100, 238
    indexes to, 98–100, 238
  definition, 228
  reference sources, 229–245
    abstract journals, 245
    bibliographies, 229–231
    biographical dictionaries, 239–241
    book digests, 238
    book reviews, 232–233
    books of quotations, 238–239
    criticism, 241–244
    dictionaries, 233–234
    encyclopedias, 233, 235–236
    guides, 229–231
    handbooks, 236–238
    indexes, 231–232
    professional journals, 244–245
    reference histories, 241–242
    yearbooks, 244
Literature of American Music in Books
  and Folk Music Collections, The,
  217
Literature of Education, The, 182
Literature of Geography, The, 254
Literature of Political Science, The,
  172

McGraw-Hill Basic Bibliography of
  Science and Technology, 196
McGraw-Hill Dictionary of Art, 214
McGraw-Hill Dictionary of Modern
  Economics, 174
McGraw-Hill Dictionary of Scientific
  and Technical Terms, 200
McGraw-Hill Dictionary of the Life
  Sciences, 200
McGraw-Hill Directory and Almanac
  of Canada, 119–120
McGraw-Hill Encyclopedia of Energy,
  204
McGraw-Hill Encyclopedia of Science
  and Technology, The, 204
McGraw-Hill Encyclopedia of Space,
  The, 205
McGraw-Hill Encyclopedia of World
  Biography, The, 106
McGraw-Hill Encyclopedia of World
  Drama, 224, 235

McGraw-Hill Modern Men of Science,
  208
McGraw-Hill Year Book of Science
  and Technology, 207
Macmillan Bible Atlas, The, 168
Magazines for Libraries, 125
Magill's Quotations in Context, 239
Mammals of the World, 207
Manual, definition, 67, 117, 153
Manual of Mathematics, 206
Manual of style, 270
Manutius, Aldus, 14
Masterpieces of Catholic Literature in
  Summary Form, 167
Masterpieces of Christian Literature in
  Summary Form, 168
Masterpieces of World Literature in
  Digest Form, 238
Masterpieces of World Philosophy in
  Summary Form, 158
Masterplots, 238
Mathematical Reviews, 210
Media Equipment: A Guide and
  Dictionary, 138
Microcard, 133
Microfiche, 134
Microfilm, 132
Microforms, 29, 132–135
  examples of, 133
Microprint, 133
Minerals Yearbook, 208
Miscellany, definition, 67, 117
MLA International Bibliography of
  Books and Articles on the Modern
  Languages and Literatures, 188
Modern American Literature, 242
Modern American Usage, 193
Modern British Literature, 243
Modern Dictionary of Electronics,
  202
Modern Dictionary of Sociology, A,
  175
Modern Encyclopedia of Basketball,
  The, 226
Modern English: A Glossary of
  Literature and Language, 234
Modern Language Journal, 194
Modern Language Quarterly, 194
Modern Schoolman, The, 159
Modern World Drama: An
  Encyclopedia, 235
Monasteries, 10–12
Monthly Catalog of United States
  Government Publications, 146

Monthly Checklist of State
  Publications, 146
  excerpts from, 144, 145
Morphology, definition, 187
Morris Dictionary of Word and Phrase
  Origins, 191
Municipal Year Book, 178
Music (see Fine arts, music)
Music Index, 217
Music Journal, 222
Music Reference and Research
  Materials: An Annotated
  Bibliography, 217
Music Since 1900, 221
Musical Quarterly, The, 222
Mythology, 169–170
Mythology of all Races, Greek and
  Roman, The, 170

National Atlas of the United States of
  America, The, 114
National Cyclopedia of American
  Biography, The, 108–109
National Geographic Atlas of the
  World, 114–115
National Union Catalog: A Cumulative
  Author List, The, 124
National Union Catalog, Pre-1956
  Imprints, The, 124
Natural History, 209
Nature, 209
NBC Handbook of Pronunciation, 191
Negro Almanac, The, 177
Negro in America: A Bibliography,
  The, 172
Negro in the United States, The, 173
Nelson's Complete Concordance of the
  Revised Standard Version of the
  Bible, 165
Networks, 18
New Cambridge Bibliography of
  English Literature, The, 231
New Cambridge Modern History, The,
  253
New Cassell's French Dictionary, 77
New Catholic Encyclopedia, The, 167
New Century Cyclopedia of Names,
  106
New Century Italian Renaissance
  Encyclopedia, The, 249–250
New College Encyclopedia of Music,
  The, 220
New Columbia Encyclopedia, The, 85

New Complete Book of the American
  Musical Theater, 224
New Dictionary & Handbook of
  Aerospace, The, 202
New Dictionary of Birds, A, 201
New Dictionary of Physics, A, 200
New Emily Post's Etiquette, The,
  121
New Encyclopedia of Sports, 226
New Encyclopedia of the Opera, The,
  219
New English Dictionary on Historical
  Principles, A, 72, 74
New Grove Dictionary of Music and
  Musicians, The, 218
New International Encyclopedia, 81
New Kobbé's Complete Opera Book,
  The, 221
New Listener's Companion and Record
  Guide, The, 220
New Orleans Times-Picayune, The,
  97–98
New Oxford Atlas, The, 115
New Revised Velázquez Spanish and
  English Dictionary, The, 78
New Schaff-Herzog Encyclopedia of
  Religious Knowledge, The, 167
New Standard Jewish Encyclopedia,
  The, 167
New Technical Books, 197
New Westminster Dictionary of the
  Bible, The, 165
New York Times Biographical Service,
  The, 107
New York Times Encyclopedia of
  Television, The, 223
New York Times Encyclopedic
  Almanac, 119
New York Times Encyclopedic
  Dictionary of the Environment,
  The, 202
New York Times Index, 97
New York Times Information Bank,
  136
Newnes Dictionary of Dates, 250
Newspaper Index, The, 97–98
Newspaper Indexes, 97–98
Newspapers, 15, 96–98
NICEM, 138
19th and 20th Century Art, Painting,
  Sculpture, Architecture, 215
Nineteenth Century Readers' Guide to
  Periodical Literature, 96, 233
Nineveh Library, 4, 5

Nonbook Information Sources, 51,
129–141
bibliographical form for, 274
determining usefulness of, 137
examples of reference materials on,
137–141
sample catalog cards for, 130
Nonbook reference sources, 68
(*See also* Nonbook Information
Sources)
*Notable American Women, 1607–1950:
A Biographical Dictionary*, 106
*Notable Names in the American
Theatre*, 225
Note-taking, 267–269
sample cards, 268

*Official Congressional Directory for the
Use of the United States Congress*,
120
Official Encyclopedia of Sports, The,
226
"Off-line," 135
"On-line," 135
ORBIT, 136
Orientation for freshmen, 32
Origins, 189
*Ottemiller's Index to Plays in
Collections*, 232
Outline Atlas of World History, An,
252
Outlining, 265, 267, 269
Oxford Bible Atlas, 168
Oxford Classical Dictionary, The, 234
*Oxford Companion to American
History, The*, 250
*Oxford Companion to American
Literature, The*, 237
Oxford Companion to Art, The, 215
*Oxford Companion to Canadian History
and Literature, The*, 238, 251
*Oxford Companion to English
Literature, The*, 237
Oxford Companion to Film, The, 224
*Oxford Companion to French
Literature, The*, 237
Oxford Companion to Music, The, 221
*Oxford Companion to Ships and the
Sea, The*, 121
*Oxford Companion to the Decorative
Arts, The*, 215
Oxford Companion to the Theatre, The,
224

*Oxford Companion to World Sports and
Games, The*, 225–226
*Oxford Dictionary of English
Etymology, The*, 189
*Oxford Dictionary of English Proverbs,
The*, 239
*Oxford Dictionary of the Christian
Church, The*, 165
Oxford Economic Atlas, 179
Oxford English Dictionary, The, 74,
191
*Oxford History of English Literature,
The*, 241
Oxford World Atlas, 115

Pamphlets, 29, 129–130
Paperbound Books in Print, 127
Papyrus, 5, 7, 13, 15
Parchment, 8, 9
*Penguin Companion to World
Literature, The*, 238
Pergamum Library, 9
Periodical indexes, 89–96, 104
examples of, 94–96
excerpts from, 91–93, 95
selection and use of, 91, 94
(*See also specific subject fields*)
Periodicals, 15, 29, 51, 68, 87–89
Peterson Field Guide Series, The, 207
*Phaidon Dictionary of Twentieth
Century Art, The*, 214
Phi Delta Kappan, 185
Philology:
definition of, 187
(*See also* Language)
Philosopher's Index, The, 157
Philosophical Dictionary, 157–158
Philosophical Review, 159
Philosophy, 156–159
definition, 156
reference sources, 157–159
bibliographies, 157
biographical dictionaries, 158–159
dictionaries, 157–158
digests, 158
encyclopedias, 157–158
indexes, 157
professional journals, 159
Phoenicians, books and libraries, 6–7
Photocopying in libraries, 28, 123
*Planet We Live On: An Illustrated
Encyclopedia of the Earth
Sciences, The*, 204

Play Index, 232

PMLA, 188, 194

Poetry, 244

Poetry Handbook: A Dictionary of
Terms, 237

Political Handbook of the World, 177

Political Science Quarterly, 180

Pollution Abstracts, 210

Poole's Index to Periodical Literature,
1802–1907, 96

Popular Composers from Revolutionary
Times to the Present, 222

Popular Guide to Government
Publications, A, 147

Popular Music, An Annotated Index of
Popular Songs, 217

Popular Names of U.S. Government
Reports: A Catalog, 148

Praeger Encyclopedia of Ancient
Greek Civilization, The, 249

Praeger Encyclopedia of Art, 214

Previews: Audiovisual Software
Reviews, 137

Primary sources, 264

Princeton Encyclopedia of Classical
Sites, The, 249

Princeton Encyclopedia of Poetry and
Poetics, 236

Printing with movable types, 13–15

Professional journals, 154
(See also specific subject fields)

Pronouncing Dictionary of American
English, A, 191

Psychiatric Dictionary, 202

Psychological Abstracts, 135, 162

Psychological Review, The, 162

Psychology, 160–162
definition, 160
reference sources in, 160–162
bibliographies, 160
biographical dictionaries, 161–162
dictionaries, 161
directories, 161–162
encyclopedias, 161
indexes, 161
professional journals, 162
yearbooks, 162

Psychology Today, 162

Public Affairs Information Service.
Bulletin, 174, 181

Public Law 94-553, 23, 28

Public Library Catalog, 126

Public Printer, The, 141

Publishers Trade List Annual, 127

"*Putnam's Nature Field Books,*" 207

Rameses II, 6

Rand McNally Commercial Atlas and
Marketing Guide, 255

Rand McNally Cosmopolitan World
Atlas, 115

Random House College Dictionary,
The, 76, 78–79

Random House Dictionary of the
English Language, The, 75

Random House Encyclopedia, The,
85

Rawlinson, Sir Henry, 5

Reader's Adviser: A Layman's Guide to
Literature, 126

Reader's Encyclopedia, The, 236

Reader's Encyclopedia of American
Literature, 235

Reader's Encyclopedia of Shakespeare,
The, 236

Reader's Encyclopedia of World
Drama, The, 235

Readers' Guide to Periodical
Literature, 91, 96

Reader's Guide to the Great Religions,
A, 164

Reader's Guide to the Social Sciences,
A, 172

Recent Publications in the Social and
Behavioral Sciences, 172

Recuyell of the Histories of Troy, 14

Reference, definition, 65

Reference books, 66–68
general, 66–68
definition, 66
subject, 68
definition, 68

Reference Encyclopedia of the
American Indian, 176

Reference Guide for Travellers, 257

Reference List of Audiovisual
Materials Produced by the United
States Government 1978, A, 138

Reference service, 27

Reference sources:
general, 66–68
judging usefulness of, 68–69
selection and use of, 69–70
subject, 66, 151–155
(See also Reference books)

Religion, 163–169
definition, 163

Religion:
  reference sources in, 164–169
    atlases, 168
    bibliographies, 164
    biographical dictionaries, 169
    books of quotations, 167
    concordances, 164–165
    dictionaries, 165–166
    digests, 167–168
    encyclopedias, 166–167
    guides, 164
    indexes, 164
    professional journals, 169
    yearbooks, 168
Religious and Theological Abstracts,
  164
Renaissance, the, 13
*Requirements for Certification of
  Teachers, Counselors, Librarians,
  and Administrators for Elementary
  Schools, Secondary Schools, Junior
  Colleges*, 184
Research, definition, 261
Research in Education, 185–186
Research paper, 261–274
  bibliography for, 265, 269–270,
    272–274
    sample cards, 266
  footnotes, 270–272
  note-taking, 267–269
    sample cards, 268
Reserve materials, 27
Resources in Education, 185–186
*Robert's Rules of Order Newly
  Revised*, 121
Roget's International Thesaurus, 192
Romans, books and libraries, 9
Rosetta Stone, 6
Russian-English Dictionary, 78

Science, 209
Science, 195–210
  definition, 195
  reference sources, 196–210
    abstract journals, 210
    bibliographies, 196–197
    biographical dictionaries, 208
    dictionaries, 199–202
    encyclopedias, 203–206
    guides, 197–198
    handbooks, 206–207
    indexes, 198–199
    professional journals, 208–210
    yearbooks, 207–208

Science Abstracts, 210
*Science and Engineering Literature: A
  Guide to Reference Sources*, 197
Science Books: A Quarterly Review,
  197
Science Reference Sources, 196
Scientific American, 210
*Scientific and Technical Books and
  Serials in Print*, 197
Scribes, 4, 6
Scriptorium, 11
Sculpture Index, 212
Sears List of Subject Headings, 58
Secondary sources, 264
*Selected U.S. Government
  Publications*, 146–147
*Selective Bibliography for the Study of
  English and American Literature*,
  229
Seligman, Edwin R. A., 171
Semantics, definition, 187
*Senior High School Library Catalog,
  The*, 126
Serial, definition, 51n.
Series, definition, 23
Sewanee Review, 244–245
Sheehy, Eugene P., x, 126
Short Story Index, 232
*Shorter Oxford English Dictionary on
  Historical Principles, The*, 76
*Six Thousand Words: A Supplement to
  Webster's Third New International
  Dictionary*, 75
Sky and Telescope, 210
Social sciences, 171–180
  definition, 171
  reference sources, 171–180
    atlases, 179
    bibliographies, 171–173
    biographical dictionaries, 179
    dictionaries, 174–175
    encyclopedias, 175–176
    guides, 171–173
    handbooks, 176–177
    indexes, 173–174
    professional journals, 179–180
    yearbooks, 177–179
Social Sciences and Humanities Index,
  174
Social Sciences Index, 92, 174, 254
Sociological Quarterly, 180
Sources of Business Information, 172
*Sources of Information in the Social
  Sciences: A Guide to the
  Literature*, 173

South American Handbook, 178
Space-Age Photographic Atlas, The, 255
Speech Index, 232
Spine, part of book, 22
Spoken Records, 139
Sports and Recreation, reference sources, 225–227
Sports Illustrated, 226
Standard Catalog Series, The, 126
Standard Education Almanac, 184
Standard Handbook for Secretaries, 120
Standard Periodical Directory, The, 125
Statesman's Yearbook, The, 118–119
Statistical Abstract of the United States, 119
Statistical Yearbook/Annuaire Statistique, 178
Statistics Sources, 173
Stedman's Medical Dictionary, 202
Steinberg's Dictionary of British History, 250–251
Strong, James, *Exhaustive Concordance of the Bible*, 165
Studies in Philology, 194
Study Abroad, 184
Subject card, 56–58
Subject Guide to Books in Print, 128
Subject Guide to Microforms in Print, 139
Subject headings, 56–59
Subject reference sources, 151–155
 definition, 151
 kinds of, 152–153
 selection and use of, 154–155
 usefulness of, 151–152
Sumerians, books and libraries, 4
Superintendent of Documents, The, 142
Superintendent of Documents Classification, 49, 144–146
Supplement to the Oxford English Dictionary, A, 75, 191
Survey of Musical Instruments, A, 221
Symbol Sourcebook: An Authoritative Guide to International Graphic Symbols, 120
Syntax, definition, 187

Table of contents, part of book, 24
Technical Book Review Index, 199
Technology, 195–210

Technology:
 definition, 195
 reference sources, 196–210
  abstract journals, 210
  bibliographies, 196–197
  biographical dictionaries, 208
  dictionaries, 199–202
  encyclopedias, 203–206
  guides, 197–198
  handbooks, 206–207
  indexes, 198–199
  professional journals, 208–210
  yearbooks, 207–208
Telescope Handbook and Star Atlas, The, 206
Telloh, 4
Text, part of book, 24
Thesaurus, 59, 87, 136
Thesaurus of ERIC Descriptors, The, 186
Thomas' Register of American Manufacturers, 120
Times Atlas of the World, The, 114
Times Atlas of the World: Comprehensive Edition, The, 114
Times Atlas of World History, 252
Timetables of History, The, 250
Title card, 56, 57
Title page, part of book, 23, 25
Today's Education, 185
Turabian, Kate L., 270
Twentieth Century Authors, 240
Twentieth Century British Literature, 243
20th Century Plays in Synopsis, 238
Twentieth Century Short Story Explication, 244

Ulpian Library, 10
Ulrich's International Periodicals Directory, 125
Union catalogs, 123, 124
Union List of Serials in Libraries of the United States and Canada, 125–126
U.S. Catalog, 128
United States Government Organization Manual, 121
Universities, medieval, 12
Use of Biological Literature, The, 197
Use of Chemical Literature, The, 197

Van Nostrand's Scientific Encyclopedia, 205

Vatican Library, 15
Vellum, 8
Vertical file, 131
Vocabulary, 72

Walford, A. J., 126
Washington Post, The, 98
Water Encyclopedia, The, 205
Webster, Noah, 72
Webster's American Biographies, 107
Webster's Biographical Dictionary, 106
Webster's Collegiate Thesaurus, 192
Webster's Dictionary of Proper Names, 121
Webster's New Collegiate Dictionary, 76, 79
Webster's New Dictionary of Synonyms, 193
Webster's New Geographical Dictionary, 115
Webster's New International Dictionary of the English Language, 75
Webster's New World Dictionary of the American Language, 76
Webster's Sports Dictionary, 226
Webster's Third New International Dictionary of the English Language, 75
Weekly Record, 128
Whitaker, Joseph, Almanack, 119
Who's Who, 109
Who's Who Among Black Americans, 109
Who's Who in American Art, 216
Who's Who in American Politics, 179

Who's Who in Architecture from 1400 to the Present, 216
Who's Who in the Theatre, 225
Who's Who in the World, 109
Who Was Who, 108
Who Was Who in America, 109
Who Was Who in America: Historical Volume 1607–1896, 109, 252–253
Wildflowers of the United States, 207
Women's Rights Almanac, 178–179
Wood-block printing, 13, 14
World Almanac and Book of Facts, The, 119
World Authors, 241
World Bibliography of Bibliographies, A, 124
World Book Encyclopedia, The, 85
World of Learning, 184
Worldmark Encyclopedia of the Nations, 176
World's Treasury of Religious Quotations, The, 167
Writing materials, 3–5, 7–9, 12
Writing styles, 3–9, 11

Yearbook of Agriculture, 208
Yearbook of American and Canadian Churches, 168
Yearbook of the United Nations, 179
Yearbook of World Affairs, The, 179
Yearbooks, 16, 116–120, 153
  definition, 67, 116
  examples of, 118–120
  selection and use of, 117–118
  types of, 116
  (See also specific subject fields)
Year's Work in English Studies, 244